The Gospel App Shape

Bill Senyard

Copyright 2015 © by William H. Senyard

All rights reserved. No part of this book shall be reproduced or transmitted in any form or by any means, electronic, mechanical, magnetic, photographic including photocopying, recording or by any information storage and retrieval system, without prior written permission of the authors.

ISBN-13: 978-1512177862

ISBN-10: 1512177865

All scripture quotations, unless otherwise indicated, are taken from the HOLY BIBLE, NEW INTERNATIONAL VERSION ®. NIV ®. Copyright © 1973, 1978, 1984, 2011 by Biblica, Inc.™ Used by permission. All rights reserved worldwide.

Scripture marked MSG is taken from The Message. Copyright © 1993, 1994, 1995, 1996, 2000, 2001, 2002. Used by permission of NavPress Publishing Group.

Cover design by Ryan Lause.

Published in United States by LE Press, Golden, Colorado.

Acknowledgments

The *Gospel App Shape* is a companion book that works in conjunction with the *Gospel App* discipleship curriculum. For many of us the key question that must be answered over and over again is "How can we as Christians recondition ourselves from our innate bent toward leaning upon our own efforts and works in order to gain God's favor and blessings? How can we individually and corporately be more aware of our desperate ongoing need of the Holy Spirit to do anything truly good? Truly Christ-like? How can we access more power from God so that we may really know today the height, width, depth and length of the love of Christ for us (Ephesians 3:14-21)?"

I would like to acknowledge the foundational influence upon my life and this *Gospel App* project, the *Sonship* curriculum (Serge.org), and specifically the decade-long friendship and hands-on discipleship efforts afforded me by Stu and Ruth Ann Batstone. Influenced by their example and encouragement, I have taught so many *Sonship* discipleship groups that there is no doubt in my mind that the lines blur between The *Gospel App* and *Sonship*. While it is my hope that the two curricula may work in creative tandem, I apologize ahead of time for any unapproved overlap. It is unintentional.

I would like to thank all who have been a part of this journey. There have been a number of churches that have enjoyed early versions of the *Gospel App*. Their feedback has been very encouraging and valuable.

I also want to acknowledge the editing prowess of my wife, Eunice. She has patiently read through the following pages multiple times. It is a much better tool due to her efforts. Similar thanks to Jeff and Aubrey Buster, John and Allison Senyard, Howie James, Eric Protzman, Ed Ragain, Scott LaPoint, Dwight Gilliland, Rick Gilmore, Leighton Cash, Jon Sharpe, Jon and Karen Gindhart, Bill Robertson, Chris McGrath, Verity Schramm, and Scott Barth who have edited or taught this material and provided very helpful feedback and comment. I also want to acknowledge the entire membership of Lookout Mountain Community Church who have been so encouraging to me with this *Gospel App* project.

May God bless His Gospel among us.

The Gospel App Shape

Contents

The Gospel App Project	1
Introduction: All We Need is Need	5
Chapter 1: The Gospel App Shape	17
Chapter 2: The Power of the Flesh	29
Chapter 3: The Testimony of Science	39
Chapter 4: The Power of the Spirit	47
Chapter 5: Guilt Versus (sin)	55
Chapter 6: Shame Versus Right	73
Chapter 7: Dealing with Shame	93
Chapter 8: Orphan Versus Adoption	115
Chapter 9: Idols Versus Spirit	141
Conclusion	163
Appendix 1	177
Bibliography	181

The Gospel App Shape

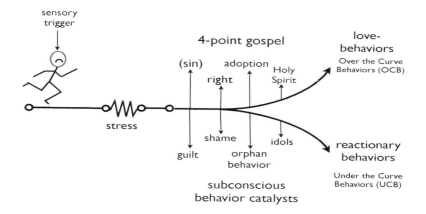

The Gospel App Project

Here I must take counsel of the gospel. I must hearken to the gospel, which teacheth me, not what I ought to do, (for that is the proper office of the law,) but what Jesus Christ the Son of God hath done for me : to wit, that He suffered and died to deliver me from sin and death. The gospel willeth me to receive this, and to believe it. And this is the truth of the gospel. It is also the principal article of all Christian doctrine, wherein the knowledge of all godliness consisteth. Most necessary it is, therefore, that we should know this article well, teach it unto others, and beat it into their heads continually."
—Martin Luther

The *Gospel App Shape* was conceived to be a companion manual to the ten-week *Gospel App* discipleship course. At the heart of The *Gospel App* is a single shape (see above), a powerful easy-to-grasp and easy-to-remember visual; designed to equip and encourage regular Jesus-followers to better "receive and apply the singular Gospel of Christ to the real lives of real people in the real world—beginning with me."

The *Gospel App* discipleship curriculum is roughly divided into two sections. The first five lessons of the discipleship course focus on the shape itself, briefly defining its twelve elements. The second five lessons shift to teaching participants how they can use the shape as a tool to recondition themselves to regularly *apply* the Gospel to their own real life challenges: e.g., addictions, unresolved conflicts, how to say you're sorry, how to forgive hurts, how to resurrect dying prayer life and how to regain a fervor for evangelizing your neighbors. These are clearly rubber-meets-the-road issues for all of us.

Most of us, even those who have been Jesus-followers for a long time, have not been intentionally trained on how to regularly apply the Gospel to our actual lives "last-week." If we were honest, many of us have largely focused on the nature of our conversion or upon the timing of Jesus' eventual return. Both good things to be sure. Unfortunately for many, the age-old question of how do I live my life in the great divide in-between remains a bit of a confusing mystery. How do we live this Gospel well? Do we just need to keep trying harder? Have we missed something?

The actual *Gospel App* discipleship curriculum is designed to train participants to bridge that important gap. It has proven to be very helpful to those participants who come weary of their struggles and ready to embrace change.

This book, the *Gospel App Shape*, is primarily for those participants in the discipleship course who want to dig deeper into the twelve elements of the shape. Teachers, facilitators, and mentors will find the material quite helpful to explain some of the more complicated elements such as guilt, shame, idols, orphanness, spiritual adoption, the nature and work of the Holy Spirit, and the double aspects of Jesus' justification.

Syncing Gospel App discipleship with Gospel App Shape

Gospel App	Gospel App Shape
Week 1	Introduction and Chap 1
Week 2	Chapters 2-4
Week 3	Chapters 5-7
Week 4	Chapter 8
Week 5	Chapter 9

Facilitators, the *Gospel App Shape* is not designed to act as a stand-alone manuscript, rather it is meant to be a helpful supplement to the *Gospel App* discipleship program. The chart above is a rough topical guide for you. The goal of both publications is to train and equip real people to learn how to really apply the Gospel to their actual lives. Such discipleship ultimately requires community and transparency. Too often Christians rely on only reading a book or attending a class to further their sanctification—to make them feel closer to God. The truth is that we can know a great deal about Christian theology and practice and still be woefully ignorant and inexperienced about how to live it out. To put it differently, many Christians do not really feel loved by God. Many of us are not daily dependent upon God and His power.

So what about you? Has your Christianity for all practical purposes flat-lined? Not lived up to your original high expectations? Are you maybe wondering if you even believe anymore? Are you just weary of the whole church-thing? Feel like you are just going through the motions?

Welcome to the *Gospel App* and the *Gospel App Shape*.

The Gospel App Shape

Introduction: All we need is need

> *Let us listen for the Spirit, confess Christ, be absolutely at His disposal. Oh, but you say to me, Are not we all that? Well, I do not know. God help us to find out for ourselves. I think we are in terrible danger of listening to the Spirit, and when His voice speaks to us, quenching Him.*
> —G. Campbell Morgan on the Welsh Revival (1904-05)

> *Wonderful things have happened in Wales in a few weeks, but these are only a beginning. The world will be swept by His Spirit as by a rushing, mighty wind. Many who are now silent Christians, negative Christians, Christians whose belief means little to them and nothing to anyone else, will lead in the movement. Groping, hesitating, half-hearted Christians will see a great Light and will reflect this Light to thousands of those in utter darkness. The whole world will hear His message of "peace, good-will toward men," and listening, will be blessed. Thousands upon thousands will do more than we have accomplished, as God gives them power. This is my earnest faith, if the churches will but learn the great lesson of obedience to the voice of the Holy Spirit. Obedience! Obedience!! Obedience!!!*[1]
> —Evan Roberts, Message to the World
> (A sermon given during the Welsh Revival)

"All we need is need," proclaimed the lecturer, "And most of the time we don't even have that."[2] The speaker was observing that nothing was more core to

---

1. "The Story of the Welsh Revival" from http://www.revival-library.org/catalogues/1904ff/goodrich.html.
2. I am indebted to Jonathan Edward scholar Dr. John Gerstner for this felicitous phrase.

the great philosopher-theologian Jonathan Edward's Gospel than a seminal and ongoing awareness of one's own desperate need. To expand the point further, any and all spiritual revival happens when normal human beings, no matter who they are, what they have done, or what has been done to them, are mysteriously made aware of their deep need for God— for His pleasure, acceptance, favor, and love. We humans flail around looking for significance, security and belonging in all the wrong places with tragically little evidence of lasting success. We have been doing it so long, we no longer question the validity of our efforts, nor lament their failures.

If we could be honest for even a moment, our relationships, even the best ones, don't give us the significance, security, and belonging that we long for. The same could be said for education, career, hobbies, sex, and even sexuality. At the end of the day, a great question could be asked of us, "So based upon all of the energies that you have invested in your *stuff* and your *being* today, how's it really going for you? Didn't you hope for more?"

But every now and then, something happens and we see clearly. We mysteriously become acutely aware that we have been underachievers with wildly high upside potential—yet unreached. We see again that the significance, belonging, and security that we desperately long for *is* available, just not from the places where we have been investing time and energy.

The source of the awareness of that need is none other than the Holy Spirit Himself. For Edwards, this was not merely a theoretical premise. He was in fact observing the actual changed lives of his church and neighbors during the historical First Great Awakening. In New England alone, ten percent of the population was added to churches between 1740 and 1742. One hundred and fifty new churches were planted in a single denomination. One historian called the work "the most glorious and extensive revival of religion and reformation of manners the country had ever known."[3]

The Great Awakening resulted in an outburst of missionary and social justice activities among Native Americans and slaves. It led to the founding of a number of academies and colleges, notably Princeton, Brown, Rutgers, and Dartmouth.

Such has been true for other historical awakenings empowered by the Holy Spirit. Here is a record of social manifestations of the 1904-'05 Welsh revival.

> "Whole communities were turned upside down, and were radically changed from depravity to glorious goodness. The crime rate dropped, often to nothing. The police force reported that they had little more to do than supervise the coming and going of the people to the chapel prayer meetings, while magistrates turned up at courts to discover no cases to try. The alcohol trade was decimated, as people were caught up more by what happened in the

---

3. J. Edwin Orr, "The Re-study of Revival and Revivalism", 1981. Retrieved from http://www.revival-library.org/pensketches/edwardsj.html.

local chapels than the local public houses and bars. Families experienced amazing renewal, where the money earning husband and father, the bread winner, had wasted away the income and sowed discord, but now under the moving power of the Holy Spirit, following the conversion to be a follower of Jesus Christ, he not only provided correctly for family needs, but was now with the family, rather than wasting his time, and wages, in the public houses of the village or town…Not only were individual lives changed by the power of the Holy Spirit, but whole communities were changed, indeed society itself was changed. Wales again was a God-fearing nation! Public houses were now almost empty. Men and women who used to waste their money getting drunk were saving it, giving it to help their churches, buying clothes and food for their families. And not only drunkenness, but stealing and other offences grew less and less, so that often a magistrate came to court, and found there were no cases for him. Men whose language had been filthy before, learnt to talk purely. It is related that not only did the colliers put in a better day's work, but also that the pit ponies were so used to being cursed and sworn at, that they just couldn't understand orders being given in kind, clean words! Yet, still the work output increased. The dark tunnels underground in the mines echoed with the sounds of prayer and hymns, instead of oaths and nasty jokes and gossip. People who had been careless about paying their bills, or paying back money they had borrowed, paid up all they owed. People who had fallen out became friends again."[4]

These were real people, living out their real normal lives with all of the real life problems that we all have—each deeply changed—in a moment. All you and I need is need. The Holy Spirit continues to make individuals, both Christians and non-Christians aware of that need. It is among His greatest ongoing works.

Have you been made aware of your desperate need for the Holy Spirit's power today for you to do anything truly *good* and *lasting*? Truly Christ-ish? Have you been made aware of the incredible unlimited significance, security, and belonging that is already yours in Christ? Accessible to you? Now? Have you been made aware that there is a real hope of actually feeling good about yourself, your relationships, your place in this world? Your identity and being? The Gospel is truly good news— better than we may have imagined.

> *"Have you been made aware of your desperate need for the Holy Spirit's power today for you to do anything truly good and lasting? Truly Christ-ish?"*

Some of you may be reading this book because you have become aware of a tragic failure in your actions, motivations, and behaviors. Your awareness of

---

4 http://truthinhistory.org/the-welsh-revival-of-1904-1905.html.

need for change is an immediate one.

Some of you may just be feeling acutely dissatisfied with your Christian experience. You had hoped for more. You had expected greater intimacy with God and with other Christians—and have been left disappointed.

Welcome to the *Gospel App Shape* and the *Gospel App* discipleship curriculum. All you need bring is your need. But that's easier said than done.

C. S. Lewis The Great Divorce

C.S. Lewis' brilliance shown never brighter than in the pages of *The Great Divorce*.[5] The storyline arose out of Lewis' deep interest in the nature of God's plan to rescue deeply needy and fiercely resistant humans—even fiercely resistant deceased men and women. He borrowed a narrative concept from the writings of the seventeenth century Anglican divine Jeremy Taylor, who introduced the ancient extra-Biblical Catholic notion of *Refrigerium*—that the deceased and damned are given opportunity for holidays, days off, from the torments of Hell.

Embracing this concept as the basis of his fictional setting, Lewis imagines a shadowy nightmarish dreamscape, a place that resembles Earth, only always dark and somber, filled with desolation and disillusionment—permanent and only expanding further outward, increasingly lonelier. This *Earth* is the place where the deceased abide but remain unattached and miserable *ghosts* forever. Those consigned to this place are truly substance-less, shadows on the wall, never real persons, never what they could have been, only lonely wanderers, empty ghosts—or better, troubled *wraiths* with no hope in their own efforts to ever improve their lot.

In the *Lord of the Rings*, written by Lewis' dear friend J.R.R Tolkien, the ringwraiths were those nine powerful rulers of men who had been corrupted by Lord Sauron, each given one of the nine Rings of Power. Their fate was beyond horrible. The ringwraiths were not allowed to die. They slowly faded into non-humanness, a living darkness, invisible to the world, enslaved to their overwhelming lusts and desires and of course subjected to the will of the evil Sauron, fated to roam Middle Earth until their end.

In the imagination of Lewis, the wraith-like ghosts who reside in the grey lifeless town that is Earth still had a single sliver of hope to become persons of substance once more. They could hop on a flying bus and mysteriously enter the very foothills of Heaven.

It sounds easy but it turns out that the task was far more difficult than it first appeared. *The deceased humans had severe challenges admitting their need.*

Once the *ghosts* arrive at heaven's foothills, they must have an audience with those of heaven, either angels or partly glorified humans, both equally

---

5. C. S. Lewis, The Great Divorce: A Dream, Harper San Francisco, 1946.

Introduction

frightening to the *ghosts* of Earth. The inhabitants of Heaven, "*Solid Spirits*" as Lewis refers to them, are to varying degrees filled with glory and light—making confrontation with the earthly wraiths quite uncomfortable for the latter. The *Solid Spirits* have no shame, no need for pretense, or even clothes for that matter. They are themselves at last, freed from shame, guilt, and idols that powerfully shaped them and their choices while alive. They now actually relish dependence upon God. Submission is no longer a nasty word. They feel loved—more than they ever felt while alive on earth—and freely love others. They fully embrace their ongoing need for God's devotion and love.

Where the earth-bound *ghosts* still struggle with appearance, worry of what others think, are concerned for success and reputation, unresolved forgiveness and the need to repent, the Heavenly residents are free. Free to love others, free to *want* to love others. In fact, these *Solid Spirits* have journeyed backwards to the bus stop strictly for the sake of the hapless, confused, frightened and still stubbornly independent *ghosts*, to invite, convict and in some cases to beg them to see their need for rescue. It is this expression of love that is so troubling to the subconsciously self-focused, fear, and shame-riddled *ghosts* who disembark from the bus. This love is frightening to Earth residents. It is offensive.

To go further on toward Heaven, the *ghosts* must first *be* loved. No matter how they try to go further by their own strengths, the *ghosts* cannot. Even the grass of the foothills is too substantive for their diminished bodies. The strange solidness of the blades of grass hurts the *ghosts'* feet. Raindrops cut through the *ghosts* like knives. Falling leaves can crush. Sunbeams hit like bricks.

Their only hope is to admit their need and finally accept the help of the *Solid Spirits* (not an easy task for we humans, alive or dead). All they need is need. In spite of their obvious inability to move toward the Celestial Kingdom, few will admit it. Tragically, most of the *ghosts* returned to the bus miserable and lonely, and took the trip back to the dehumanizing shadows of Earth.

One of the heavenly *Solid Spirits* is the late theologian Gordon MacDonald. Lewis' protagonist, a ghost on his first bus trip, asks MacDonald,

> "But I don't understand. Is judgment not final? Is there really a way out of Hell into Heaven?"

To the protagonist, Spirit MacDonald replies,

> "It depends on the way you're using the words. If they leave that grey town behind it will not have been Hell. To any that leaves it, it is Purgatory. And perhaps ye had better not call this country Heaven. Not Deep Heaven, ye understand." (Here he smiled at me). "Ye can call it the Valley of the Shadow of Life. And yet to those who stay here it will have been Heaven from the first. And ye can call those sad streets in the town yonder the Valley of the Shadow of Death: but to those who remain there it will have been Hell even from the

beginning…Never fear. There are only two kinds of people in the end: those who say to God, 'Thy will be done,' and those to whom God says, in the end, 'Thy will be done.' All that are in Hell, choose it. Without that self-choice there could be no Hell. No soul that seriously and constantly desires joy will ever miss it. Those who seek find. To those who knock it is opened."

Here is the question. Are we humans-yet-living so differently from these fictional largely deceased wraiths? Meaning this. Is living humanity of far less substance than we imagine, burdened with far more shame and guilt, enslaved more than we care to admit to conscious and subconscious idols, more in denial of our need for God to really live now, and driven by a deep ongoing hatred of anything that smacks of dependence and submission to God's power? Are we, relative to our post-Cross potential, mere ghosts, shadows on the wall, wraiths, not subject to Lord Sauron, but to our own flesh—too stubborn, afraid, or ignorant to admit our ongoing need for God's power to truly live?

> *"Never fear. There are only two kinds of people in the end: those who say to God, 'Thy will be done,' and those to whom God says, in the end, 'Thy will be done.'"*
>
> **C.S. Lewis**

Could it really be that we are unable, on our own, to truly forgive or to fully repent, or to love others; though each of us imagines that if only we would work a bit harder, do a few more things right, or read another Christian book, we would at long last be successful and at long last really earn God's favor and devotion that we have been missing. Are we habitual underachievers relative to our great potential?

There is a provocative scene in *The Great Divorce* where a woman *Solid Spirit* who resides in Heaven comes across her newly deceased husband—a twisted ghost—who provocatively appears as a shrunken dwarf holding on to a erudite actor by a chain. The tragedian is the enfleshed dislocated voice of the diminished man, imagined as an over-the-top British actor on a grand stage. Lewis' protagonist describes the scene[6],

> "I turned and saw an oddly-shaped phantom approaching. Or rather two phantoms: a great tall Ghost, horribly thin and shaky, who seemed to be leading on a chain another Ghost no bigger than an organ-grinder's monkey."

Thus begins a dialogue on the nature of love: a contrast between earthly love and the substantively different frightening love that is of Heaven.

"Love!" said the Tragedian striking his forehead with his hand: then, a few

---

6. Lewis, The Great Divorce: A Dream, 120.

Introduction

notes deeper, "Love! Do you know the meaning of the word?"

"How should I not?" said the Lady. "I am in love. In love, do you understand? Yes, now I love truly."

"You mean," said the Tragedian, "You mean—you did not love me truly in the old days?"

"Only in a poor sort of way," she answered. "I have asked you to forgive me. There was a little real love in it. But what we called love down there was mostly the craving to be loved. In the main I loved you for my own sake: because I needed you."

"And now!" said the Tragedian with a hackneyed gesture of despair. "Now, you need me no more?"

"But of course not!" said the Lady; and her smile made me wonder how both the phantoms could refrain from crying out with joy.

"What needs could I have," she said, "now that I have all? I am full now, not empty. I am in Love Himself, not lonely. Strong, not weak. You shall be the same. Come and see. We shall have no need for one another now: we can begin to love truly."

As you begin the *Gospel App* discipleship curriculum, ask yourself this question, "What is the true nature of your love, your very best love? Is it this high? Is it this glorious?" Have you chosen to love God, or chosen to believe that He loves you? Good, but are you living day-to-day *in* that palpable mysterious love? There is a difference. Consider Jesus' words:

"Love the Lord your God with all your heart and with all your soul and with all your mind and with all your strength.' The second is this: 'Love your neighbor as yourself.' There is no commandment greater than these." (Mark 12:30-31 NIV)

Do you suspect that He is referring to your very best love on your very best day? Or do you now see, if you were honest, that He is speaking of a much higher, as Lewis coins it, "less needy" love—i.e., His love in and through you? The answer is obvious in this passage from John.

"A new command I give you: Love one another. As I have loved you, so you must love one another. By this all men will know that you are my disciples, if you love one another." (John 13:34-35 NIV)

Have you felt such higher "other" love toward you recently? Are you *in* such a vast dynamic love? Have you ever been? Have you been filled with such an alien love for *others* recently? It would be noticeable. That's what Jesus is saying.

Others will notice the difference and comment to you that you must be a follower of Jesus Christ. What would such a love possibly look like that would be so noticeable and such a distraction to others? Would it be a miraculous mysterious loving attitude and motivation toward your family? Friends? Co-workers? Neighbors? That irritating neighbor? Some enemy of yours?

Jesus is expecting something more oozing from your pores, something strikingly other than your best love on your best day. It is so strikingly *other* that others—and I assume this would include those *others* who are not even Jesus-followers—will see clear evidence and conclude that you must be of Jesus; for what other explanation could there possibly be? That is Jesus' present expectation of you and me—in Him—in His love. He would have us frequently access His ongoing heavenly love for us and for others through us, yesterday, today, and tomorrow. It should be noticeable.

How can you access such a love today? Answer. All you need is need. If you attempt to try harder, to discipline yourself to do more loving acts, to be more patient with people—to choose to not be critical—no doubt people will appreciate the difference.

But Jesus makes us aware of the present possibility of so much more, even more than you can do on your own, on your very best day. In order to love, really love, others, friends, family neighbors, allies and enemies, you need His love in and through you. Until, then, like Lewis' *Solid Spirit* testifies, you are too *needy* to love others.

> *"But Jesus makes us aware of the present possibility of so much more—even more than you can do on your own, on your very best day. In order to love, really love, others, friends, family neighbors, allies and enemies, you need His love in and through you. Until, then, like Lewis' Solid Spirit testifies, you are too needy to love others."*

Whew, there, it has been said. You cannot love your enemy. It is not in you. You can't even really love your friends. Not with your love. Your love is too needy. Your love is far more conditional than you really want to admit.

Good news. There is such a love. It is accessible by faith, now, from God, through the Holy Spirit in you. How can you get such a love? Easy, just receive it (Eph 3:14-21).

Most Christians, at one time or another, live in a fantasy world that looks and feels more like Lewis' shadowy earth unaware of the glorious foothills of the Heavenly Mountains. In

Introduction

such a shadowy stupor, we *ghosts* are yet convinced that if we only try harder, we will achieve heavenly goals. We imagine to ourselves that if we were only better prepared, or would just concentrate more we would *do* Jesus.

That is the arrogance and ignorance of the late "What Would Jesus Do?" campaign. On the surface it was well meaning. Of course that would be good for us to lean into. Unfortunately, the results were most often very short term.

There is a better way to begin to accomplish WWJD. We can humbly admit that the core desire to *want* to do what Jesus would do is not in us—that is—in our hapless *free* will and deceptive flesh. Our will is way too compromised, our flesh too self-focused. So much of our actions are actually subconscious reactionary behaviors that bypass our brain at light speed (more on this topic in Chapter 3).

To love my family, I need the "love that surpasses knowledge" (Eph 3:19) regularly. Likewise, I need an externally accessed justice in order to forgive the person that hurt me so much, even if he or she does it again, seventy-times seven times? Honestly, lets face it, I can't—I will not. There is a heavenly power that I can, by faith, access that will empower me to want to forgive. First, I must *need*.

How can I "be perfect, even as my heavenly Father is perfect" (Matt 5:48)? Or are you one of those Type A earth-bound wraiths in denial? Truth be told, you cannot be perfect, or to be biblically specific, you *will* not be perfect—at least not by your own will and strength. Your will, and mine, is far too compromised.

We often have little idea how much in need of God's external power we are on an ongoing basis. The good news is that our upside potential is very high, if only we would just *need*. *The Gospel App* is built on this foundation.

The Spirit MacDonald says of the earth confined wraiths, the "damned souls" but could just as easily speak functionally about us:

> "For a damned soul is nearly nothing: it is shrunk, shut up in itself. Good beats upon the damned incessantly as sound waves beat on the ears of the deaf, but they cannot receive it. Their fists are clenched, their teeth are clenched, their eyes fast shut. First they will not, in the end they cannot, open their hands for gifts, or their mouths for food, or their eyes to see."

Lewis' protagonist asks MacDonald, *"Then no one can ever reach them?"* That's the right question isn't it? Are we children of God who are functionally existing as if we were only living *ghosts*, reachable? Of course. The *Gospel App* is for those whose eyes are even slightly cracked open to see their real need.

Are you one of those people who dare jump on the Heaven-bound uber-bus? Are you realizing that your experience of the Christian walk has not lived up to its potential—nowhere near. Are you realizing, even a little bit, that your experience of Christ is far less than you had hoped for when you signed up? Are you realizing that the fruit of this earthly place—even the best fruit is far from truly satisfying? Even the hits are no more than the hit that an alcoholic gets from a shot of cheap well-bourbon.

Are you among the few Jesus-followers that would dare admit that you can relate to those tragic underachieving dwellers in Lewis' abode of the damned? Those consigned to that place are truly substance-less shadows on the wall, never real persons, never what they could have been, only lonely wanderers, empty *ghosts*—or better, troubled wraiths with no hope in their own efforts to ever improve their lot. Is this you?

If you say to yourself, "Well that is all good perhaps, but isn't this a bit harsh? A bit too much? I mean, sure, my Christian walk has struggled, my prayer life is in the toilet, my quiet time is truly that: quiet. I have given up on finding a church that meets my expectations and needs, but I am still a Jesus-follower. After all, He died for my sins right?"

Well God bless you, yes. Jesus' death was a tremendous gift for you—and took you to a place where you could never go on your own. And when you finally pass on, you will be pleased and surprised just how wonderful Jesus' death was and what it accomplished for you.

But why wait? The foothills of the Heavenly Kingdom are yours to begin to explore now. Jesus has already purchased your full entry fee. Heaven for you begins now, proclaims Lewis. Why live as an underachiever in this world—lazily waiting for the high joys of the next? If you are a Spirit-filled child of God, these earth-born paths are for you the Valley of the Shadow of *Life*. Why dismiss the power of the Holy Spirit to give you joy now, today, and tomorrow and the next day? What arguments are you making to yourself to *not* avail yourself of life now?

Spirit MacDonald brilliantly describes the pitiful nature of the shadowy damned earth, those who dwell in the Valley of the Shadow of Death.

> "And yet all loneliness, angers, hatreds, envies and itchings that it contains, if rolled into one single experience and put into the scale against the least moment of the joy that is felt by the least in Heaven, would have no weight that could be registered at all. Bad cannot succeed even in being bad as truly as good is good. If all Hell's miseries together entered the consciousness of yon wee yellow bird on the bough there, they would be swallowed up without trace, as if one drop of ink had been dropped into that Great Ocean to which your terrestrial Pacific itself is only a molecule."

Have you have come to believe again, for perhaps just a moment, that there is such a mind-bending joy that is, at least partially, accessible by you now for the asking. You have not because you ask not, the Apostle James once said (James 4:2). It's simple.

"But what of the poor Ghosts who never get into the omnibus at all?"

Introduction

"Everyone who wishes it does. Never fear. There are only two kinds of people in the end: those who say to God, 'Thy will be done,' and those to whom God says, in the end, 'Thy will be done.' All that are in Hell, choose it. Without that self-choice there could be no Hell. No soul that seriously and constantly desires joy will ever miss it. Those who seek find. To those who knock it is opened."

So hop on the *Gospel App* bus. There is plenty of room. Buckle up, you are in for the ride of a lifetime. Bring your fears, doubts, shame and unresolved guilt. All you need is need.

It is such stunning good news. Discipleship is poorly described as the effort required to become more like Jesus. Better, discipleship is a function of becoming more *dependent* upon Jesus' Spirit. These are two different strategies.

The Gospel App Shape

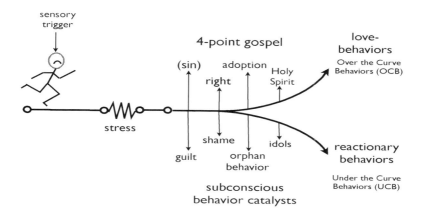

Chapter 1: Quick Overview of the Gospel App

> *For the sinful nature desires what is contrary to the Spirit, and the Spirit what is contrary to the sinful nature. They are in conflict with each other, so that you do not do what you want.*
> —Galatians 5:17 NIV

> *For when we were controlled by the sinful nature, the sinful passions aroused by the law were at work in our bodies, so that we bore fruit for death. But now, by dying to what once bound us, we have been released from the law so that we serve in the new way of the Spirit, and not in the old way of the written code. What shall we say, then? Is the law sin? Certainly not! Indeed I would not have known what sin was except through the law. or I would not have known what coveting really was if the law had not said, "Do not covet." But sin, seizing the opportunity afforded by the commandment, produced in me every kind of covetous desire. For apart from law, sin is dead.*
> —Romans 7:5-8 NIV

The *Gospel App* is meant to be a simple, easy-to-remember shape that any Christian can use to equip themselves to receive and apply the singular Gospel of Christ to their own lives. It portrays in clear, relevant, and simple terminology the real Gospel for real people with real issues living in the real world.

The goal is for the disciple of Christ to grow more and more dependent upon Him and His Spirit in them. Paul models such dependence in his letter to the Ephesians. In Eph 3:14-21, he speaks of the Christian's ongoing need for alien, external power from God, available upon the asking, to even *know* that they are loved by God—much less to be empowered toward any Kingdom effort on behalf of others.

The implication is that this "exercise of need" is designed to be a daily occurrence. Disciple, you need regular power available solely from God to do anything remotely Christ-like today, tomorrow or the next day. This *need* is at the very core foundation of the *Gospel App* discipleship curriculum. This need will remain until you and I enter the Heavenly portals. Step One? Be more and more aware of your ongoing need.

The Gospel App Shape Overview

Let's begin by looking at the twelve core elements of the *Gospel App*. Consider the Stick figure on the previous page. We will call him (or her), Stick. Stick is just going about his daily routine. A good Christian, Stick wakes up in the morning asking that God would bless him today. He meant it, he thinks—at least as much as he means it when he prays every morning—well most mornings, at least most mornings when he remembers.

So he is on the freeway, running a tad bit late to work, and he notices that his gas tank is almost empty. He growls to himself, "Didn't I tell my wife to fill the car up yesterday? I did, I know I did. Well apparently she forgot! Now I am for sure going to be late."

He pulls into the usual 7-11 to get gas, but realizes that he left his wallet on the bed stand. He has no money to pay for gas. Though it is hard for him to logically blame his wife for that, he divines a way. Now he's going to be *really* late—and clearly it is *her* fault.

When he finally arrives at work, after going all the way back home, yelling at his wife for being self-centered and uncaring, getting back in traffic, being cut off at least a dozen times—"Don't they know that I am late to work?"—He arrives at work only to be criticized for being late again.

It's a pretty bad day for Stick. You may argue that these are all "First World problems," but nevertheless for Stick, these stimulus triggers cause him a great deal of stress. He is observably not oozing with love for his wife in these moments—much less other folk who he runs into. He is out of sync with God, or more specifically with the Spirit of God within him. What is the present Gospel for Stick?

Sensory Trigger and Stress

Using this tale of woe as a backdrop, let us consider the first two elements of the *Gospel App* (See figure on pg. 17). The *Sensory Trigger* is anything that initiates a reaction. It could be a criticism. It could be someone cutting you off in traffic.

Triggers are everywhere and happen all the time. The *Trigger* initiates *Stress*. *Stress* is a normal chemical reaction ignited within your brain which necessitates subconscious fight, flight or freeze responses (More on this in Chapter 3).

Let me tell you a little bit about stressed-Stick. The *Trigger* initiated a powerful toxic cocktail of chemicals to be released into his brain which suppressed his normal ability to concentrate, his short-term memory, and his ability to think rationally and compassionately toward others.

No matter how mature a Christian Stick may be, in these post-*Stress* moments, he is naturally engorged with self-focused motivations and will be largely indifferent to others. He is not evil—at least not necessarily—just normal-Stick-under-*Stress*. If the *Stress* is large enough or chronic enough, Stick will further react as if his very survival is at stake. He may do or say something that he will deeply regret later.

Under the Curve Behaviors (UCB)

It is almost inevitable, all other things equal, that such a chemically motivated transformation would drive Stick to habitual reactionary behaviors or better *Under the Curve Behaviors (UCB)*.

His wife noticed Stick's reaction to her well-meaning oversight of not filling the car with gas. It was not an act of deliberate contempt or abuse on her part most likely. It was a mistake, a well-meaning and unfortunate mistake. If an outsider would judge Stick's overreaction, they might think that something really horrible had gone down. In Stick's chemically suppressed reality, post-stress cocktail, it was that large to him. In his *altered* state, it felt *very* hurtful. He no doubt reasoned that such disrespect required a reaction of equal magnitude.

> "What were you thinking? Didn't you remember me asking you to fill the car up yesterday? This is not the first time. This is a habit. You just don't care if I am late. You don't care about my reputation at work. All you care about is you and your stuff. We will talk more tonight. Now I have to go get gas and be even more late."

Every Stick is unique, yet it not uncommon for Sticks to truly emote with rage, anger, guilt trips, overstatements, blameshifting, or accusations of others—much chemically initiated. These *Under the Curve Behaviors (UCB)* are quite common, largely subconscious, and deeply habitual

Stick will most likely calm down eventually. He will slowly come to see and perhaps admit that he overreacted. Hopefully. Then the next time—it will happen again. It is chemical, subconscious, habitual, and bypasses the rational will at light speed.

Everyone has this reactionary capacity. Not everyone has the same *Trigger* or same level of reaction. A person who has known significant trauma in their lives will typically have hair *Triggers* and will trip into fear-based reactionary behaviors quickly and linger there much longer. Others require more significant or sustained *Triggers* to "flip their lids".[7]

> *"...this reactionary behavior is not controlled by our reason, our hapless, bypassed "free" wills, or our usual desire to do good."*

Having said that, this is normal human behavior; subconscious, chemically motivated, and empowered. It usually happens at virtual light speed and by-passes our frontal cortex where rational and strategic functions happen.

In other words, this reactionary behavior is not controlled by our reason, our hapless, bypassed "free" wills, or our usual desire to do good.

Most of our daily confrontations and relational issues are related to such *Triggered* chemicals within us blown on by the world, flesh, and the Devil (Eph 6:12).

Remember the commercial where someone is frying an egg. The voice over says, "This is your brain!" The next scene is the egg all scrambled. "And this is your brain on drugs!" Your reactionary behavior is your brain on drugs, in this case natural chemicals that are "good" not "evil," nevertheless they can ignite horrific, uncaring, self-centered destructive behavior. Paul's testimony of such struggle is brilliantly put:

> "For I don't understand what I am doing. For I do not do what I want—instead, I do what I hate. But if I do what I don't want, I agree that the law is good. But now it is no longer me doing it, but sin that lives in me. For I know that nothing good lives in me, that is, in my flesh. For I want to do the good, but I cannot do it. For I do not do the good I want, but I do the very evil I do not want! Now if I do what I do not want, it is no longer me doing it but sin that lives in me." (Rom 7:15-20 NIV)

The Flesh and Under the Curve Behavior (UCB)

Biblically, this *Under the Curve Reactionary Behavior (UCB)* happens within the realm of our flesh. This is the place where such knee jerk reactions and habitual behaviors like addictions are not only at home, they are coddled and encouraged. There, in my flesh, the focus is solely on myself and my own well-being. To put it another way, there in my flesh is an all-too natural disinterest in the well-being of others.

---

7 For more info on this topic see Seigel, Dan (2012). Flipping Your Lids: A Scientific Explanation [Video] Retrieved March 15, 2015, from https://www.youtube.com/watch?v=G0T_2N-NoC68.

Quick Overview

This flesh is the realm where statements like, "Well, I would certainly never do anything like that!" are regularly mocked and dismantled one self-righteous plank at a time (Matt 7:1-5).

Reactionary behaviors happen as long as the flesh, our sinful nature, exists. Our sinful nature remains viable until we die. Paul refers to these reactionary behaviors as the "works of the flesh."

> "For the sinful nature desires what is contrary to the Spirit, and the Spirit what is contrary to the sinful nature. They are in conflict with each other, so that you do not do what you want…The acts of the sinful nature are obvious: sexual immorality, impurity and debauchery; idolatry and witchcraft; hatred, discord, jealousy, fits of rage, selfish ambition, dissensions, factions and envy; drunkenness, orgies, and the like." (Gal 5:17-21 NIV)

For our purposes, don't think of these as necessarily evil. They can be. They can lead to evil *UCB*, but they are best understood as normal human reactionary behavior, the stuff that occurs on any given day when the myriad of daily *Triggers* happen. It is sad to say that these are our go-to strategies, or better, our go-to knee-jerk reactions.

We have developed clear predictable go-to habitual *UCBs* that we enter into without thinking. It is what we do when we are triggered.

Here's the point, unchecked and unchallenged, these are the behaviors that will "happen" in your life. They don't work—not really. They may offer you short-term benefits, short term hits. At the end of the day, these reactionary behaviors will leave you dissatisfied, still riddled with shame and guilt, still needing to find value somewhere, your relationships left stressed and in tatters.

Triggers will happen. *Stress* will also happen. All things equal, when they do, you will react the way that you have always reacted—for days, months, years and decades before. If you really objectively consider your *UCBs* you would never have done it that way. But, it is you.

In addition to your brain's reactionary system, the flesh has four identifiable powers or catalysts that exacerbate *UCBs*, if unaddressed and unchallenged.

The Flesh's Catalysts

Guilt (Chapter 5). *Guilt* is that normal human emotional power surge, largely subconscious that happens when Stick has done something wrong or has not done something right.

Most of us will do whatever we need to in order to get rid of the *Guilt* quickly. To that end, we will either consciously or subconsciously launch into a multitude of predictable human reactionary behaviors: defensiveness, excuses, justification, blameshifting, arguing, deflecting, anger or rage at the one who is making you feel *guilty*. The implied hope of such *UCBs* is to relieve us of *Guilt*.

They rarely, if ever, work.

Shame (Chapters 6-7). *Shame* is that normal human emotional power surge often accompanying *Guilt*. Whatever went down, Stick now wonders if something is just wrong with him or her. Not only didn't he do right, there is something not right with him. He wonders if he is a loser, unlovable, not worthy of success, honor, relationship, or compliments. The normal person doesn't deal with *Shame* well and will often enter into habitually conditioned *UCBs* (largely subconscious) to diminish the harsh feelings related to *Shame*. *Shame* is very powerful, and as we will see, very antithetical to the Gospel.

Orphan Behavior (Chapter 8). Imagine being an *Orphan* living on an impoverished inner-city street. The *Orphan's* sense of well-being, identity, name, validation, reputation, and value is dependent upon what he or she does or does not do in the next fifteen minutes. All the *Orphan* knows is that if he or she is going to not only survive but feel good again about themselves and their lot in life, they are going to have to make something happen urgently on their own.

Our flesh is riddled with such *Orphan* intentionality and fears. It is orphanness that will generally tend to take charge and not wait for God or anyone else. Here is the voice of our inner-*Orphan*. "It's all up to me. If I am going to get rid of this nasty guilt and shame, I must do something quick. If I am going to feel significance, security, and belonging, it is all up to me."

Like the other downward power vectors, this *Orphan* catalyst is largely subconscious and reactionary. None of us sit down and plan out a strategy to recover our reputations in the moment. Rather, over the years each of us has a set of habitual *UCBs* that surge out of us, some very self-focused and even destructive. We are each conditioned over years to react in a predictable way. We may make excuses, employ blameshifting strategies, generate creative explanations and justifications. We may quickly change the topic. We may even attack the one who "attacked" us.

Orphan, there are infinite *UCBs* at your disposal. They are strategically designed to serve you, not anyone else. You will even use others if you have to in order to feel good about yourself again. These reactions are not necessarily evil. You will no doubt feel justified when you do them. Otherwise, why would you keep doing them?

Idols (Chapter 9). *Idols* are anything you run to in order to feel right (or less wrong) about yourself—other than God. They measure you and tell you that you are "right," Or they measure you and tell you "you are not right." Either way, you run to your particular set of *Idols* needing them to measure and define you.

Anything can be idols. Your emotions can be idols. The law can be an *Idol*. Religion, work, hobbies, recreation, drugs, alcohol, relationships—all can be *Idols*. What others think of you can be an *Idol*. What you think that others think about you can be an *Idol*. Ultimately, you are a slave to whoever or whatever you have made your *Idol*. *Idols* are everywhere; we all have hundreds, maybe thousands. They do not really work. They have no power or capability to give you the significance, belonging, and security that you so deeply desire. They may offer short-term, often powerful hits, but Jesus purchased so much more for you.

The Gospel and Over the Curve Behavior (OCB)

Unchecked, or better put, unchallenged, the four under the curve catalysts will always lead to self-centered, unsatisfying, behaviors: "works of the flesh." These *UCBs* are the normal status quo of all humanity. Jesus came to rescue us from this present evil age motivations and actions (Gal 1:4).

The *Gospel App* has divided the vast singular Gospel of Christ into four categories of upward motivating powers that can be received and applied by faith to our daily *Stressors*.

(Sin)(Chapter 5). First, in the *Gospel App* diagram at the beginning of the Chapter, note that *Guilt* is juxtaposed by another opposite power: *(sin)*. The word "sin" within parentheses is the *Gospel App's* way of communicating God's *removal* of my sin (mathematical use of parentheses to denote subtraction from an account) and consequences of sin (in particular, guilt) from my legal account.

Child of God, Jesus died for all of your crimes against Heaven, humanity and creation 2000 years ago. It is finished. All of the times that you sought your identity, value, worth, justice, and wholeness from any source other than the Triune God—i.e., sin—have been perfectly addressed.

So now when you become aware of *Guilt* within you for some sin, you can look up and by faith, through the power of the Holy Spirit in you, run to God, be reminded and assured that the very crime was objectively and legally dealt with two millennia ago. You were found guilty and sentenced to death. Jesus, mysteriously and wonderfully, took your death on Himself. It is finished. Theologians use the term *justification* to describe this aspect of Jesus' work on your behalf.

What about the *Guilt* that you feel? Do you wonder if God is still judging you? Holding you in contempt due to something that you did or didn't do? Do you feel that God is being critical toward you? It cannot be so. He was already infinitely critical toward Jesus on your behalf. It would be an unjust double jeopardy for God to re-judge you for the same crime. So hold up your guilt-ridden hands and proclaim your need for God to intervene on your behalf to remove its power over you now (Heb 10:1-4).

In the *Gospel App* shape, *(Sin)* is a power that is rightly positioned opposite of *Guilt*. The more that you really comprehend what Jesus did related to your crimes against God, creation, and humanity, the less power *Guilt* will have over you day-to-day. Or to put it a different way, if you are guilt-ridden today, the only real cure is to have the truth of *(Sin)* hammered into your head over and over. Receive it and be assured of its immediate validity for you now.

Right (Chapters 6-7). Justification has two aspects: *(Sin)* and *Right*. A second mysterious miracle occurred for you as a result of Jesus' life and death. Jesus, we know, was perfectly faithful to the Father. He did everything that the Father desired for him to do. More than that, He wanted to. His motivations were in line with the Father's. If He didn't already have it, that level of perfect faithfulness would have earned Jesus all of the undying unwavering love of the Father for all time. Often we Christians toss around the phrase "unconditional love" to describe God's love for His children. Nothing could be further from the truth.

God's love is *perfectly* conditional. God's blessings are *perfectly* conditional (Dt 28:1-15). It is just that Jesus has already accomplished all of the conditions *perfectly* on your behalf. Because of Jesus' work alone, the Law is your best friend.

Why is that good news for you? In a surprise move, Jesus' record of 100% faithfulness is put into your resume. His record of perfect righteousness, His faithfulness, and everything that such perfection earned, is now mysteriously yours. This *imputed* alien *Right* means that now you *must* be treated as if you had been perfectly faithful.

Upshot? You get all of the heavenly blessings due Jesus. They are irrevocably yours, including all of the love and favor of God. God can't love you any more or any less than He does right now. You can't mess it up, no matter what you do or what has been done to you. It may not feel like it, but that is a lie.

God the Father irrevocably loves you as much as He loves His own Son, as much as the Son loves the Father. This Gospel power is the opposite of the flesh's power of *Shame*.

In the *Gospel App* shape, *Right* is presented as a vector in the opposite direction from *Shame*. The more you experientially comprehend the *Righteousness* of Jesus is yours, the less power that your innate *Shame* will have over you.

Or to put it a different way, if you are ashamed of something that you have done, or not done, something that was done to you, or you did to someone else, the only real cure is to remember and be assured afresh that Jesus' *Right* is now yours, along with the love, adoration, honor, and benevolence of God that such *Right* earns. Note how the Psalmist in Psalm 31 juxtaposes the powerful human experience of *Shame* with the *Righteousness* of God. They are natural enemies.

> In you, O LORD, I have taken refuge; let me never be put to *Shame*; deliver me in your *Righteousness*. (Psalm 31:1 NIV)

Adoption (Chapter 8). In addition to your two-fold justification, you have been given the greatest honor that you can *never* earn. *Adoption* refers to the declaration by God, strictly as a result of Jesus life and death, that you are a full-card-carrying son or daughter of the Lord of Lords, a prince or princess in the Heavenly

Kingdom. That honored position can never be removed from you. There are no possible grounds for demotions. The honor is yours, strictly because of what Jesus has already accomplished.

This is a hard one for people who have been deeply wounded. It may feel like the perpetrator robbed you of honor. But they cannot. Your honor as an *Adopted* child of God remains untarnished and undiminished. This is great news, isn't it?

This power is placed opposite of *Orphan* behavior in the *Gospel App* shape. The *Orphan* must find significance, security, and belonging by means of their own independent daily actions on the street. No matter how hard *Orphans* work at it, they will never achieve the significance, security, and belonging that they desire down deep. Their efforts may help, may slightly diminish that nagging murmur of discontent that they feel, but it is only temporary. Paul puts it colorfully. "All creation groans" (Rom 8:19-22).

Good news. The more that you remember and are powerfully and presently assured that you have already received the significance, security, and belonging that you have longed for in Christ—i.e., the power of your *Adoption*—the less you will feel the need to live like an *Orphan*—striving to find crumbs of each in this fallen stingy world.

Or to put it a different way, if you have been looking for significance, security, and belonging today in all the wrong places and still feel alone, diminished, unloved, marginalized, and a lone-wolf outsider, the only real cure is to run to God, hold up your empty and scarred *Orphan* hands and plead that God would make you be assured of your *Adoption* now.

Holy Spirit (Chapter 9). Fourth, you have also been given first-hand access to the *Holy Spirit*—including His fruit, power, fullness, and gifts.

There is no such thing as a child of God who is without the *Spirit* of God. On the other hand, believers may have varying present *awareness* and *empowerment* of the *Holy Spirit* in them.

Paul teaches that Jesus-Followers at the same time mysteriously *have* the *Holy Spirit* and can be presently filled with *more* of Him (Eph 5:18). The difference between the two should be palpable and observable.

One of the fruit of the *Holy Spirit* in you is "faith," perhaps the most critical of the fruit absolutely required in re-conditioning your reactionary behavior into love behaviors. Consider faith that "secret working"[8] from God capable of making you experientially assured that the first three aspects of the Gospel are really true for you *now*. It is this enigmatic and necessary gift of the *Holy Spirit*, available to you anytime you desire that alone can assure you how much the Father, Son and Spirit adore you, right now, as you are.

In the *Gospel App* shape, all that is entailed by the gift of the *Holy Spirit* in

---

8. John Calvin, Calvin: Institutes of the Christian Religion 1, trans. Ford Lewis Battles, ed. John T. McNeill, vol. 20 of Library of Christian Classics (Philadelphia: Westminster Press, 1960), 537.

you is presented as a vector in the opposite direction from *Idols*. The more you access the power of the *Holy Spirit* in you, the less urgency you will feel to run to other lesser measuring entities to define who you are. You will feel like a son or daughter of the living God, filled to the full with the fullness of God (Eph 3:14-21).

> *"If this doctrine is lost, then the whole knowledge of truth, life and salvation is also lost and gone. On the other hand, if this doctrine flourishes, then all good things flourish; religion, the true service of God, the glory of God, the right knowledge of all things and states of life."*
>
> **Martin Luther**

Or to put it a different way, if people, emotions, success, or anything other than the *Holy Spirit* in you is defining who you are, and you are aware how unsatisfying that really is, run to God and ask to be filled afresh, to the full with His *Holy Spirit*, and your *Idols* will have far less influence on you today. Having "more" of the *Holy Spirit* is the only real competition for *Idolatry*.

Our hope is that we can recondition ourselves to access by faith through the Holy Spirit in us these four powerful aspects of the Gospel resulting in observable pro-social Over-the-Curve Behaviors.

Under the powerful sway of such Gospel power, Stick might react differently to his deteriorating situation. He may be filled with God's love for his wife. He may feel new devotion and compassion for her and her busy schedule. He may desire to forgive her for her oversight. He may need the approval of his co-workers that comes from being on time *less*. He may have patience and long-suffering with other drivers. He may laugh at his own weaknesses and misfortunes. He may think of other people more.

It is possible. The Gospel is that powerful. Our role is simple. We are invited to begin to recondition ourselves to receive and apply the Gospel on a regular basis so that when *Triggers*, *Stress*, *Guilt*, *Shame*, *Orphan Behaviors* and *Idols* happen, there are competing powers that kick in to resist our flesh. This is the goal of the *Gospel App* discipleship curriculum.

How are we to lean into the four aspects of the Gospel more and more so that not only will we feel more loved and adored by God, but we will also begin to feel more love for others?

Martin Luther referred to the four aspects of the *Gospel App* collectively as the "doctrine of received righteousness."

"Therefore it is very necessary, that this doctrine be kept in continual practice and public exercise; read and heard over and over again. And no matter how well we think that we know it, or have learned it, the devil, our adversary, continually wanders about seeking to devour us. He is not dead. Likewise, our flesh and old man is still very much alive. To make our situation even more dangerous, we are aggravated and oppressed on every side by all kinds of temptations. So you see why I say again that this doctrine of received righteousness can never be taught, urged, and repeated enough. If this doctrine is lost, then the whole knowledge of truth, life and salvation is also lost and gone. On the other hand, if this doctrine flourishes, then all good things flourish; religion, the true service of God, the glory of God, the right knowledge of all things and states of life."

By faith, ask. Each aspect of the Gospel is a supernatural predator to each of the four aspects of the flesh. Paul calls the behaviors empowered by the Spirit, "fruit of the Spirit."

"But the fruit of the Spirit is love, joy, peace, patience, kindness, goodness, faithfulness, gentleness and self-control. Against such things there is no law. Those who belong to Christ Jesus have crucified the sinful nature with its passions and desires. Since we live by the Spirit, let us keep in step with the Spirit." (Gal 5:22-25 NIV)

The Gospel simply put

With the *Gospel App* now banged in your frontal cortex at least once, may I remind you of the stunning Gospel of Jesus Christ for you? You know all of this, or probably do. I am honored to merely remind you of the height, width, length and breadth of the singular Gospel again.

First, Jesus died for all of your sins, every single crime against God creation and humanity. Your trial was accomplished two thousand years ago. You were found to be guilty, the sentence was death, and someone else died in your place. Justice's demands are perfectly satisfied forever.

What does this first aspect of the Gospel, *(Sin)* mean to you today? Eternity in heaven—sure. But it also means that you never ever need to fear God judging you again. He will not. You have already been judged. You never have to fear that judgmental or even critical look in the eyes of God. He never rolls his eyes at you. Ever.

Second, you have been imputed with the righteousness of Jesus. What does that mean? Jesus did everything right. As a reward, he earned all of the heavenly blessings. Seems only fair. What is *not* fair is that His record of right has been imputed to you. It is now shoved into your resume, your unauthorized biography. That means that you have all of the heavenly blessings that He earned. God loves you as much as He loves His Son. He actually likes you. He can't love or like you any more or any less. You cannot change that no matter what you do, or do not do. This unchanging love is yours no matter whether you feel it right now or not. Huge!

Third, you have been irreversibly adopted as the son or daughter of the

King of Kings. You have already been given the greatest honor in all the universe that you can *never* earn. Again, nothing can change that, ever. You are a prince or princess in the Kingdom of God. Your greatest accomplishment, you didn't even accomplish. Granted it is a bit counter-cultural for many in North America to receive such a grossly undeserved honor. Nevertheless, it is already yours no matter what you do or don't do from this point onward.

Lastly, you have been given access to the *Holy Spirit*: including His endless supply of heavenly power, the fullness of God, fruit, love joy, peace, patience, and perhaps the most helpful in your day to day walk: *faith*. *Faith* is the power that alone can make you really believe this stuff is true for you right now. *Faith* is powerful enough to make you believe it is true even after stress hits you and all internal chemical hell breaks loose. That's when God's power is clearly necessary.

If you are a Spirit-filled follower of Jesus, these four powers—and they are clearly *powers*—are already yours by decree, and can be personally experienced today by faith through the *Holy Spirit* in you. You may access all four Gospel powers any day, anytime.

If you begin to make a habit of accessing the four powers by faith regularly during the day—or in Luther's term, hammering the Gospel into your head daily—and in particular when life's many *Triggers* and *Stress* happen, you should begin to see and feel a difference.

If this makes sense, take a few minutes right now and meditate on the four over-the-curve aspects of the Gospel. Ask God to make them experientially yours right now. Write down any thoughts. We will hit this multiple times on your journey. It does no good to just rationally *know* about these four powers. These powers will only affect your life, your reactionary behavior, if they are received and applied regularly—today, tomorrow, and the day after that.

Chapter 2- The Overwhelming Power of the Flesh

Since we live by the Spirit, let us keep in step with the Spirit.
—Galatians 5:25 NIV

You may be one who still feels sufficient for the task of loving others as Jesus did.

> "Do I really need all of this shape-stuff? I am not convinced that I don't just need to try harder, make more resolutions, get into an accountability group—just do it!"

God bless you. Please, just bookmark this page and put the book in a safe accessible place, so when you do fail again to live up to Jesus-standards—or even your standards, you can return here and begin this safe powerful journey. To put it differently, when you again realize your desperate need, welcome back to the *Gospel App*.

Why is it so hard to get along? Why does such a utopian peace seem so far from our grasp? Certainly peace is a rational goal for both the Israelis and

Palestinians? Wouldn't peaceful co-existence be mutually beneficial?[9] Of course. Then why is such an end so elusive?

What about Democrats and Republicans actually working across the aisle to accomplish important things that serve the greater population—that would be beneficial to both constituencies?

Why can't husbands and wives—who deeply loved each other once—process hurts and wounds—find some loving resolution? Didn't they say, and really mean, "In sickness or in health?"

Why so many denominations? According to one count, there are over twelve hundred denominations in the US alone. I understand why some exist apart. There are essentials of our faith that are worth dividing over—yet doesn't twelve hundred seem excessive?

Jesus taught that the outwardly observable core of His church would be love for others, particularly love for enemies (Luke 6:35). The will of the Father that Jesus embraced in the garden was to die for his enemies. We find such radical other-oriented movements very difficult, almost impossible. What is wrong with this picture?

The Dawn of the Planet of the Apes

I learn so much from movies. Some do a great job helping me understand real life—in this case, the real-life insurmountable difficulties in working through issues.

The context of "The Dawn of the Planet of the Apes?" There are two *Homo Sapien* tribes, separated, afraid, and highly suspicious of each other. There has been a history of mistreatment between the two. Each is traumatized, living out of deeply conditioned fear-behavior. Neither community would sacrifice for the other—both are focused on their own safety and survival.

If you asked the apes how it got to this point, they could tell you. It wasn't that long ago that the apes had been kidnapped, held against their will in small unsanitary laboratory cages. They would use the emotion-laden term *torture*. The older apes remember it as if it were yesterday.

That's why they are afraid of humans. Humans experimented upon them, mistreated them, and then hunted them down when they escaped captivity. Hopes of peace are unlikely while such wounds remain unaddressed and unhealed. They will not—they cannot trust the humans.

Even when they aren't thinking about the humans, in their gut, at a subconscious level anger rages, an us-versus-them mentality, and terror thinking of

---

9. According to a recent Rand study, peace between Israel and Palestine could lead to huge financial benefits. Israel would gain $123 billion over a decade, while Palestine would gain $50 billion. On the other hand failure to do anything would lead to losses of $250 billion and $46 billion, respectively. See http://airport-exposed.beforeitsnews.com/middle-east/2015/06/%E2%80%8Bpeace-between-israel-palestine-could-bring-173bn-in-economic-benefits-study-2491126.html.

ever being made vulnerable to humans again. Racism abounds in such a context. "We are good and right, they are evil." "We are the oppressed victims here. They are the oppressors. Nobody ever changes their stripes, ever."

"We must attack them before they attack us!"

"From humans, Koba learned to hate."

"Humans lie."

Just beneath the surface, the apes are living with inflammatory hair-triggers that even a minimal stress could ignite into severe and immediate under the curve reactionary behaviors.

The humans—only a few miles away—are also very tribal—also self-absorbed and worried about their own survival. The few that remain are the lone survivors of the Simian Flu that destroyed the majority of the human race—including many of their families and friends. They are hunkered down in a highly armed and protected enclosure in San Francisco, not really free, constantly worried that the race may still perish, and afraid of catching the Simian Flu.

Like the apes, humans are terrified and will kill to protect the survivors.

"It's us versus them."

"They're apes, man. They don't understand what you are saying."

"Are you telling me that you don't get sick to your stomach when you see them?"

"We are survivors, they are animals."

At the beginning of the movie there appeared to be some minute hope for peace and relationship between the two *tribes*, yet it only took a single misunderstanding to ignite the unresolved, subconscious fear, anger, rage, bigotry, and racism which roiled just beneath the surface.

No doubt none of the movie viewers were in any way surprised that it only took a microscopic incident to inflame the bone-dry kindling, which would inevitably lead to another incident, which would inevitably lead to another—and another.

And so it happened. In a mere three days, there was an unavoidable war between the apes and humans. Everyone in the theater knew it was inevitable. Those who instigated the war felt fully justified—perfectly righteous.

What Happened?

Everyone who is even the slightest bit honest understands what happened. Each of us could admit scores of times when we unnecessarily overreacted, causing harm to people that we were supposed to love, resulting in fractures to relationships that were supposed to be not only permanent but honoring to others.

Many times, reactions just seem to happen. It wasn't like you thought about the plan, the strategy, weighed the consequences, or prayed for wisdom first.

I can recall cases where I was just as surprised as the object of my vitriol at what came out of my mouth and how it surged, carried forward by a deluge of rage that was out of line, over the top, and not justifiable at all. When I look back on such episodes I would testify that it was not really me. That is just not how I talk, not how I process events. I am usually cool and collected—in a word, reasonable.

Sometimes after the moment, I want to immediately take it back, get a re-do, but the hair-trigger rage had a mind of its own. That's not totally accurate. The rage did come from me, from somewhere deep inside of me. Paul calls that place—that power source—the flesh or the sinful nature (Gal 5:19-21). The flesh is indeed me, but mysteriously seems to have its own mind, and do its own thing. It rarely asks for my opinion, as it stealthily bypasses my brain. I don't seem to have a muscle group that controls my flesh. Do you? Unfortunately, this is normal fallen human behavior. Christians are not immune from the flesh's vast overreach.

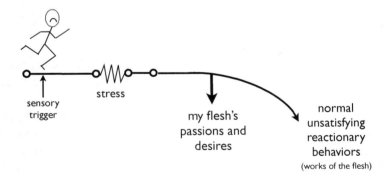

Ekporeuomai Happens

Jesus, the master teacher put His artistic, yet earthy spin to this very same phenomenon. In Mark 7, He is answering the very transparent criticisms of the Pharisees and the teachers of the law concerning what is it that makes a human unclean; that is, unacceptable to God and subject to His disfavor.

In their tradition, eating etiquette was one of the hotly contested battleground issues. Jesus blows the lid off of their hypocritical blind spots related to

God's standards of acceptability.

> "Again Jesus called the crowd to him and said, 'Listen to me, everyone, and understand this. Nothing outside a man can make him 'unclean' by going into him. Rather, it is what comes out of a man that makes him 'unclean.'" After he had left the crowd and entered the house, his disciples asked him about this parable. 'Are you so dull?' he asked. 'Don't you see that nothing that enters a man from the outside can make him 'unclean'? For it doesn't go into his heart but into his stomach, and then out of his body.' (In saying this, Jesus declared all foods 'clean.') He went on: 'What comes out of a man is what makes him 'unclean.' For from within, out of men's hearts, come evil thoughts, sexual immorality, theft, murder, adultery, greed, malice, deceit, lewdness, envy, slander, arrogance and folly. All these evils come from inside and make a man 'unclean.'" (Mark 7:14-23 NIV)

In a bit of populist's humor, Jesus begins with a point of universal agreement. Defecation makes a human unclean. No doubt a discernible chuckle erupted from the crowd. Jesus uses the word *ekporeuomai*, a "going forth from one area to another" as a euphemism for the normal day-to-day bowel movements that makes the person unclean.

In the Law, there were clear regulations that governed the out-of-camp location of the toilet (Dt. 23:9, 12-13). Everyone got the metaphor. You go out of the camp to relieve yourself. If not, the entire camp becomes unclean.

Jesus then swings the euphemism back onto the self-righteous legalists. Just like everyone's bowels daily soil them, there is another regular bowel movement common to all humanity—that also soils us all.

This *ekporeuomai* is the exiting from our "heart."

In those days, the heart was considered to be the composite of a person's mind, will, and emotions. Jesus imagines the "heart" as just another colon, working by internal reflexes out of the control of the mind and will.

What does my heart defecate? Nothing good—evil thoughts, sexual immorality, theft, murder, adultery, greed, malice, deceit, lewdness, envy, slander, arrogance and folly—expurgates out of my heart. Its release of these toxins to the world is as regular a function as going to the bathroom. No point denying it Pharisees.

Jesus brilliantly imagines our heart as another excrement-producing colon. What triggers the defecation process? What manages and controls it? Not clear. *Ekporeuomai* happens. Yet everyone does it. Everyone.

Paul calls that source of these toxic behaviors, the *flesh* or the *sinful nature (Gr: sarx)*. Paul imagines the flesh as a power source within all of us that unilaterally launches us on a trajectory of selfishness and immorality, even if our mind doesn't want to go there. There is energy behind it, often overwhelming energy. Here is Paul's abbreviated list of the *ekporeuomai* of the flesh from Eugene Peterson's The Message.

"It is obvious what kind of life develops out of trying to get your own way all the time: repetitive, loveless, cheap sex; a stinking accumulation of mental and emotional garbage; frenzied and joyless grabs for happiness; trinket gods; magic-show religion; paranoid loneliness; cutthroat competition; all-consuming-yet-never-satisfied wants; a brutal temper; an impotence to love or be loved; divided homes and divided lives; small-minded and lopsided pursuits; the vicious habit of depersonalizing everyone into a rival; uncontrolled and uncontrollable addictions; ugly parodies of community. I could go on." (Gal 5:19-21 MSG)

Is it fair to observe that this is one area of Christian discipleship where most of us have fallen short? Have we failed to manage our own heart's public bowel movements or even dared to regularly be willing to consider the possibility that we have a severe digestive problem unaware?

Why might that be? Perhaps we have failed to understand that our *flesh* is largely autonomic and so functions below our level of consciousness. Imagine other autonomic functions such as heart rate, breathing, swallowing, or perspiration. The flesh simply does its own thing. So the works of the sinful nature *happen*. We are relatively passive carriers, controlled by our sinful nature's passions and desires.

For when we were controlled by the sinful nature, the sinful passions aroused by the law were at work in our bodies, so that we bore fruit for death. (Rom 7:5)

These *death-fruit* are often not rational, or objective, or even under our control. As far as I can tell, they have no discernible off-on switch. There are no known muscle groups that are effective enough to make a dent in them. And they rage on all the time, 24/7. They are not tidal fluctuations, they are tidal waves. When they are triggered, and the triggers happen all the time in life, they will rise up and more than not, swallow all other lesser motivations to do good underneath their muscular crashing waves. Thus, in this light consider:

- What is it that drives a normally respectable human being into hours and hours of looking at pornography on their computer—when they know it is destructive and would have just minutes before said they were committed to a life free of porn?
- What is it that makes that very same person boldly lie to their spouse over and over again?
- What is it that happens within a normally calm, thoughtful mother that would cause her to erupt in rage at her crying child—even knowing at a

certain level in her psyche that her reaction was ugly and harmful to the child that she loves?
- What is it that causes a rational normally calm person to become part of an angry mob bent on destruction and mayhem?
- What is it that gets into that person who is so emotionally concerned about their weight that they purge themselves after every meal—knowing rationally that they will never be satisfied?
- What is it that causes a once loving married couple who swore to stay in love until "death due them part," to flood their relationship with erratic and often irrational rage and accusations?
- What is it that happens to once happy children that changes them into prodigals?
- Why is forgiveness so hard to nail down?
- Why are divorce rates among conservative Christians significantly higher than for other faith groups, higher than Atheists and Agnostics experience?[10]
- Where does that impatience come from that causes such arguments again and again?
- How can we explain the reportedly 1200 *Christian* denominations in the US alone?
- What gets into nominally intelligent folk that ignites them into clearly dangerous even destructive behaviors (cutting, drugs, radical sexualization, gangs, etc.)?

The answers to the questions above are probably complex and context specific. There are no doubt emotional and physical dysfunctions involved, childhood trauma issues, chemical addictions, and the like, at work.

How many of your choices of behavior, responses, things said or not said, done or not done were intentionally made by your conscious will this week? Ten percent? Twenty percent? My guess is that for the most part, those choices that you would most like to take back, the ones that got you in the most trouble, that led to the biggest arguments, were in the non-conscious—or subconscious category. These behavioral choices bypassed your conscious brain and therefore bypassed your will. Your most insensitive comments, the most self-centered and destructive behaviors were not even put before your reason (or will) for consideration at all. Listen to Paul's similar struggle.

"I do not understand what I do. For what I want to do I do not do, but what I hate I do. And if I do what I do not want to do, I agree that the law is good. As it is, it is no longer I myself who do it, but it is sin living in me. I know that

---

10. "Christians Are More Likely to Experience Divorce Than Are Non-Christians," Barna Research Group, December 21, 1999, http://www.barna.org/. Barna no longer has this report online. However, a review of the report is at: http://www.adherents.com/.

nothing good lives in me, that is, in my sinful nature. For I have the desire to do what is good, but I cannot carry it out. For what I do is not the good I want to do; no, the evil I do not want to do—this I keep on doing. Now if I do what I do not want to do, it is no longer I who do it, but it is sin living in me that does it. So I find this law at work: When I want to do good, evil is right there with me. For in my inner being I delight in God's law; but I see another law at work in the members of my body, waging war against the law of my mind and making me a prisoner of the law of sin at work within my members. What a wretched man I am! Who will rescue me from this body of death?" (Rom 7:15-24 NIV)

Paul, I totally get it. Me too. There are times, usually after an argument—or having been criticized—that I fall into a bit of depression ruminating how I was treated unfairly or with disrespect. It may take a while for me to come to my senses and cry out to God,

"What is wrong with me? I want to love my neighbors, my spouse, my kids, my parents and my congregation. I am committed to it. I read a lot about it. I go to conferences to learn how. I pray for You to help me accomplish it, and yet it takes something as simple as a single word, or a single look—or the absence of either—for my flesh to override all other instructions and do its own thing—to do my own thing."

So why is peace so difficult? Why can't or won't the Israelis and Palestinians find a mutually beneficial path to a healthy co-existence? Why can't or won't Democrats and Republicans work for the common good? Why can't the apes and humans figure something out? It would make sense to make these things happen. That's the problem in a nutshell. Our frontal lobes are not in control over our autonomic reactionary systems. Our problem is that we are far more out of control than we want to ever imagine. *Ekporeuomai* happens! We need a rescuer. We need a redeemer.

We are invested in thinking that with enough education, intentionality, and effort, my will can overcome my flesh and gut out OCB (over the curve behavior). This is reflected in most recent philosophies of Christian discipleship. A good discipleship program is one designed to teach me how to be more *like* Jesus. With the truths learned in the program, with enough accountability, and consistent intentionality I can choose to love others, including my enemies. I can choose to not take that next drink, or cut myself, or slide into the next pornographic site. I can choose to not participate in gossip, even the good stuff. I can choose to forgive. I can do it. Nike lives today in Evangelicalism. Most discipleship courses are geared toward equipping the participants into stepping up to be more like Jesus, to choose to do what Jesus would do.

Honestly, it sounds right and even Biblical. But what if good discipleship opens my eyes to really see again that I am far more needy than I want to admit? I realize that I cannot, on my own, love my friends, much less my enemies—not to the level that Christ commands. What if I cannot really forgive? Or repent when I hurt others? What if true Biblical discipleship is learning to be more *dependent* upon Christ and His Spirit? This is a very different philosophical approach to discipleship.

Truth? Our flesh, the source of constant downward powers noted in the *Gospel App*, hammers us 24/7, most of it subconscious, by-passing our cognitive will.

> *"We are invested in thinking that with enough education, intentionality, and effort, my will can overcome my flesh and gut out OCB. The underlying philosophy is that good discipleship makes me more like Jesus. But what if good discipleship makes me more dependent upon Jesus? Those are two different philosophical approaches."*

We have a choice. Our flesh does indeed have a powerful enemy, more than capable to neuter its effect upon us, our motivations, and actions on a daily basis. That enemy is none other than the Holy Spirit who indwells believers.

> "For the sinful nature desires what is contrary to the Spirit, and the Spirit what is contrary to the sinful nature. They are in conflict with each other, so that you do not do what you want." (Gal 5:17 NIV)

The person who is indeed tired of being dragged to and fro, from reactionary behavior to reactionary behavior may run to God in their need and ask for more of the Holy Spirit's power now. We are not left as orphans in our day-to-day struggle. We are called to participate. But our participation is largely passive. We can recognize our need to run by faith to the Holy Spirit in us and ask for power in order to be loved and to love others. To the extent that I own and admit my lack of capacity to wage war against my flesh, I can by faith access counter-agents to my flesh's onslaught. I can receive and apply the four aspects of the Gospel and be changed, be loved, and be filled with the capacity to want to love others. All I need is need.

Louis Pasteur's Discovery of Our Invisible Need

It wasn't until the end of the 19th century that the research of Robert Koch and Louis Pasteur discovered that the main source of cholera and other bacteria diseases was contaminated drinking water. Before that time, an untold number of people throughout the world had died unaware by merely doing something reasonable and good—drinking water. In their defense, before Koch and Pasteur's

The Gospel App Shape

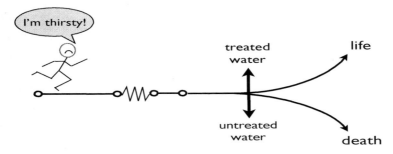

research no one knew that water could be the source of an *invisible* bacteria that could kill.

The visitors to the 1893 Chicago's World Columbian Exposition had a choice. In Chicago of the late 19th century, most people got their drinking water from a pumping station set-up in Lake Michigan which regularly included raw sewage runoff from the nearby Chicago River. Engineers tried to fix the situation a couple of decades before by reversing the river's flow. Unfortunately prolonged rains, not uncommon to Chicago, "routinely caused the Chicago River to regress and again pour dead cats and fecal matter into the lake, and in such volume that tendrils of black water reached all the way to the intake cribs of the city water system."[11]

For the first time in history visitors to the 1893 Exposition had a choice. William S. MacHarg designed and constructed a water purification plant on the grounds of Exposition and made clean, disease free-water available to all attendees. For the first time in history, people could choose to drink water from the lake that was no doubt riddled with deadly bacteria, or, they could choose to drink clean sterilized water from MacHarg's new purification plant—free.

To put it another way, visitors to the Exhibition could continue to do what they had always done, quench their thirst by drinking contaminated Lake Michigan water that could lead to their death, or they could admit their need and choose to quench their thirst with clean water.

Would you be surprised to hear that many attendees still chose to drink Lake Michigan water? Habits and conditioned behaviors are very hard to admit, much less break. All they needed was need, and most of them could not admit need.

Child of God, now you know. All you need is need.

---

11 Erik Larson, The Devil in the White City (New York: Vintage Books, 2003), 138.

Chapter 3: The Testimony of Science

I do not understand what I do. For what I want to do I do not do, but what I hate I do.
And if I do what I do not want to do, I agree that the law is good.
As it is, it is no longer I myself who do it, but it is sin living in me.
I know that nothing good lives in me, that is, in my sinful nature.
For I have the desire to do what is good, but I cannot carry it out.
For what I do is not the good I want to do; no, the evil I do not want to do—
this I keep on doing. Now if I do what I do not want to do,
it is no longer I who do it, but it is sin living in me that does it.
So I find this law at work: When I want to do good, evil is right there with me.
—Romans 7:15-21 NIV

Many of our ongoing behaviors are not managed by our reason or our will. Actions such as walking, swallowing, or breathing are generally accomplished by our autonomic response system. These are things that you do not think about doing. Your autonomic system just manages it on its own.

Likewise, there is another system in your body that is designed to respond to stress, to danger, and to survival. When this system kicks in, chemicals are released that are designed to specifically shut down your cognitive capacity. In a phrase, it shuts down your *will*.

Hear this. Most of your bad behavior is initiated by this system—completely bypassing your will.

The Chemistry of Stress[12]

According to recent science, stress triggers activate the hypothalamic-pituitary-adrenal HPA axis system, releasing catecholamines—neurotransmitters such as dopamine, norepinephrine, and epinephrine. These chemicals activate the amygdala and suppress concentration, short-term memory, rational thought, and inhibition. To put it in more laymen terminology, when a stressor happens, your body automatically releases a chemical cocktail that shuts down your reason and lasts for a time. All that's left are the fight, flight, or freeze reactions.

Almost everyone is familiar with the physical symptoms of intense stress: racing heart, sweaty palms, butterfly-filled stomach. Yet there are dramatic subconscious changes as well.

In layman's terms, after a stress trigger, your body shifts away from rational control. You no longer can thoughtfully strategize your next measured appropriate loving response. Your body shifts into reactionary gear, the domain of your flesh with its powerful passions and desires.

Also, in this new mode, your former inhibitions ("I will never respond that way") are virtually gone. Your will as well as your capacity to think and reason are chemically suppressed. This suppression of normal brain responses allows you to engage fully in fight or flight without your brain intruding.

This chemical reaction can be very good to your community. A lifeguard, in response to the chemicals surging within her, may heroically plunge into shark-filled water to save a swimmer, and afterwards say she "went on auto-pilot." Without the chemicals, she may have paused to consider all of the dangers and consequences of such a heroic act. That split second could have been fatal to the helpless victim. But ripped with the newly injected chemicals, she didn't react logically; she just rushed into a place that was quite dangerous to her own well-being.

Why? She experienced an extreme stress trigger imagining the swimmer in imminent danger, and that information entered her brain with such force and urgency that it bypassed her prefrontal cortex and other higher brain centers. Instead, it went directly into her limbic system, the seat of her emotion and reactionary behaviors. Essentially, her reason and judgment temporarily went off-line. Scientists understand that under such a stress trigger, the instinct and survival center of her brain, located in the brain stem, took over. It is this part of the brain that controls all autonomous bodily functions such as heartbeats and breathing. She literally reacts sub-consciously.

The Stress Model

One of the research sources that informed the *Gospel App* is the Stress Model

---

12. For those who are following along with the *Gospel App* discipleship curriculum, the material below comes from the "Going Beyond: Stress" article in Week 2 (pages 22-25).

developed by Forbes and Post.[13] They are working with traumatized children, attempting to better understand the things that drive behaviors such as hitting, bullying, fighting, arguing, lying, stealing, defiance, and other hostilities.

They counsel that if we understand what motivates such destructive behaviors, we can work toward changing it at a root level one child at a time. We can, with enough patience and consistent effort, re-condition even the most traumatized child. Very encouraging work.

Examples of Childhood Trauma?

Almost all of the children diagnosed with reactive attachment disorder, oppositional-defiant disorder, bipolar, and other such psychiatric diagnoses have experienced some degree of trauma in their lifetimes. Here is a partial list of events that will produce trauma in people. Without minimizing the horrific trauma that many have to live with, it is fair to observe that no one escapes trauma. No one lives trauma-free.

> Physical Abuse
> Sexual Abuse
> Emotional Abuse
> Neglect
> Adoption
> Foster Care
> Surrogacy
> Frequent Moves
> Automobile Accident
> Pre and Perinatal Birth Trauma
> Loss of Caregiver
> Depressed Parental Care
> Prolonged Experiences of Unmet Needs
> Bullying
> Domestic Violence
> Medical Trauma

Forbes and Post observe,

> "When a child experiences trauma, the child's ability to develop a sufficient regulatory system is severely compromised…For these children, their internal survival mechanisms then become activated, dedicating all the body's resources to remain alert in 'survival mode.' These children perceive the world as threatening…They operate from a paradigm of fear to ensure their safety and

13. Heather Forbes and Bryan Post, Beyond Consequences Logic and Control: A Love-Based Approach to Helping Children with Severe Behaviors (Boulder, Co.: BCI, 2009), 3-10.

security. Hence, what is seen is an overly stressed-out child who has difficulty interacting in relationships, who struggles to behave in a loving way, who quite often cannot think clearly, and who swings back and forth in his emotional states...[A] child of trauma is essentially a scared child—a stressed child living out of a primal, survival mode in order to maintain his existence."[14]

Of course, this also applies to adults that you know, maybe some close to you—perhaps even you last week. It has certainly applied to me. "The vast majority of negative behavior arises from an unconscious, fear-based state of stress."

Am I saying that our wills are less free than we want to imagine? The *Gospel App* assumes that whether our wills are free or not, bad behavior happens all the same. It is science. It is largely subconscious reactionary behavior that has been conditioned over years and decades. Can we push back against the loop? Of course. We will look at our hope of reacting differently in a future chapter.

Before we do that, let's go a bit deeper to better understand our need. We each have four "memory states" that when activated direct and dominate our behavior. *Cognitive memory* is where we store all data and facts. Then there is *Emotional memory*. For every data stored in cognitive memory, there is an emotion attached. That's why everyone remembers where they were when they heard about 9/11. Not only were facts involved, but there was an emotional significance to them. *Motor memory* is the body's automatic pilot; why you can walk without thinking about each step.

Last, there is *State memory*.

> "[State] is responsible for processing raw data from the environment and sending immediate signals of fight, flee, or freeze...When a person reaches a heightened state of stress, this state memory gets triggered, thereby releasing all previous relevant memories into the upper memory banks. In this manner, when a child with a traumatic history is confronted with a situation which heightens his level of stress, the child's state memory becomes activated. Rapid-fire communications to the other areas of the memory system are initiated, informing the child that the current situation is threatening. Additionally, this rapid-fire communication is also telling the child that this situation is almost guaranteed to work out like a previously stored experience...In other words, in the midst of a stressful or perceived threatening event, this child...is likely to believe deep within the very cells of his body that if he doesn't convince this person right now that he is telling the truth, then in all likelihood he might be abused, abandoned, neglected, or worse—he might die! Faced with this looming threat, this child is most likely going to tell a lie, despite his understanding at the cognitive level that lies are morally and ethically wrong. In the midst of stress and threat, the state memory can

---

14. Forbes and Post, Beyond Consequences, 5.

completely override all other memory states."[15]

Do you remember times when you were caught, busted, embarrassed, your safety or safety of those close to you threatened, and immediately this surge of fight, flight or freeze took over and you lied, or covered-up, or accused, or attacked. In the moment, you said or did something that was hardly "rational" or well thought out—but at the time, it made perfect sense to you. In the end it was destructive.

Husbands and wives can live out of this heightened traumatized state for long periods of time; a heightened awareness of the dangers when the other is in the room or in the conversation. The discussions between them, as seen by outside observers, can be wildly destructive, things overstated, colored to protect the speaker, exaggerated, accusing, hardly any sense that they are working on behalf of the relationship. A survival mentality has kicked in.

Entire churches can be caught in a fear state. When this traumatization occurs, the heightened awareness of stress and fear responses is palpable. Normally caring Christians fall into vulgar reactionary behaviors that have no place in the church: knee jerk criticism, paranoia, consumeristic demands, fears, fatigue, and looking for persons or persons to blame. In some circles, such churches are referred to as "pastor-killing" churches. In reality, they are traumatized and are acting out of their corporate State memories where there is no peace, no trust, no submitting to the process until a re-conditioning takes place.

> "In times of stress, our thinking processes become confused and distorted. Not only are we not thinking clearly when stressed, but the very framework of our understanding is challenged in that moment by what we can believe and remember…This means that when children act out in a disturbing manner, they are not only confused and overwhelmed, but they cannot even remember what is safe and what is not safe…Traditionally, we have seen children as being willfully disobedient and manipulative. This stems from a belief that in the moments of being disobedient and manipulative, they also have full cognitive and conscious awareness of their actions. Unfortunately for both parents and children, this could not be further from the truth. Stress constricts their thinking, distorts their perspective, and short-circuits their short-term memory."[16]

In these times, we are working out of subconscious motivations that by-pass our reason. Our will, free or not, is bypassed—often a hapless observer.

Here's the point. If it's true for children, it is even truer for adults, because our State memory is jammed packed with memories of previous stress and trauma. Some of us more and some of us less. Many of us have experienced loss

15. Forbes and Post, Beyond Consequences, 6-7.
16. Forbes and Post, Beyond Consequences, 4.

of loved ones, emotionally distant or critical parents, emotional, physical, spiritual abuse, etc. We are left traumatized.

When incoming perceptions bypass the rational part of the brain, a normally good person may act without the regulating effect of wisdom, memory or judgment. At that moment, logic is simply unavailable, and reactions are based on raw emotions, passions, and desires. To speak Biblically, under these situations, the person's flesh is in almost sovereign control.

This is perhaps a large reason why so many who have been beat-up or disappointed by organized churches become angry and very critical of "church" and "God." They are more than likely reacting from their very powerful State Memory. Their anger, criticism, and fears seem right and rational to them. But likely the cognitive memory is bypassed. What they are *feeling* is very emotional, not so much rational, though they will quickly *rationalize* the feeling, justifying it. In the end, their actions hardly measure up to the height, width, length and depth of the love of Christ for others.

Couples, both loaded with triggers from their childhood, adolescence and teen years, are ready to fire—sometimes after seemingly innocuous triggers: money, sex, use of authority, things said, things not said, a time of year (Valentines, anniversary of loss)—and boom—a rush of stress and emotion that leads to immediate survival instincts, defensive mechanisms, excuses, exaggerations, lies, fears, boundaries, arguments, flight or fight.

How is all of this practical to you? This is also the very same mental process that occurs when pornography just happens to pop up on your computer. It is a powerful surge of desires and passions that subconsciously overwhelms your normal hatred of this action.

This is the same mental process that occurs during many crimes of passion. You were committed to faithfulness to your husband or wife, but something happened within you and every fiber of your being justified adultery.

This is the same mental process that ignited over-the-top anger and rage in response to some very small insignificant trigger.

It is the very same mental process that caused you to feel unreasonable and inexplicable fear and anxiety last week. Depression. Revenge. Your inability to let go of unforgiveness. The former process initiates such hatred of that other person or people group.

If you are Republican, you may have become subconsciously conditioned to mistrust all Democrats. If you are a Democrat, to dislike all Republicans.

Where does that paranoid loneliness happen, where you in unreasonable anger and fear push away the very person that moments before you wanted close—and then blame them for your loneliness?

When incoming perceptions bypass the rational part of the brain, a normally good person may act without the regulating effect of wisdom, memory or judgment. At that moment, logic is simply unavailable, and reactions are based on raw emotions, passions, and desires. To speak Biblically, under these situations, the person's flesh is almost in sovereign control.

Doesn't this explain why you reacted the way you did? Your flesh, fed by natural chemicals that suppress your reason and inhibitions, then does what it does best. You find yourself choosing to do and say things that you would never do or say under normal conditions when you were more rational and objective.

In the *Gospel App*, this reaction to normal stress-triggers is represented by the downward vector. Don't mistake this. This Under the Curve Behavior (UCB) is normal fallen human behavior. It may or may not be harmful and destructive. It does not need to be labeled *evil* necessarily—but could be. It is normal.

It is what humans—Christians and non-Christians alike—do apart from a present intervention of other power from God. It may even appear to be good, and certainly you may argue that your reaction felt justifiable, but it is not loving. To clarify, it is not loving of others—only self.

Augustine of Hippo is credited with describing all sin by the Latin phrase "*Incurvatus in se*" which literally means the self-turned/curved inward on oneself. *Incurvatus in se* is a good image of the bent of the flesh toward self-centeredness. Jesus taught that all of the law can be summed up in two outward movements, loving God and loving others. *Incurvatus in se* is the opposite of both. To one degree or another all sin is a result of a life lived *inward* for self rather than *outward* for God and others.

In his lecture on Romans, Luther expands:

> "Our nature, by the corruption of the first sin, [being] so deeply curved in on itself that it not only bends the best gifts of God towards itself and enjoys them (as is plain in the works-righteous and hypocrites), or rather even uses God himself in order to attain these gifts, but it also fails to realize that it so wickedly, curvedly, and viciously seeks all things, even God, for its own sake."[17]

The *Gospel App* imagines a different outcome available to Christians: the Over the Curve Behavior (OCB) represented by an alternative upward vector.

This outcome is also driven by a power that can motivate different desires and passions within hapless Stick: God's very desires and passions.

Filled with these alien heavenly motivations, Stick would experience new

---

17. Martin Luther, Lectures on Romans, quoted in Mark Johnston, Saving God: Religion After Idolatry, (Princeton: Princeton University Press, 2009), 88.

desires directionally opposite the normal longings of his or her flesh. Stick would even be passionately motivated to love the "other" with this passionate love of God. It is pretty clear that the outcome behaviors will be quite different, right?

OCB doesn't just happen in the life of a Christian. In fact, it is the UCB that is inevitable. UCB happens. To see more OCB in his or her life, the Christian disciple must lean into accessing the passions and desires of God constantly to have any real hope of experiencing such love-behaviors.

> *"In the Gospel App, this reaction to normal stress-triggers is represented by the downward vector. Don't mistake this. This under-the-curve-behavior (UCB) is normal fallen human behavior. It may or not be harmful and destructive. It does not need to be labeled "evil" necessarily—but could be. It is normal."*

"So I say, live by the Spirit, and you will not gratify the desires of the sinful nature. For the sinful nature desires what is contrary to the Spirit, and the Spirit what is contrary to the sinful nature. They are in conflict with each other, so that you do not do what you want...Those who belong to Christ Jesus have crucified the sinful nature with its passions and desires. Since we live by the Spirit, let us keep in step with the Spirit. Let us not become conceited, provoking and envying each other." (Gal 5:16-26 NIV)

The *Gospel App* is a helpful tool to guide the Christian disciple how to access the power of the Spirit on a daily basis so that he or she will witness more OCB. The fruit of this practice will be noticeable. The *Gospel App* is designed to be that much-needed tool for this generation's ever-growing hope to make and become miraculous disciples.

Chapter 4: The Power of the Spirit

So I say, live by the Spirit, and you will not gratify the desires of the sinful nature. For the sinful nature desires what is contrary to the Spirit, and the Spirit what is contrary to the sinful nature. They are in conflict with each other, so that you do not do what you want. But if you are led by the Spirit, you are not under law. The acts of the sinful nature are obvious: sexual immorality, impurity and debauchery; idolatry and witchcraft; hatred, discord, jealousy, fits of rage, selfish ambition, dissensions, factions and envy; drunkenness, orgies, and the like. I warn you, as I did before, that those who live like this will not inherit the kingdom of God. But the fruit of the Spirit is love, joy, peace, patience, kindness, goodness, faithfulness, gentleness and self-control. Against such things there is no law. Those who belong to Christ Jesus have crucified the sinful nature with its passions and desires. Since we live by the Spirit, let us keep in step with the Spirit.
—Galatians 5:16-25 NIV

At any point in your Christian life, were you told that you need to daily, perhaps hourly, ask God to give you His power before you can even begin to feel like a real Christian? I do not recall being instructed that my daily personal experience of being loved by Jesus involved dependence by me. I think that I assumed that when I became a Christian, I got it all. Now it was up to me to work hard to live right, to do what Jesus would do. I couldn't have been more wrong.

I suppose you could argue that I was partly right. I am commanded to love my neighbors. In fact, I am supposed to *want* to love my neighbors. I am commanded to go and make disciples. I am supposed to *want* to go and make disciples. All true.

Yet what I missed—and this is a critical aspect of the Kingdom of God's inner workings is that I can't do it. Whew, I said it. The dirty little secret of my day-to-day walking with Jesus. I can't do it. My situation is even worse than that. I don't *want* to do it—otherwise I would. Right? This is just Logic 101.

> *"I have really good news for you. You were never designed to do the Christian life on your own strength. Your flesh—even though redeemed—is still far too powerful and deceptive. You will not win. Your record will be hit or miss at best—hardly miraculous."*

I have really good news for you. You were never designed to do the Christian life in your own strength. Your flesh, even though redeemed, is still far too powerful and deceptive. You will not win. Your record will be hit or miss at best, hardly miraculous. Hardly superior. Few people will see your good works and be converted in your wake. That seems to be what Jesus had in mind when he told the first disciple:

> "In the same way, let your light shine before men, that they may see your good deeds and praise your Father in heaven." (Matt 5:16 NIV)

How good would your "good deeds" really have to be for a non-Christian to respond by praising the God in whom they previously didn't believe? We don't have the right stuff to make such a miracle happen.

What you and I need is power—a power beyond our human capabilities. Did you know that God has assured you that such power is yours upon asking (Eph 3:14-21)? All you need is need.

Letter to the Ephesians

Though scholars differ, the letter to the church in Ephesus was likely penned by the Apostle Paul in the early 60's CE. That would place the letter some three decades after Jesus death and resurrection. Many suggest that it was written by Paul while he was imprisoned, perhaps in Rome. He probably wrote his epistles to the Colossians and Philemon just before this letter.

What do we know about the church in Ephesus? Not very much. We can surmise that it was still a mere church plant, made up of recently converted Jews and Gentiles. We know that it was in a very secular, very pagan cosmopolitan city, one of the largest and most diverse in the Roman Empire.

Ephesus was the gate city between the eastern and western portions of the Empire. Humanly speaking, it was a critical place for the Church to be. It was also in a precarious position with lots of alternative conversations to the Christian

Gospel—and no doubt many who viscerally opposed the Gospel of Christ.

We do have a unique look into how well they did their calling. Perhaps thirty or so years later, there is another missive written by the Apostle John to this very same church. It is a scathing rebuke from Christ Himself.

> "To the angel of the church in Ephesus write: These are the words of Him who holds the seven stars in his right hand and walks among the seven golden lampstands: I know your deeds, your hard work and your perseverance. I know that you cannot tolerate wicked men, that you have tested those who claim to be apostles but are not, and have found them false. You have persevered and have endured hardships for my name, and have not grown weary. Yet I hold this against you: You have forsaken your first love. Remember the height from which you have fallen! Repent and do the things you did at first. If you do not repent, I will come to you and remove your lampstand from its place." (Rev 2:1-5 NIV)

It would appear that the church in Ephesus did everything right, except the one thing that truly made a difference. They forsook their first love. The Greek word for forsaken is better understood to be released themselves from— i.e., separated from. This is damning.

They implicitly, probably over many years, concluded that they could do church on their own and didn't explicitly "need" Jesus' love anymore. I am sure that this was not a decision that they came to overnight. My guess is that they were far more well-meaning than that. The shift away from needing Jesus' love probably happened over months and years. It just happened while they were unaware, like the erosion of a rock by years and years of the sun's heat and the incessant blowing of the wind. Here is how the discussion might have gone down.

Jesus: Go and make disciples everywhere you work and play.

Ephesians: We will do that.

Jesus: But first come to Me. Receive My love for you and My love for your neighbors.

Ephesians: No need Master. We've got this. We have the writings. We have listened to a bunch of sermons on loving others. We choose to love them. We will get back to You if we really, really need Your help.

Paul seemed to have a premonition of this danger as he penned these verses in Ephesians 3.

"For this reason I kneel before the Father, from whom his whole family in heaven and on earth derives its name. I pray that out of his glorious riches he may strengthen you with power through his Spirit in your inner being, so that Christ may dwell in your hearts through faith." (Eph 3:14-17 NIV)

What would you write to a church that you suspect is going to go through hell on earth? Imagine that you are Paul, in jail, perhaps suspecting that you will never get out alive. You are thinking about some of the churches that you started and feel responsible for them. You know how the world persecutes those of your faith. You are in jail—helpless, humanly speaking. You naturally would be concerned about those fragile gatherings that are teetering in very dangerous places—like Ephesus.

Paper is rare, ink is expensive. You don't have a lot of space to communicate all of the things that you want to say. So you distill your instructions into as few words as possible. Your hope, if they only adhere to these instructions, is that the church will thrive. Keep it simple, succinct, and applicable.

"So let me pray just one thing for you my spiritual children…"

If it were me, I might be tempted to pray for God's protection, for the rise of solid leadership, new growth in converts, capital to find suitable meeting space, a qualified worship leader, etc. All good things. Yet Paul knows that what these baby Christians need—the one thing—is not among those *good* things. They are secondary—good but not critical.

What did the Apostle Paul believe to be so critical to Christians then and today? They needed power. Not just any self-generated effort, but a specific power that comes not from within men and women, their strength of character and will; rather an external enigmatic power that is sourced singularly from God's celestial riches alone. Paul is emphatic. This is the first of three references to "power" (two Greek words "*exischuo*" and "*dunamis*") in this short section of the epistle.

Paul understood that we all-too-human Jesus-followers need ongoing power to live a vibrant Christian life. Did you know that you need ongoing power to love your spouse, your children, and your neighbors? Or to obey your parent, to not bicker, or to not be jealous? Or to even know experientially that you are a child of God right now. You know it in your head that you were adopted. But in

> *"What did the Apostle Paul believe to be so critical to Christians then and today? They need power. Not just any self-generated effort, but a specific power that comes not from within men and women, their strength of character and will; an external enigmatic power that is sourced singularly from God's celestial riches alone."*

your "inner being" (Eph 3:16) where you desperately want to know that God isn't judging you *today* and is perfectly pleased with you today, you still need ongoing power.

On the surface, it would appear that Paul has lost his theological mind. He writes that we Christians need an external power, all the time, "so that Christ may dwell in your hearts through faith." Wait a minute. He already dwells in my heart. That is one of the great gifts of my salvation. That is irrevocable. I can't mess it up, right?

Yes and no. Here is the way to unravel this Gordian knot. All Christians have the Spirit of Christ dwelling in them—but not all Christians are presently *experiencing* the Spirit of Christ in them as real. To experience, to know beyond comprehension the Spirit of Jesus within you, you will need power right now. Could this be why you may have not really experienced the joy of your salvation, the powerful presence of the Holy Spirit in your life for days, weeks or months?

Paul continues:

> "And I pray that you, being rooted and established in love, may have power, together with all the saints, to grasp how wide and long and high and deep is the love of Christ, and to know this love that surpasses knowledge — that you may be filled to the measure of all the fullness of God..."(Eph 3:17-19 NIV)

In his determination that we not miss this, Paul repeats our need for present power. This time, he links the need for power with our experience or non-experience of the vastness of Jesus love.

The word for "grasp" here is interesting. *Katalambano* typically means to requisition for oneself, to appropriate intentionally and by force, or to seize. It could have been translated to "take down by force." Imagine a military siege being laid around a huge impregnable city. The conquering army is using all its technology and strategy to find a weakness in the walls and to take advantage of it. Then once the walls are breached, the army goes door-to-door to conquer the city. Surprisingly in this case, the city is not an enemy city, but the height, width, length and depth of the love of Christ.

That is a shocking choice of words by Paul. As above, I thought that I had all of the love of Jesus when I was saved. Why in the world would I be required to lay siege around the love of Christ, as if it was a fortified city that strives to resist my embrace?

So do I or don't I have Christ's love? Yes and no. It is true. I am the recipient of all of the love of Jesus. He can't love me any more or any less than He does right now. I can do nothing to diminish that love—no matter what I do, or do not do, no matter how I feel or don't feel. Yet, as in the above case, I may not be experiencing that love right now. Instead I may feel shame, guilt, unbelief—very powerful works of the flesh that may overwhelm my present experience of the love of Christ for me.

How long has it been since you really felt the height, width, length and depth of the love of Christ for you? Hours? Days? Weeks? Years? Paul says that you haven't been experiencing such a love because you haven't been asking for power from God first. When was the last time you asked for power from God in order to feel how much He loves you?

> *"That is a shocking choice of words by Paul. As above, I thought that I had all of the love of Jesus when I was saved. Why in the world would I be required to lay siege around the love of Christ, as if it was a fortified city that strives to resist my embrace?"*

The Ephesians were just like us in some ways. Within them was a contrary power that bred shame and guilt—a lying feeling that doubted that God loved them. Also, as in each of them, there was that subconscious power that motivated them to be independent—orphans—to imagine that they were good-to-go on their own.

Do you see the difference between us *having* the love of Christ, based upon Jesus' work alone, and us *experiencing* the love of Christ, by faith, through the Holy Spirit today?

The Ephesians forgot that the way to regain this love was to run to God every day and ask, by faith, through the Holy Spirit in them, for "His glorious riches" (Eph 3:14).

Instead, they no doubt did what we tend to do. We look for that love or some reasonable substitute in all the wrong places. We can be amazingly persistent attempting to earn love from God that we long forgot cannot be earned. The love of Christ is already perfectly given to those who did not earn it.

Notice also that there is no limit put on the love of Christ. It is as high, wide, long and deep as can be. It is not limited to feeling God's vast perfect love for me.

It must also include experiencing God's love for others as well. Husbands, how are you to love your wives with a love equal to the love of Christ for the church (Eph 5:25)? Easy. You access power from God, by faith, through the Holy Spirit in you. Then you will become a glorious conduit of His love for your wife. That's it. She will notice the difference. That's the only way; and it is within your reach of faith. Simple, right?

How would your Christian life change today if you were flooded with the height, width, length and depth of the love of Christ for you and for others? It would be dramatic. Your worship? Off the charts. Your evangelistic efforts? You would actually love your neighbor. That makes a huge difference. Your quiet time? Energized. Your relationships? Miraculous. It is so easy that a child could do it. Imagine a church community filled with such other-oriented power? Such love for others (Phil 2:3-5). It would be noticeably different.

How? First, I need to recognize that I can't do the Christian walk. I can't do what Jesus would do. In fact, I can now see the reason that I haven't been living the Christian life is that at some level I don't *want* to.

All I need is need, most of the time, I don't even have that. I need power even to begin to love God, to be loved by God, and certainly to love others. With that power, I can love the irritating, the unlovable, those who will never love me back. I am finally doing the love of Christ. This power must be accessed by faith, from the Holy Spirit in me, now. And now. And now.

> "Now to him who is able to do immeasurably more than all we ask or imagine, according to his power that is at work within us, to him be glory in the church and in Christ Jesus throughout all generations, for ever and ever! Amen." (Eph 3:20-21 NIV)

This is Paul's vision for you as well. Your behaviors, your relationships, and your emotions should be indescribable by human means. How are you to pull off this task? It must be a result of a miracle. Not by you at all. He gets all the credit (1 Cor 1:31; 2 Cor 10:17, 11:30, 12:9; Gal 6:14). You wouldn't have it any other way.

Isn't this remarkably good news for you, no matter how long you have been a Christian? You can right now, no matter who you are, what you have done, or what's been done to you, receive and apply power from God, already purchased for you by Jesus, that can make you experience and channel to others, the height, width, length and depth of the love of Christ.

Further, when you recondition yourself to lean into this power over and over, you will begin to see a noticeable change in your behavior day-in-and-day-out. Do not think that you can wait for the inevitable sensory trigger to go off and then even imagine that you will be motivated to run to God and ask for power. It's too late then. If you wait until chemicals are surging through your brain, taking over, you are most likely *not* going to think, "Hey, I should go and ask for the Holy Spirit to empower me with love right now." No more than Eve in the garden thought, "Hey, I should go and ask Yahweh about this snake."

The Ephesians forgot their need for God's singular love and pursued, no doubt, *good* counterfeits. Without such a unique and powerful love, they could not do the task given them by Jesus. Listen to the judgment against them in God's courtroom only a couple of decades after Paul's letter. Jesus concludes:

> "Yet I hold this against you: You have forsaken your first love. Remember the height from which you have fallen! Repent and do the things you did at first. If you do not repent, I will come to you and remove your lampstand from its place." (Rev 2:4-5 NIV)

Luther's Received Righteousness

The great reformer Martin Luther understood this need for power: God's love for self and others purchased by Christ. He labeled it "received righteousness." Listen to this paraphrase of his preface to his commentary of Paul to the Galatians.

> "So you see why I say again that this doctrine of received righteousness can never be taught, urged, and repeated enough. If this doctrine is lost, then the whole knowledge of truth, life and salvation is also lost and gone. On the other hand, if this doctrine flourishes, then all good things flourish; religion, the true service of God, the glory of God, the right knowledge of all things and states of life…This received righteousness is a righteousness hidden in a mystery, which the world does not know. In fact, Christians themselves do not thoroughly understand it, and can hardly take hold of it in their day-to-day struggles. Therefore it must be diligently taught and continually practiced. And whoever does not understand or apprehend this righteousness in afflictions and terrors of conscience, will be overthrown, will fall away, will get caught up into consumerism, will become discouraged in their Christian walk, will not find intimacy and purpose and joy. For there is no comfort of conscience so firm and so sure, as this received righteousness."[18]

To summarize: if we access such received righteousness, there will be revival; individual and corporate. If not, there will only be confusion, need, and anxiety.

> "Most necessary it is, therefore, that we should know this article well, teach it unto others, and beat it into their heads continually."[11]

Bottom line, for the most part, we have—in our ignorance—been living as unfortunate underachievers as Christians. We've been working really hard, with very little to show for it. Nevertheless, the good news is that there is a very high upside potential.

---

18. Martin Luther, St. Paul's Epistle to the Galatians (Philadelphia: Smith, English & Co., 1860), 206.

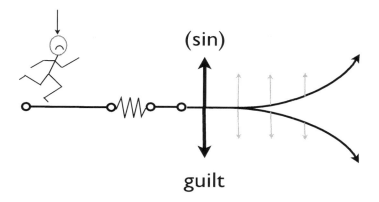

Chapter 5: The Power of Guilt versus (sin)

> *Therefore, brothers, since we have confidence to enter the Most Holy Place by the blood of Jesus, by a new and living way opened for us through the curtain, that is, his body, and since we have a great priest over the house of God, let us draw near to God with a sincere heart in full assurance of faith, having our hearts sprinkled to cleanse us from a guilty conscience and having our bodies washed with pure water.*
> —Hebrews 10:19-22 NIV

While *guilt* is normally described as an emotion, it is better understood to be an emotive *power*, often subconscious, below reason's radar, that necessarily initiates a broad range of normal human reactionary behaviors, some good (confession, remorse, desire to do restitution, and reconciliation), but others, quite destructive.

The Gospel provides for all believers a powerful *counter-agent* to guilt. The more that I can, by faith, in the moment, through the Holy Spirit in me, truly grasp that Jesus has already paid the price for all of my sins, in *Gospel App* terminology, "*(sin),*" the *less* my internal guilt will empower my habitual anti-social, self-destructive behaviors—my under the curve reactionary behaviors (see diagram above).

What is sin?

In the *Gospel App*, we consider both aspects of "sin." In common parlance, "sin" is mainly understood in negative terms, "Don't do _____." While that is legitimate, we find it helpful to expand the notion of sin in positive terms.

In its broadest sense, "sin" includes any attempt to find personal significance, security, and belonging anywhere other than God. Conceptualized in that manner, it should be clear that we sin all the time. If I consciously or subconsciously in any way come to expect that my career, health, finances, sex, sexuality, home, relationships, religion, government, or church should provide peace, security, significance, intimacy, and identity, I have veered away from the only real source of such things. I have substituted infinitely less powerful false deities for the one God. I sin. Framed in this manner, it should be clear how tragic sin really can be.

Are the two sin categories different? Upon closer inspection, it should be obvious that they are two ways of looking at the same separation from God. Why do people commit crimes? Why do people typically gossip, argue, fight, betray and lie? Their expected sources of significance, belonging, and security have failed them, so they must react to recover by other means—often by doing something they would never have done under other circumstances. Then guilt happens.

It has been my experience that if we frame sin in only negative terms, "Don't do _____," many of us will imagine that the cure for the subsequent guilt is to stop doing _____, and to say you are sorry. But honestly, how has that gone for you?

It is far better to see that at the root of my sinful behaviors is a lack and longing for the significance, security and belonging that I can only access from God, already fully purchased for every Jesus-follower. We need and have been given access to the fullness of God. If we were experiencing such fullness, we would look for filling from other sources—even good ones—less.

The Powerful Ever-present Force of Guilt

Where does my guilt come from? Guilt is a nasty emotional feeling that erupts from within us when we have done something wrong or have not done something right. Susan Krauss Whitbourne lists five typical categories of guilt.[19]

Guilt Cause #1: Guilt for something you did. This is the most obvious category. You did something that led to harm to someone else, perhaps physical or psychological pain. Maybe your feelings of guilt are exacerbated because you violated your own ethical or moral codes, or did something that you had resolved to never do again. Guilt in such cases is not evil; rather it is a normal human response to your actions. In fact, to not feel guilt would be a sign of psychopathy of some kind.

---

19. Susan Krauss Whitbourne, August 11, 2012, "The Definitive Guide to Guilt: The Five Types of Guilt and How You Can Cope With Each" https://www.psychologytoday.com/blog/fulfillment-any-age/201208/the-definitive-guide-guilt.

Guilt Cause #2: Guilt for something you didn't do, but wanted to. Remember the infamous Playboy interview of then President Jimmy Carter, where he confessed to mentally lusting after another woman? He did not actually commit adultery, yet his guilt reared its ugly head anyway because he was tempted to play around. This is a difficult guilt to process. On the one hand, you feel guilty, but on the other hand, you remain less-than-firmly planted on moral high ground because you did not actually engage in sin.

Guilt Cause #3: Guilt for something you *think* you did. Imagine a time when you left a conversation or a situation and felt guilt even though you just couldn't put your finger on what you could have possibly done. You think that you did something wrong yet you were not sure what it was. How do you know? Simply put, you feel guilt.

Guilt Cause #4: Guilt that you didn't do enough to help someone. Imagine a situation where you have conflicting "good" activities. It would be good to go and visit an ailing friend who is in the hospital. On the other hand, it is also a good activity to go and spend time with your family. For many, no matter which good activity you choose, you will likely feel some guilt emotions for not picking the other path.

Guilt Cause #5: Guilt that you're doing better than someone else. People in higher socio-economic categories may feel guilt over their success which can lead to stress, anxiety, and even avoidance of others in lower financial strata. Combat veterans who have survived conflict while friends did not may have "survivor guilt." Good students may feel guilt over their innate ability to do well on tests or in classes.

> *"We have done something, or not done something, intentional or not intentional, that results in hurt, pain, anguish, disappointment, loss, indignity, anxiety and harm to another. In such cases, normal human response is to feel some level of remorse and regret, in a word, guilt, for the actual or imagined hurt and disappointment that we have or believed we have caused by our actions or inactions."*

No matter which of the above categories of guilt with which you resonate, we have all been there. We have *done* something, or not *done* something, intentional or not intentional, that results in hurt, pain, anguish, disappointment, loss, indignity, anxiety and harm to another. In such cases, *normal* human response is to feel some level of remorse and regret, in a word, guilt, for the actual or imagined hurt and disappointment that we have or believed we have caused by our actions or inactions.[20]

Like most, I have self-expectations of doing right things and avoiding doing non-right things. When I have, or suspect that I have not done right, there is a normal rush to one degree or another of negative emotions, such as remorse, regret, and disappointment that I did not achieve behavior that I expected I could and should have done. I come to see that my choices and actions have not lived up to my own, my community's and God's expectations of my choices. I had implicitly or explicitly determined to treat others the way they should be treated and I did not succeed.

Put simply, my guilt is related to my action or inaction—what I did or did not do. In guilt, the self is not the central object of negative evaluation. In my assessment, what I did was either bad and immoral, or good and moral. It was either right or *not*-right. Guilt explicitly or implicitly asks these self-oriented questions:

> What did I do?
>
> Why did I do what I did?
>
> Why didn't I do something different?
>
> Can my crime be repaired? Forgiven?
>
> Can I avoid the same choice in the future?
>
> Am I still forgiven by God even though I did something wrong?

Guilt is that distressful and often agonizing feeling of regret and responsibility for my actions, both conscious and subconscious. I did not do right by the other person. I either intentionally or unintentionally disappointed the other person or inflicted pain to him or her through my actions. It is normal human behavior to feel guilty about our wrongdoing.

Lonesome Dove: A Novel

Larry McMurtry brilliantly provides the image of a man struggling with years of guilt. Rough and tough cowboy Call had a dark secret in his past, a secret that he had failed to make right. Now years later, he could only carry the guilt.

As a young cowpoke, he fathered a child with a prostitute Maggie. It wasn't the dalliance that so much caused the guilt for Call. Call had never admitted being the boy's real father. In the years since, Maggie had died leaving Call with unresolvable feelings of self-reproach and anguish over what he had done and not done. Here is how McMurtry describes the deep guilt in Call's psyche.

---

20. There are a variety of personality disorders that exhibit a diminished ability to feel remorse or guilt. A psychopath, for instance, would not feel such guilt after disappointing or harming another person.

Guilt vs. (Sin)

"A time or two [Call] even stood up to go to [Maggie], but his resolve always broke. He just could not go back. The night he heard she was dead he left the town without a word to anyone and rode up the river alone for a week. He knew at once that he had forever lost the chance to right himself, that he would never again be able to feel that he was the man he had wanted to be. The man he had wanted to be would never have gone to Maggie in the first place. He felt like a cheat—he was the most respected man on the border, and yet a whore had a claim on him. He had ignored the claim, and the woman died, but somehow the claim remained, like a weight he had to carry forever."

"The boy, growing up in the village, first with a Mexican family and then with the Hat Creek outfit, was a living reminder of his failure. With the boy there he could never be free of the memory and the guilt. He would have given almost anything just to erase the memory, not to have it part of his past, or in his mind, but of course he couldn't do that. It was his forever, like the long scar on his back, the result of having let a horse throw him through a glass window. Occasionally Gus would try to get him to claim the boy, but Call wouldn't. He knew that he probably should, not out of certainty so much as decency, but he couldn't. It meant an admission he couldn't make—an admission that he had failed someone. It had never happened in battle, such failure. Yet it had happened in a little room over a saloon, because of a small woman who couldn't keep her hair fixed. It was strange to him that such a failure could seem so terrible, and yet it did. It was such a torment when he thought of it that he eventually tried to avoid all situations in which women were mentioned—only that way could he keep the matter out of mind for a stretch of time."[21]

Hear the guilt? The sense of having failed, not done right, not taken actions to repair the situation, and the unrealized "should-ofs." By his unwillingness to deal with the guilt, Call carried the dehumanizing weight of guilt and remorse for the rest of his life.

Healthy Guilt

Healthy guilt and its associated remorse can, and often does, evoke a pro-social desire to restore the relationship to the way things were before the harmful actions or inactions. In order to make things right again and to right the crippled relationship, I may confess my motivations and actions, seek to bring restitution, make resolutions of future good behavior, or other conciliatory actions. *Healthy* guilt often leads to a longing to be seen as a "right-doer" in the eyes of the other again—to remove the label of "wrongdoer." It can motivate a desire for appropri-

21. Larry McMurtry, Lonesome Dove: The Novel, New York: Simon & Schuster, 2010, 363-364.

ate reconciliation (of course where it is safe and wise to do so).

Healthy guilt *can* lead to healthy steps toward consolation. These could include:

- facing and accepting privately and publicly what you did without trying to justify, minimize, shift blame or avoid ownership.
- finding ways to better understand *why* you did what you did.
- if other people were involved, exploring with them the consequences of your actions to them. The goal is for you to better understand the harm you caused them from their perspective.
- beginning to take appropriate short and long-term actions to repair the damage.
- committing to yourself and others your resolve to not repeat the harm.

While these are arguably pro-social and healing, three observations are worth considering.

First, while the above five actions would certainly, on their face, appear pro-social and good things to do, my problem is that I often don't *want* to do them. Otherwise, I would have already moved in that direction. When push comes to shove, I still—like Call—often hesitate to do the right and loving thing.

Why? I don't do these things, frankly because I subconsciously don't *want* to do them. It is only logical. I do the things that I both prioritize and want to. Whether it is denial, blind spots, self-centeredness, indifference to others, or pure cowardice, I have a long list of unresolved stuff.

The *Gospel App* recognizes that many of us are in the same boat. We don't do things that might relieve guilt and restore community ultimately because we don't *want* to. When all is said and done, my inner decision making processes have subconsciously or consciously weighed the pros and cons of either doing something or not doing something and have landed on the latter. Consider this. If I had indeed prioritized the resolving of my guilt above reputation, risks, and fears, I would have leaned into the situation until a satisfactory resolution was achieved. I have a motivation problem.

The good news is that there is a powerful source of new motivation for me that has the fresh alien other-oriented power to make me want to do the right thing. This new motivational power is available to followers of Jesus 24/7. I must request it by faith through the Holy Spirit in me.

> *"The good news is that there is a powerful source of new motivation for me that has the fresh alien other-oriented power to make me want do the right thing. This new motivational power is available to followers of Jesus 24/7. I must request it by faith through the Holy Spirit in me."*

Guilt vs. (Sin)

Second, I can find ways to do many of those pro-social actions for the wrong reason. I can do repentance selfishly. I am pretty good at it. I am willing to do just about anything within reason to get rid of that nagging feeling of guilt inside of me. My actions may even look, and to outside observers, feel like Jesus, but just beneath the surface, they could be very self-serving. Paul sets a higher standard in Phil 2.

> "If you have any encouragement from being united with Christ, if any comfort from his love, if any fellowship with the Spirit, if any tenderness and compassion, then make my joy complete by being *like-minded*, having the same love, being one in spirit and purpose. Do nothing out of selfish ambition or vain conceit, but in humility consider others better than yourselves. Each of you should look not only to your own interests, but also to the interests of others. Your attitude should be the same as that of Christ Jesus: Who, being in very nature God, did not consider equality with God something to be grasped, but made himself nothing, taking the very nature of a servant, being made in human likeness. And being found in appearance as a man, he humbled himself and became obedient to death — even death on a cross!" (Phil 2:1-8 NIV)

To put Paul's words in the context of repenting of guilt, "Don't just do pro-social works of repentance for public show, or to satiate the pangs of your own guilt. Your attitude should be to truly *want* to raise the person that you dishonored back to pre-crime honor and worth—for their sakes, their well-being—not primarily your own."

If I were indeed "like-minded" with Christ, I would surely feel deep regret for the pain and loss that I caused the other. My driving motivation to repent of my actions would be to restore *them*, to honor *them*. Getting rid of the ugly feeling of my own guilt would be largely secondary.

Perhaps you are like me. I would love to think that I am like-minded with Christ—but even a cursory overview of my past repentances testify that I often am far more concerned with my own guilty conscience, my own raging feelings. My knee-jerk UCB response is to put my interests—getting rid of the horrible feeling of guilt—over the interests of others.

Third, even if I were given such a powerful Celestial other-oriented motivation to fix what I broke, really admitted blame, publicly repented, offered restitution, these pro-social efforts will only, at their best, partially reduce that nagging inner feeling of guilt. We will discuss that more below. Suffice it to say here that guilt is a deep-rooted power often inextricably intertwined with shame that cannot be effectively dismantled by our actions, even good ones like the above.

The Old Testament had legislated every detailed pro-social action that guilty persons should do once they were aware of their specific crimes and were truly remorseful. There were trials before the elders. There were court-divined confession, restitution, offerings and, of course, punishment. And yet, none of these right actions were sufficient to relieve guilty consciences. Here is how the author of Hebrews puts it.

> "The law is only a shadow of the good things that are coming—not the realities themselves. For this reason it can never, by the same sacrifices repeated endlessly year after year, make perfect those who draw near to worship. If it could, would they not have stopped being offered? For the worshipers would have been cleansed once for all, and would no longer have felt guilty for their sins. But those sacrifices are an annual reminder of sins, because it is impossible for the blood of bulls and goats to take away sins." (Heb 10:1-4 NIV)

> "This is an illustration for the present time, indicating that the gifts and sacrifices being offered were *not* able to clear the conscience of the worshipper." (Heb 9:9 NIV)

Indeed, it had no power to do so. Here's the dirty little secret. All of the many legislated reparatory actions that were divined by the Torah didn't work—not completely. They helped, no doubt. Yet the guilty conscience remained even after concerted well-meaning pro-social efforts to reconcile. Even after all of the effort defined by the Torah, the worshippers still "felt guilty for their sins" (Heb 1:3 NIV).

Why? Guilt—and related shame—are very powerful and harder to weed out of our flesh than we want to admit. The above restorative actions may have initially felt helpful and may have even diminished feelings of guilt somewhat. But none of my motivations or actions have the intrinsic power to scrub my conscience clean. Apart from the existence and involvement of a loving God, who alone has such capacity to scrub hardened residual plaque off my worn and guilty conscience, these actions are as good as it gets.

However, the good news of the Bible—and of course the *Gospel App*—is that even the most powerful and pervasive guilt has an even more powerful enemy—all the more so after the Cross. There is a personal God who is invested in cleansing and diminishing my guilt.

The Spiritual Enemy of Guilt

In the *Gospel App* diagram at the beginning of this chapter, note that guilt is juxtaposed by another opposite power: *(Sin)*. The word "*sin*" within parentheses is the *Gospel App*'s way of communicating God's removal of my sin (mathematical use of parentheses to denote subtraction from an account) and consequences of sin (in particular, guilt) from my legal account.

When I become aware of my guilt, I can look up and by faith, through the power of the Holy Spirit in me run to God, hold up guilt-ridden hands and proclaim my need for God to intervene on my behalf in three specific areas; that God would...

- remind me of the finished trial on my behalf,
- remind me that the Judge Himself has personally underwritten all payment for all of my debts,
- give me Godly sorrow, that powerful fruit that moves me out of myself and focuses me on the needs of others, in particular the other that I dishonored.

The Power of Finished Justice

As I preach the Gospel to myself and in particular, the Gospel related to Jesus' work on the Cross to satisfy the Law's demand due to my sins, my guilt is observably diminished within me.

Imagine your guilt overwhelming you again. You know that you did harm to someone and are unable to process the ugly emotions of shame. You remember that Jesus not only died for all of your sin, but also for that specific sin that is causing you remorse. By faith, run to the singular courtroom of the only Lord and objective Judge—ready to submit your case to His jurisdiction and fully and totally accept His justice.

It is the wildly wonderful dynamic theology of the work of Jesus on the Cross. Two thousand years ago, Jesus died on the Cross for all of the sins of people like me—*everyone* of the sins. On that bared lumber, there was a functional trial before God for all of *my* crimes against God, humanity and creation, including of course, the very crime for which I feel such guilt and remorse.

It was a unique trial. Evidence was not necessary as the Judge already knew the full extent of the crime. There was no need for a slick defense attorney to present my side of the story. God already knew it. The Judge knew exactly what went down: all motivations, all contexts and extenuating circumstances, anything that might get me off the hook in today's courts.

After all was said and done, I was found 100% guilty for a myriad of crimes against God, humanity and creation. To tell you the truth, I am not questioning the finding of the court at all. No appeal is necessary. I fully concur. My feeling of guilt is enough evidence for me. I *am* guilty.

The trial then entered the second phase, the verdict. Once again different from modern trials where extenuating circumstances, precedents, or judicial mercy and subjectivity may lead to a reduced sentence—with time off for good behavior. In my trial, two thousand years ago, none of those had any sway. The wages of sin—all sin—is death (per Rom 6:23).

God's courtroom has no mercy—at least in the modern context where mercy refers to the possibility of lesser sentences. The *Law* is the law. Period. For all of my crimes—or for any of them, the appropriate legal sentence is death. Today's coddled and confused judicial consciences may revile at such workings of this court, but guilt must be taken seriously. Remember, the goal is the removal of guilt and the restoration to fellowship with God that had been bartered away in the Garden. This is severe surgery that must remove deadly, dehumanizing anti-social guilt.

Enter the third phase of the trial: penalty phase. It turns out that God's courtroom has a vast alien mercy after all. In the mystery of the Gospel, something unexpected, strange and wonderful happened. God's Son Jesus, who never sinned—ever—never looked for value, worth, identity or glory in any other place than His Father's eyes, willingly stepped up in my place and took upon His own shoulders all of the punishment (i.e., death) due me. He died in my place to perfectly and permanently satisfy *all* of celestial justice's demands.

He willingly took my death—Justice's rightful sentence—on His innocent shoulders and perished in my stead.

This is the nature of God's mercy. There are no loopholes in the Law that I can cling to in order to receive a reduced sentence. God's plan is so much higher and more mysterious.

Once my guilty inner-being realizes that all of the requirements of God's law have been fully satisfied, my innate fear of further consequences is drastically diminished for a moment. The Law and God's courtroom have become my friend and supporter.

No matter what I do, or do not do, what I say, or do not say, or even how I feel, God the Judge can never ever judge me again. That would be celestial double jeopardy.

All of this is incorporated in the first upward power vector on the *Gospel App: (Sin)*. Jesus died to take away my sins and to carry away on his shoulders the deep powerful guilt associated with my sins against God, humanity and creation, including the guilt that I feel for any particular sin (Ps. 103:11-12). All I need to do when I feel any of the five categories of guilt is to, by faith through the Holy Spirit in me, access this aspect of the Gospel which Luther is credited with calling the "Great Exchange."

> "This is that mystery which is rich in divine grace to sinners: wherein by a wonderful exchange our sins are no longer ours but Christ's, and the righteousness of Christ not Christ's but ours. He has emptied himself of his righteousness that he might clothe us with it and fill us with it; and he has taken our evils upon himself that he might deliver us from them."[22]

Paul puts it succinctly.

---

22. Martin Luther, Commentary on Galatians, Grand Rapids: Fleming H. Revell, 1988, 182.

Guilt vs. (Sin)

"God made him who had no sin to be sin for us, so that in him we might become the righteousness of God." (2Cor 5:21)

God made (ordained/charged/planned ahead of time) Jesus who had no acquaintance (participation of any kind) with sin (and the many dehumanizing consequences of any and all of my sin: i.e., guilt, shame, loneliness and alienation from perfect intimacy with the Father, or finding his value in other lesser gazes), to take on *all* of the consequences of *my* sin including all appropriate legal punishments (i.e., death), so that I, on the very solid legal basis of His substitutionary death (my rightful penalty already *perfectly* satisfied on my behalf by another) would immediately be fully and permanently established as perfectly legally *right* with God—as *right* with the Father as Jesus is right.

"Our most merciful Father…sent his only Son into the world and laid upon him the sins of all men, saying, "Be thou Peter, that denier; Paul that persecutor, blasphemer and cruel oppressor; David that adulterer; that sinner that did eat the apple in Paradise; that thief that hanged upon the cross; and be thou the person which hath committed the sins of all; see therefore that thou pay and satisfy for them."[23]

So for the purposes of the *Gospel App*, this first aspect of the upward Gospel arrow reminds me that Jesus took away the ultimate consequences of every one of my betrayals against God, humanity and creation—every single one. This action is irrevocable no matter what I do or do not do. My record of sin was permanently taken away from my record and put in His. Simply put, Jesus perfectly died for all of my sin—all of it. It is done.

"When the guilt of sin affrighteth us from God, and we are thinking that God will not accept such great offenders as we have been, then Christ is our remedy, who hath paid our debt, and borne our stripes, and procured and sealed us a pardon by his blood. Shall pardoned sins drive us from him that pardoneth them? He hath justified us by his righteousness. The curse and damnation are terrible indeed; but he hath taken them away, and given us a free discharge."[24]

God's Underwriting of My Debt

There is a second aspect of this upward Gospel arrow. In modern insurance policies, an underwriter signs their name, thereby becoming liable in case of certain losses specified in the policy. Jesus-Follower, God has underwritten your entire myriad of debts. The first *Gospel App* arrow focuses on your debt accrued against

---

23. Martin Luther, Commentary on Galatians, Grand Rapids: Fleming H. Revell, 1988, 182.
24. Richard Baxter, Christian Directory, Soli Deo Gloria Publications, 1990, 66.

God. Like the Magnanimous King in the Parable of the Unforgiving Servant, the King even before the Servant asks cuts a check to Himself for the servant's vast un-payable debt owed (Mt. 18:21-35).

Still your God's grace extends even further. It would be sub-human to be satisfied with a resolution of your trial until the person that you hurt is satisfied as well. How can you feel guiltless while the consequences of your crimes linger?

Good news. The first arrow reminds us that God by nature restores *all* losses, including all of the losses that I have caused other people. God will cover all of my myriad of debts. This is really good news to all involved. I don't have pockets deep enough to make a dent in my debt. God does. Here are a collection of verses that teach this restorative nature of God's character.

God's justice reflected in Old Testament case law includes reparation for losses. Throughout the Old Testament case law, justice involves both an objective trial as well as defined attempts to restore the plaintiff to wholeness.

> "If men quarrel and one hits the other with a stone or with his fist and he does not die but is confined to bed, the one who struck the blow will not be held responsible if the other gets up and walks around outside with his staff; however, he must pay the injured man for the loss of his time and see that he is completely healed." (Ex 21:18-19, see also 21:22, 27, 30-36)

God prophetically promises to remove disgrace caused by crimes.

> "On this mountain the LORD Almighty will prepare a feast of rich food for all peoples, a banquet of aged wine — the best of meats and the finest of wines. On this mountain he will destroy the shroud that enfolds all peoples, the sheet that covers all nations; he will swallow up death forever. The Sovereign LORD will wipe away the tears from all faces; he will remove the disgrace of his people from all the earth. The LORD has spoken." (Isa 25:6-8 NIV)

God promises to restore sinful Israel for all losses that they incurred from outside enemies including losses that were consequences from their own rebellion against Him.

> "I will repay you for the years the locusts have eaten—the great locust and the young locust, the other locusts and the locust swarm—my great army that I sent among you." (Joel 2:25 NIV)

The evidence of the Bible is that it is part of God's innate nature to proactively pay every restorative debt owed to all Plaintiffs—Himself. It is intuitive to suggest that God will pay all debts due Christian plaintiffs. Certainly heaven will be made up of all Christian plaintiffs made whole. All losses that they have ever incurred due to any crimes committed against them fully and completely paid by the Celestial Account Settler on behalf of the perpetrator—all perpetrators. Heaven will be a place where they will be whole again. No debts overlooked, large or small.

A strong case could also be made, based upon the proclaimed nature of God reflected in many verses similar to those above, that He will equally restore all Hell-bound plaintiffs to wholeness as well. I am not referring here to extended salvation to those who reject the person and work of Christ.

Rather, I am speaking about those unresolved debts, hurts, and losses that have been incurred by any and all crimes committed against them by others. In Joel, God unilaterally promises to chronically unfaithful Israel to make them whole—not based upon anything that they did, or will do right. It is a unilateral promise made to deeply rebellious people who habitually rejected covenantal intimacy with God over and over, who intentionally ran after other gods and flaunted them in Yahweh's face, and made deals with the nations around them. God is basically saying, "Whether you deserve it or not, whether you ask for it or not, whether you repent for your idolatry and return to Me ever, still I plan on paying you back for everything that you have lost. I alone will restore to you everything you lost to your other gods, not just what was falsely taken from you, or robbed from you by force, but also all that you willingly gave away to buy the favor of other spiritual lovers. Why? Because that is my nature. I make people whole."

Arguably both Heaven and Hell (whatever Hell might be) will be filled with people made whole by God. This is the final grace of God—even to those hell-bound who refuse to be embraced by Jesus.

Access the Fruit of Godly Sorrow

The third aspect of this singular Gospel arrow *(Sin)* is also critically important. If my justice has been fully paid by Jesus on my behalf, and I am convinced that God will ultimately restore my victims to wholeness, why would I lean into reconciliation? The reason that I didn't pursue resolution of my guilt at the beginning was that I just didn't want to—whether out of insensitivity, cowardice, selfishness, fear of making it worse, or whatever. Why would I want to move toward the person that I hurt now? Paul defines a new source of hope for those who want restoration of fractured relationships.

> "Godly sorrow brings repentance that leads to salvation and leaves no regret, but worldly sorrow brings death. See what this godly sorrow has produced in you: what earnestness, what eagerness to clear yourselves, what indignation, what alarm, what longing, what concern, what readiness to see justice done. At every point you have proved yourselves to be innocent in this matter." (2 Cor 7:10-11 NIV)

Paul speaks of two sorrows, two remorses, two very differing motivations to process our guilt. They come from two very opposite sources: the world and God.

Worldly Sorrow

Worldly sorrow is remorse that naturally comes from our own sinful natures. It only produces relational death. It has no capacity or power to truly reconcile broken community, period.

Why? Such "sorrow" is a *pseudo*-guilt that is driven by self-centered goals and motivation. I have done something wrong to someone and feel the consequences and will do whatever it takes to feel better again. It is all about *me* and how I am feeling. This unhealthy guilt is not focused on the well-being of the person I hurt, not interested in justice or doing the right thing. It wants relief at any cost for my own pain and consequences.

The *Gospel App* recognizes that quite often I experience such an unhealthy *guilt* that subconsciously by-passes my will and higher judgment and instead initiates my flesh's habitual self-focused reactionary behaviors—powerfully mobilizing all of my emotional resources to "fix" the guilt by any means available to me. In such a reaction, I am normally concerned less for the other person's well-being and restoration to rightness and more focused on alleviating the nagging discomfort of my guilty conscience, i.e., making myself feel right again. Unless challenged and exposed, I will most often assume that I am pursuing Godly sorrow of course. "Just look at me. I said I was sorry after all." This is a very hard thing for people, including *good* people to at last admit.

Everyone's habitual knee-jerk response to such unhealthy guilt is unique. One person may try to minimize their feelings of guilt by defending their actions. Another may try to accomplish the same goal by making excuses. Another may lie, or cover-up, or deflect attention to others—even the one hurt. Another's guilt may ignite rage, depression, self-medication, or even self-destructive behaviors like overeating, cutting, slander, gossip, and public self-loathing.

I have witnessed one very effective strategy by a very angry man who would regularly emotionally abuse his poor wife. When his berating was noticed by someone else and challenged, he would immediately apologize for his harsh words to his wife. She readily participated in his madness, as any good co-dependent would, by quickly accepting the apology, letting him off the hook—again.

Godly Sorrow

Then there is the miraculous Heaven-sourced sorrow that leads to relational life. Paul calls it "Godly sorrow." Godly sorrow, once the switch is flipped on, is a regular manufacturing plant, even apart from your will and reason, producing

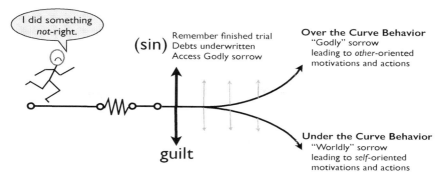

brand new other oriented motivations that did not exist within you moments before: earnestness, readiness to see real justice accomplished, concern for the other, urgency to make amends, and the like. This heavenly-birthed "sorrow" is both salvific and unregretful. How does one access such a sorrow vital to healthy community? You have not because you ask not. All you need is need.

Conclusion

In conclusion, guilt is an offense-related response which in its healthier form naturally leads to sorrow and regret. Guilt is normal, not always evil. Healthy guilt can, and often does, motivate us to pro-social responses: a healthy internal review of what went wrong, a fresh authentic humility (i.e., clear-headed awareness of my need for healing and repair), a desire to accept responsibility for the crime free from debilitating self-condemnation, an other-oriented repentance, and a pro-social desire to restore and repair broken relationships.[25] Even healthy guilt by itself is powerless to remove guilt. The Gospel invites us to regularly access a powerful counter agent to healthy and unhealthy strains of guilt.

Now we can see why all three aspects of the *Gospel App* arrow, *(Sin)*, stands in such powerful conflict with any guilt. The more that I truly understand what Jesus did for me two millennia ago, the less power my guilty conscious has over me. The present forces of guilt within me, which are very powerful and as shown earlier, will lead to a great deal of reactionary self-focused UCB can be greatly diminished, to the extent that I *presently* am empowered by faith through the Holy Spirit to *believe* that what Jesus did was not only true, but permanent.

The magnitude of this substitutionary action of Jesus is vast. John Newton puts it well in his hymn "Justice smiles and asks no more"[26]—ever. The upshot of this decisive action by Jesus, not based upon anything I did at all, is that now I *can* presently and experientially know that God isn't judging me—and nev-

---

25. See Fischer M. L. & Exline, J. (2006). Self-Forgiveness versus Excusing: The Roles of Remorse, Effort, and Acceptance of Responsibility, Self and Identity, 5, 127-129.
26. Newton, John. Let us Love and Sing and Wonder, Twenty Six Letters on Religious Subjects, by Omicron, 1774, alt. accessed December 8, 2014 from http://www.cyberhymnal.org/htm/l/e/letuslov.html.

er will, no matter what I do or do not do, what I say or do not say or what I feel or do not feel. All of my sin is already paid for. Period. That can never change.

I never have to worry about what I will see when I look into the eyes of my God. There will never be any sense of criticism from Him. Jesus took all of the court's criticism of me already. It would be the most egregious double jeopardy for God to judge the crime twice. God will never lean back in heaven disgusted at me, with His holy arms crossed, shaking his head in contempt. Jesus took all of that contempt that was due me.

I may feel like God is angry or critical of me at times. That is a lie spewed into my brain by my own flesh in cahoots with the vile whispers of Satan. Anytime, and every time I feel such guilt, I can through the Holy Spirit in me access the faith (a wonderful fruit of the Spirit in Galatians 5) to really believe that this is true for me today.

> *"Godly sorrow, once the switch is flipped on, is a regular manufacturing plant, even apart from your will and reason, producing brand new other oriented motivations that did not exist within you moments before: earnestness, readiness to see real justice accomplished, concern for the other, urgency to make amends, and the like. This heavenly-birthed "sorrow" is both salvific and unregretful. How does one access such a sorrow vital to healthy community? You have not because you ask not."*

How great is this? Apart from this wonderful and mysterious transaction done on my behalf, I would never be freed from the powerful subconscious guilt that drives my UCB. I would never feel right with God or others. I would always to some degree, perhaps subconsciously, still feel guilty. I would always hesitate to access the healing, life-giving gaze of God.

There is only one way that a guilty conscious can be cleansed.

> "How much more, then, will the blood of Christ, who through the eternal Spirit offered himself unblemished to God, cleanse our consciences from acts that lead to death, so that we may serve the living God!...Let us draw near to God with a sincere heart in full assurance of faith, having our hearts sprinkled to cleanse us from a guilty conscience and having our bodies washed with pure water." (Hebrews 9:14; 10:22)

Suffice it to say at this point, that once that nagging guilt is observably diminished (an ongoing battle day after day, hour by hour), I will, I can boldly do what Adam and Eve could have done, but did not do. I can look up into God's gaze and feel whole once more, or at least a powerful experience of feeling more

Guilt vs. (Sin)

whole than moments before. Drawing near to God with a sincere guilt-cleansed heart opens the door to many other possibility, other "powers" that will motivate me to truly love myself and others, including the person that I have hurt, in the same way that God loves them. That is a game changer.

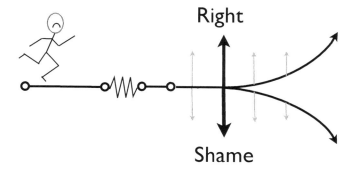

Chapter 6: The Power of Shame versus Right

> *"What? Must I hold a candle to my shames?"*
> —Shakespeare, *The Merchant of Venice.*

> *"We must courageously face our character under the gentle yet truthful guidance of the Holy Spirit. We are all imperfect."*
> —Everett Worthington.

> *"The supreme happiness of life is the conviction that we are loved; loved for ourselves—say rather, loved in spite of ourselves."*
> —Victor Hugo, *Les Miserables.*

> *"The gospel does not make sense unless you have a heart to enter your own shame. And you will not have the work of the Kingdom of God guiding your mind and heart unless you have the courage to enter even into your own simple, broken stories of shame. Who will pursue you?"*
> —Dan Allender

The Power of Shame

As debilitating and as powerful as guilt feels, shame is worse.[27] Unlike guilt, shame is less *offense* and more *self*-focused. Shame wonders if I am this way or I did what

---

27. June. P. Tangney and Ronda L. Dearing, Shame and Guilt, New York: Guilford Press, 2002 and Tangney, J., Steuwig, J. & Hafez, L. Shame, Guilt, and Remorse: Implications for Offender Populations. The Journal of Forensic Psychiatry & Psychology, 22 (5) October 2011, 707).

I did because I am innately not-right, not sensitive, not caring, unethical, unfaithful, immoral, or ugly. This can be a shocking assessment of my own identity.

I did non-right, because at a certain level, I *am* not right. My actions reflect something of my character and I do not like what I see. Something must be innately wrong with me that I would do something like this—or that I couldn't, or worse, wouldn't stop some horrible thing from happening to myself or someone close to me. Some researchers prefer to speak of shame as "self-condemnation."

Shame is

> "that feeling of self-castigation which arises when we are convinced that there is something about ourselves that is wrong, inferior, flawed, weak, or dirty. Shame is fundamentally a feeling of loathing against ourselves; a hateful vision of ourselves through our own eyes—although this vision may be determined by how we expect or believe other people are experiencing us. Generally speaking, this self-vision is accompanied by self-consciousness, and by a conviction of important failure that often generates a wish to hide or conceal. A common reaction to shame may be expressed as "I could have sunk into the ground" or, analogously, "I could have died!" The reference to death brings to mind a common synonym of shame—mortification...As guilt generates confession and the goal of forgiveness, shame generates concealment and hiding, and the wish for acceptance (by self or other)."[28]

Most of us *want* to believe that, at our core, we are generally good, kind, caring and responsible people who *want* to treat others with honor and fairness. We *want* to believe that we can and will make wise and moral decisions for the good of our loved ones. We *want* to believe that we can prevent harm to those we care for and to ourselves.

Yet when that doesn't happen, shame automatically erupts from within us. You can see how this would lead to dangerous self-condemnation.[29] Shame is more than a feeling. Shame is a negative self-destructive physiological motivator, most often at the subconscious level, that bypasses the reason and the will initiating habitual reactionary behaviors: fight, flight or freeze. It is appropriate to describe shame as a *power* initiated by a myriad of stress triggers (See Chapter 3). Bottom-line? Shame is a very powerful catalyst of behavior, more than most of us know.[23]

---

28. Morrison, p. 13-14. Shame is "self-conscious" in that it requires a concept of the self, or an ability to see the self as an object of evaluation that reflects both identity and worth. One study found that shame and guilt emerge only after children are able to recognize themselves in the mirror.
29. June. P. Tangney and Ronda L. Dearing, Shame and Guilt, New York: Guilford Press, 2002,3..

Shame vs. Right

"Shame is an extremely painful and ugly feeling that has a negative impact on interpersonal behavior. Shame-prone individuals appear relatively more likely to blame others (as well as themselves) for negative events, more prone to a seething, bitter, resentful kind of anger and hostility, and less able to empathize with others in general."[30]

Shame consciously or subconsciously asks these self-oriented questions:

> What is wrong with me?
> How can I get rid of this self-condemnation?
> Can I ever be fixed?
> Am I lovable?
> How can God ever love someone like me or even begin to forgive me?

Faces of Shame

In one scene in C.S. Lewis' *The Great Divorce*, a heavenly resident (Lewis refers to them as *Solid Spirits* or *bright* people) has a confrontation with a terrified female *ghost* who has ventured to the foothills of the Heavenly mountains, but finds that she cannot stand being in the presence of the *Solid Spirit* who has come for her.

To remind the reader of the premise of Lewis' fictional account, there is a great divide in the realm of the departed. All deceased humans first go to a dark, depressing city, where they, if they choose to remain, will slowly lose what is left of their mortal identities and value, becoming more isolated, and more vaporous. They become *ghosts*, persons of less substance than they once had—but far less substance than they could gain if they would only submit to travel on to the Heavenly Kingdom. All they need is need. Having need is harder than it appears on the surface.

A special bus is provided for all *ghosts* who would choose to begin the journey from Earth to Heaven. As the few willing Heaven-bound *ghosts* step off the bus, they are met by friendly *Solid Spirits* whose sole desire is to lead the *ghosts* on to glory. These *Solid Spirits* were once *ghosts* themselves who chose to pursue Heaven. The meetings between the *ghosts* and *former-ghosts-now-Solid-Spirits* is recorded for us by Lewis' protagonist.[31]

> A ghost hobbled across the clearing…looking over its shoulder as if it were being pursued…I saw that it had been a woman, a well dressed woman and I thought that its shadows of finery looked ghastly in the morning light. It was making for the bushes…it seemed to believe it was hiding. A moment later I

---

30. See Worthington, E. L. and Langberg, D. (2012). Religious Considerations and Self-Forgiveness in Treating Complex Trauma and Moral Injury in Present and Former Soldiers. Journal of Psychology and Theology, 40(4), 274-288.
31. Lewis, Great Divorce, 59..

heard the sound of feet and one of the bright people came in sight. One always noticed that sound there for we ghosts made no sound when we walked.

"Go away," squealed the ghost, "Go away, can't you see that I want to be alone."

"But you need help," said the solid one.

"If you have the least trace of decent feeling left, you'll keep away," said the ghost. "I don't want help, I want to be left alone. Do go away. You know I can't walk fast enough on those horrible spikes to get away from you. It's abominable for you to take advantage."

"Oh that," said the Spirit, "That will soon come right. But you are going in the wrong direction. It's back there to the mountains you need to go. You can lean on me all the way. I can't absolutely carry you. But you need have almost no weight on your own feet. And it will hurt less at every step."

"…Can't you understand anything? Do you really suppose that I am going out there among all those people, like this?…I'd never have come at all if I had known that you all would be dressed like that."

"Friend, you see I'm not dressed at all?"

"I didn't mean that. Do go away…How can I go out like this? Among a lot of people with real solid bodies? It's far worse than going out with nothing on would have been on earth. Have everyone staring through me?"

"Oh I see, but we were all a bit ghostly when we first arrived you know, that will wear off. Just come out and try."

"But they'll see me."

"What will it matter if they do?"

"I'd rather die."

"But you've died already…"

"…I wish I'd never been born…what are we born for?"

"For infinite happiness," said the Spirit, "You can step out into it at any moment."

"But I tell you, they'll see me."

"An hour hence and you will not care. A day hence and you will laugh at it. Don't you remember on earth there were things too hot to touch with your finger? But you could drink them all right. Shame is like that. If you will accept it—if you will drink the cup to the bottom, you will find it very nourishing. But if you try to do anything else with it, and it scalds…Friend, could you only for a moment fix your mind on something not yourself."

    The shame-infected female *ghost* was so terrified of what others might think about her appearance, how she was dressed, and her translucency, that she could not submit for help. A child could do it. She could not. Shame is that debilitating. Her expectation of negative gaze of the others withered her.
    Why the absurd and tragic response? Why not, "Sure let's do this thing?" Perhaps she had suffered under years of thoughtless salvos from a critical parent? Perhaps she had been chronically mocked due to some physical feature. Whatever the source of her shame, whatever the nature of her specific conscious or unconscious *uglies*, this diminished wraith was terrified of the opinions of others.
    Shame's ugly irony is apparent. This Earth-affected woman was terrified of the only way for her to become truly dressed. Her real glory would have to come from God. This latter-day glory has no place for even the least infinitesimal clinging shame.
    Up until that point, she believed that her value, worth, glory and beauty had been determined by her efforts in make-up, hair-do, dress, adornment, Spanx or the many masks donned to display acceptable personality and charm. She was so afraid of being seen for who she was—a person that she did not ultimately see as worthy or beautiful, rather riddled with stains, flaws, and innate ugliness—that she could only push away the only one who had the power to lead her into an experience of real substance and worth. She couldn't—or better was too ashamed—to drink from the only stream of living water. Her shame prevented her rescue.

"Shame is ubiquitous. It is everywhere and it is pervasive, that is, it touches every component of our lives. Our shame experiences may be isolated. We may even now be able to remember a few of those moments where we felt significant exposure, but the reality is for most of us we've learned over many, many years to be able to manage shame so that we actually avoid people, prophesies, worlds where there might actually be that experience of that shudder that we once knew many, many, many moons ago. But this is going to affect your sexuality. It's going to affect who you choose to marry. Its going to affect often how you chose a career…The reality for each and every one of us is that we know shame. We know something of the searing profound entry

The Gospel App Shape

Shame and guilt have almost identical facial expressions. The person tends to look down and to the side to avoid meeting the eyes of other people. The eyebrows arch outwards in a non-aggressive expression and the mouth droops in apparent sorrow. Often the head is tilted forward, the body posture stooped, shoulders are slack and the gait is slow and shuffling.

of that kind of darkness, and we know that it is an exposure of something so basically raw and naked about us that exposes what we fear to be true and that is that there is something deeply foul and ugly about us. And shame as exposure that gets to the very core of who we are or fear we are actually sends most of us on a flight—many ways a rampaging flight—from even the prospect of being known or seen that way ever again."[32]

The Origins of Shame: Adam and Eve

"When the woman saw that the fruit of the tree was good for food and pleasing to the eye, and also desirable for gaining wisdom, she took some and ate it. She also gave some to her husband, who was with her, and he ate it. Then the eyes of both of them were opened, and they realized they were naked; so they sewed fig leaves together and made coverings for themselves. Then the man and his wife heard the sound of the Lord God as he was walking in the garden in the cool of the day, and they hid from the Lord God among the trees of the garden. But the Lord God called to the man, "Where are you?" He answered, "I heard you in the garden, and I was afraid because I was naked; so I hid." And he said, "Who told you that you were naked? Have you

32. Allender, Dan (2014). On Shame: Jubilee 2014 Main Session [Video] Retrieved March 15, 2015, from https://youtu.be/6QiHzlwqeOE.

Shame vs. Right

eaten from the tree that I commanded you not to eat from?" The man said, "The woman you put here with me—she gave me some fruit from the tree, and I ate it." Then the Lord God said to the woman, "What is this you have done?" The woman said, "The serpent deceived me, and I ate"…The Lord God made garments of skin for Adam and his wife and clothed them." (Gen 3:6-21 NIV)

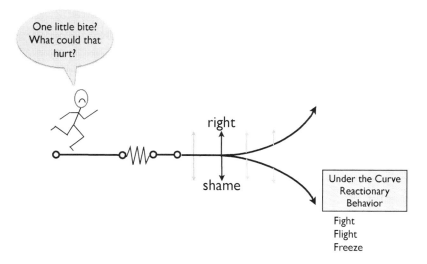

Consider the *Gospel App* shape above. The Stick figure represents Eve immediately after her fatal bite. Up until this moment, as far as we know, Adam and Eve had only been subjected to perfect love, resulting in only love behaviors. All they have ever done was to love themselves, each other, creation and God, and be loved by all of the above.

There had been no experience of shame yet. There was not even the slightest concept of shame on the horizon, consciously or subconsciously. There was no bickering, no jealousy, or selfishness. No awkwardness with God. No wondering if God actually loved them as they were. No wondering if the "other" didn't like me. Only humans filled with joy. No us-versus-them. No shame at all. It is hard to imagine.

Consider this quote from an Old Testament scholar Carleen Mandolfo:

"As a human being, I am "finished" by others; I have no independent identity apart from the "gaze" of others."[33]

Mandolfo rightly concludes that no man or woman is an island. We are

---

33. Carleen R. Mandolfo, Daughter Zion Talks Back to the Prophets: A Dialogic Theology of the Book of Lamentations, SBL, 2007, 12.

relational to the core. "I am" is to a large degree a function of who I am in relationship to you and others; and to that end, your's and God's assessment of me and my worth.

This was good news for Adam and Eve pre-Fall. All they did was enjoy the life-giving, value-creating gaze of each other and, in particular, of God Himself. Such a powerful assessing gaze finished them, made them whole, and fulfilled them. In the imagery of Lewis's *Great Divorce*, the gaze of God made them *Solid Spirits*.

What "finished" Adam and Eve alike? It was the necessary result of each gazing unhindered and without hesitation into God's adoring gaze—enhanced only secondarily by the gaze of each other. If Adam wondered who he *was* related to God and to Eve, he only had to look into their eyes. There was always only adoration and appreciation for his "Adam-ness"—his God-likeness. Likewise, Eve only had to look into God's eyes or Adam's and she would be assured of her unchanging glory, value, identity and worth—her "Eve-ness"—her God-likeness.

This is so strange for us to imagine. At the end of our day, the self-assessment of our own well-being, worth, success, purpose, name—in Great Divorce terminology: our *solid*-ness—comes from a variety of disjointed, inconsistent, and lesser sources: our work, any words of encouragement or "critique" from others—someone we just happened to bump into on the subway or who cut us off in traffic—or worse, one's inconsistent and largely unverifiable feelings. These *gazes* from the many others that we run into are often not encouraging or life-giving at all. Our judgment of worth is driven by so many data points, many of which are out of our control.

Whose gaze did you drink in today? Yesterday? Two decades ago? What identity did their gaze attribute to you? Did you earn it? Did you not deserve it? Of course, the evaluation process begins again tomorrow.

Back to the Garden. Before the Fall, Eve was wonderfully dependent upon Yahweh for her sense of worth. She knew nothing other than her valuation in God's eyes every time she looked up and *heard* with her eyes, "Well done good and faithful servant." His valuation was consistent and positive.

This relationship was the old normal. It's fruit? Eve was never more Eve than when she was with Yahweh, in His gaze. As a fruit of such Eve-ness, she could—and was motivated to—love God and Adam nakedly, fearlessly, and freely. In the cast light of God's constant positive assessment, Eve didn't even *need* Adam's assessment of her value. I assume that his second opinion, also constantly positive and adoring, was quite a confirmation of God's assessment of her. Pre-Fall Adam would have been totally in-sync with God on this topic. "Eve, there is nothing about you that could not be described as *right*. You are indeed good very good."

Orphaned Eve

Then, along came Satan and his all-too-successful strategy to manipulate a psychic and emotional wedge between Eve and her Maker's gaze. Perhaps the first thing she felt after "Fruit-gate," was an immediate exhilarating sense of independence—not freedom. Freedom is what we experience when we are *with* God and He is *with* us. In such a freedom we are more who we were meant to be.

Independence is the drive of those apart from the gaze of God who must find their valuation, their "finishing" from the gaze of so many other sources. Freedom and independence are two very different things.

In this first millisecond of the Fall, Eve experiences independence. There are no recorded thoughts that she desired to go and ask Yahweh what to do, or to tell Him of the conversation. She shifted from a living dependence upon Yahweh's freedom—to acting as if she were an orphan living alone on the street. She experienced for the very first time in human history being Eve-without-Yahweh—a whole new creation—something far less than Eve-with-Yahweh.[34]

In this scene we also witness the first tragic subconscious act of idolatry. Idols are those gazes, other than God's that we look toward to measure our present significance, security, and belonging. We look to idols for our "rightness," our being and feeling right.[35]

Before this very moment in the Garden, how were good and bad, right or wrong, smart or dumb measured? Arguably, God determined all of the above. He was seen as being very reliable.

> "Is this good? Is this right? Is this the right thing to do? Will this give me pleasure? Will this make me more Eve? I don't know. Ask Yah."

In a single tragic moment, Eve discovered exciting new measurement devices to determine her sense of rightness: including her own visual assessment, her expectation of what would give her pleasure, and her "belief" (based upon the Serpent's testimony) of the result—that she would be wiser than she was before.

These measuring devices were way out of alignment with God and His gaze.

When did God step down as the arbiter of what was right for Eve? God, by nature, was into pleasure for her. When did the source of wisdom shift from God to eating a fruit? This was a huge deviation in procedure.

In the end, in a mere moment of time, Eve's longing-to-be-measured-and-assessed fell to the gaze of created things. Unknowingly, so did her assessment of her own value. In Lewis-speak, she became a ghost, a coreless wraith.

The Christian philosopher Kierkegaard called this misalignment of ac-

---

34. We will cover orphanness in Chapter 8.
35. We will cover idolatry in Chapter 9.

tions and motivations "sickness unto death."[36] To the degree that Eve lived out of calibration with God's measurement and assessment, she was sick, miserable, not truly Eve anymore. The same could be said of Adam's fall.

Eyes Wide Opened

This misalignment is the fundamental root of sin. Sin is looking for my significance, security, and belonging in any other place than God's assessing eyes.

Immediately, humanity experienced the most tragic event that has ever occurred. "Then the eyes of both of them were opened." Once Eve's gaze was no longer toward God's adoring loving eyes, an emotional measurement-vacuum occurred, not consciously, but rather subconsciously. Her present measurement of value and worth now fell to things and persons other than God. For the first time in her life she had to wonder if she was wonderful. She had to find some measuring device that gave her the answer to the questions, "Who am I? Am I a person of honor? Worth?"

"We can now speculate what happened at a scientific level immediately after Fruit-Gate. Eve was not thinking, she was reacting. Her limbic system did exactly what it was designed to do. For the very first time in human history—but certainly not the last—a chemical cocktail was immediately released from her brain, virtually shutting down her frontal lobes, her ability to reason, to think strategically, or to think of others. Her God-created reactionary survival system kicked in igniting three choices: fight, flight or freeze."

Unfortunately all created gazes are lesser gazes, some good, some bad, but all lesser. So Eve and Adam now felt naked—no longer aware or sure of their beauty and attractiveness in the eyes of each other. Seminal shame and guilt erupted from within perfect humanity.

What might they have sensed? I would imagine that it would have felt like their very identities were for the first time exposed and very vulnerable to criticism. They had shifted from solidness to wraith-ness in a nanosecond. They had no way of knowing, post Fruit-Gate if they were still beautiful, pleasing, good, or worthy. Why? They just separated themselves from the only previously accepted judge of beauty and value and worth: the gaze of Yahweh.

We can now speculate what happened at a scientific level immediately after Fruit-Gate. Eve was not thinking, she was reacting. Her limbic system did

---

36. "For so it is with men in this world: first a man sins from frailty and weakness; and then -- yes, then perhaps he learns to flee to God and to be helped by faith which saves from all sin... And for the whole of Christianity it is one of the most decisive definitions that the opposite of sin is not virtue but faith." Soren Kierkegaard, The Sickness Unto Death, (Princeton: Princeton University Press) accessed on March 15, 2015, Religion Online.org.

exactly what it was designed to do. For the very first time in human history—but certainly not the last—a chemical cocktail was immediately released from her brain, virtually shutting down her frontal lobes, her ability to reason, to think strategically, or to think of others. Her God-created reactionary survival system kicked in igniting three choices: fight, flight or freeze.

How do we know? We can observe her foolish strategy to still shame's condemning voice. Eve's pathetic plan involved covering herself with leaves. Laughable, of course; quite unreasonable. Clearly, the initial launch of the first human's fight, flight and freeze systems was a notable success. Eve's well-designed limbic system did what it will do thousands of time subsequent to this moment.

Eve, everyone can see that the leaves could not relieve your shame. If you could for a moment be reasonable, not ashamed, or afraid, you could see that too. Your shame is far too powerful, far too subconscious.

She and Adam had bigger problems of course. For now, they were reacting emotionally. Eventually each had to wonder, "What does God now think of me? Is God angry at me? Is God disappointed in me? Does He no longer like me? Is God disgusted with me?"

All of this was new for Adam and Eve, internally generated—subconscious, irrational, overwhelming, and accomplished at near light-speed. They had to urgently discover another mirror to assess themselves.[37] They had never felt God angry before, never felt disappointment from Him, and never wondered if He was disgusted at them. That is what they experienced now. As a result, they no longer dared to look into His eyes. This is the devastating power of shame. They hid.[38] They hid from the only one who could or would save them.

It was the first in a subsequent long line of fear driven subconscious self-destructive choices. We, the readers, see that. In their thinking there was an immediate need to hide. Absurdly, these two hide behind a tree to escape the all-knowing, all-seeing God. This is a powerful narrative image of how irrational shame motivation can be. Imagine, if the first sin led to such insanity and craziness, what our umpteenth sin with all of the residual State Memory might cause us to do.

Where are you, Oh Man?

The tsunami of shame subconsciously by-passed Adam and Eve's capacity to reason and horribly misled them. They were irrationally wrong about God's response. His words were not harsh, or angry. God's call, "Where are you O man?" (Gen 3:9) should be read as a warm loving invitation to his guilty and ashamed

---

37. Shame is a feeling "associated with being negatively evaluated (either by the self or others) because one has failed to meet standards and norms regarding what is good, right, appropriate, and desirable." Wong, Y., Tsai, J. (2007) "Cultural models of Shame and Guilt." In J.L. Tracy, R.W. Robins, & J.P. Tangney (Eds.) The Self-Conscious Emotions: Theory and Research (209-223). New York: Guilford Press. 210.
38. "Shame makes us hide. Shame makes us mean." Allender (2014), On Shame.

children to look into His eyes again. God already knew where they were and what had happened to their gaze. God asked an engaging question to His two beloved children, newly riddled and crippled with *de-God-imaging* shame and guilt; now dangerously deceived by a myriad of faulty internal and external measuring devices. They no longer knew who they were. They no longer had any way of fixing it, not by their own efforts anyway.

What hope did they have? The singular and most obvious answer to reasonably calm people clear of shame and fear is *God*—or more specifically God's unwavering adoring gaze toward them. Unfortunately, as a tragic result of the rush of toxic chemicals racing through their fight, flight and freeze limbic systems, they either *forgot* that God still loved them as they were or they were afraid that He had negatively reassessed His devotion.

Truth be told, God didn't love them any less than He had two minutes before. All they needed to do in order to unravel all of the fear-based behaviors and shame consequences was to, by faith, throw themselves back into the warm and loving arms of Yahweh. All they needed to do was to re-attach to the adoring gaze of God. Just look up, Adam and Eve. They could not. They would not.

Apart from the surge of guilt and shame, why wouldn't they look up? All they had ever known was the love and acceptance of Yahweh. Previously, ten times out of ten, God was there for them. He was always good, trustworthy, and loving. His assessment was always—always—life giving.

This time *felt* different. Both Adam and Eve would have agreed. This time, they were filled with something formerly foreign to them. In this *new* place, they somehow just knew that God could not love them anymore—not after what they had done. Witness the birth of guilt and shame. All of this devolution of perfect community happened in a matter of moments.

This breakdown led to even *more* reactionary unreasonable behaviors: excuses, blaming of each other, the inability or unwillingness to listen, unbelief, and amnesia of the constant never-changing nature of the love of God (Gen 3:7-18). This was novel, a powerful rush of fear, guilt, and shame from within the soul of perfect humanity. In the end, God's calm and loving evangelistic invitation had no sway over these two miserable anthropomorphic petri dishes.

Adam and Eve's shame was a powerful emotive force, debilitating, not evil, yet hardly reasonable either. Their previously *free*-wills were for the first time in human history far less free. Their once pristine ability to choose had been highly compromised. In other situations, shame, and guilt in particular, can lead to an awareness of need for a rescue. Not in this case. All Adam and Eve needed was need. Instead they circled the wagons, unfortunately with their Savior on the outside.

The point is that if such irrational and powerful forces can surge through perfectly loved previously non-traumatized folk in the perfect context of the Garden, imagine our vulnerabilities. It would certainly explain a lot.

Sin happens—and subsequent shame—when I gaze into lesser gazes to be measured, to see how worthy I am. I look away from God as my measurement and submit to the measuring authority of others. This is arguably the heart of all sin.

At the writing of this chapter, I have had 58 years of serious conditioning to look at lesser gazes and only a spotty 37 years of conditioning to forsake the latter and to look up again. If the truth were known, it has only been in the last decade that I have concertedly tried to reprogram my knee-jerk reaction to stressors by looking up into God's gaze more often. It is slow-going—but noticeable and encouraging gains are being made.

Why have an affair? People look into the eyes of his or her spouse and don't *feel* valued. They look into the eyes of another partner and *feel* valued, loved, and appreciated. Sin happens.

Why gossip? People don't feel valued and appreciated so he or she subconsciously comes up with a strategy. If they can be the source of some information that draws attention upon themselves, he or she might just *feel* just a little bit more substantive. They are desperately looking for some worth in the eyes of others who turn their gaze to enjoy the little juicy tidbits of information. At that moment, probably subconsciously, the person appraises that feeling of value from others over the possible destruction that might happen through gossiping.

> *"In the end, God's calm and loving rhetoric had no sway over these two miserable anthropomorphic petri dishes."*

In that moment, the person is out-of-sync with the love of God. He or she is also out of sync with how much God adores and loves them. If they felt the height, width, length, and depth of the love of Christ, they wouldn't *need* to resort to gossip.

The core of sin is to look into other gazes for one's present sense of being valued as being lovable, honorable, and worthy. He or she is not feeling right about themselves and need to glean rightness from some gaze, some experience, and some measurement. Ultimately sin is not finding those from God—rather attempting to find them from other lesser sources. Needless to say, we "sin" hundreds of times daily.

All of us suffer from shame to one degree or another. Our subconscious knee jerk reaction? We will hide, cover up our shame, make excuses and at times go on the offensive if that would remove from us the negative gazes of others. "Shame is difficult to treat because, so often, it is difficult to find. We hide our shame behind the guises of anger, contempt, depression, denial, or superiority."[39]

Personal Testimony: State Shame

I have struggled with body image for a long time. I was quite a chubby child and

39. Andrew Morrison, The Culture of Shame. New York: Ballantine. 1996, 10.

for years thought others agreed. Perhaps they did, perhaps they didn't. I'm not so sure now. All I know is that I did not like my body, and largely assumed that others thought I was an unfortunate character as well. This largely subconscious self-loathing was a great hindrance for me, in sports, relationships, and happiness in general. I became someone overly concerned with people liking me. I put a lot of effort into it. Experts call this "state shame." My shame was not about what I did. I was ashamed of me.

At one point I seriously thought about becoming a stand-up comedian. I adored Robin Williams and Steve Martin. I did a couple of stand-up sets with great reviews. I can see now, for me to have pursued that career would have been committing myself to a lifetime of servitude to the laughter of others as a measuring stick of my worth and being *right*. My sense of self and well-being would have likely been ruled by questions asked at the end of the day: "Was I a person of value today? Did people like my routine? Did they laugh at my jokes? Do they think that I am funny today?" Or even darker questions? "Are they just laughing at me, the chubby guy on stage?" That would have been self-imposed slavery for me—nothing to laugh at.

Shame has already happened when one finds oneself afraid of gazing into the eyes of anyone because he or she is far too afraid to see his or her reflection in their eyes. Shame looks away. Shame looks downward. It is part of the nature of shame.

We Live in a Shame-Based Culture

We all know shame. We are all affected by it, every individual, every family, and every culture. As I write this, many urban centers in the US are ablaze with marches to raise awareness of supposed double standards in the justice system. "The police and the courts have an innate bias against people of color," the demonstrators argue, "Black lives matter." Recent events in Baltimore, Staten Island, New York and Ferguson, Missouri are put forth as proof in their assessment.

While I do not want to argue the case here, I would present another line of dialogue related to the arguable division between the white and black communities that may just lead to more pro-social results for both. I would suggest that the inner-city black community, individually and corporately have endured decades of shaming—certainly some from the outside but a significant amount from inside their ranks as well. Both create a culture of shame.

The core issue in the current racial divide is less justice or injustice, or even racism (though these are critically important and relevant topics to be sure). The foundational issue is generational and cultural shame. Until this core State Memory shame is intentionally diminished by a greater power, there will only be ongoing divisions and degradation. This is a serious issue for all the population, white and black.

Am I saying that welfare (too much or too little) is, or is not, the problem?

Shame vs. Right

Government policy? Unemployment? Ongoing prejudice by white corporate America? Education or lack thereof? The violent and degrading lyrics of some Hip Hop music? The growing percentage of single-parent families in certain subcultures? While these issues are important, I am arguing that for the most part, these are not the roots of the problem but among the many fruit of the singular toxic tree.

At its core hides shame. Shamed people often resist being raised up, resist education, may even resist succeeding in careers and life in general. Subconsciously they may feel that they deserve to be treated as unworthy. Shamed people, no matter what race, nationality, subculture, sex, or socio-economic status can quickly deteriorate into their own negative caricatures. They can become their own *uglies*.

In an interesting blog, Xavier James points out five televisions shows that in his opinion most shame the black community. They include The Flavor of Love, Tyler Perry's House of Payne, The Jerry Springer Show, The Maury Show, and B.E.T. (Black Entertainment Television).[40] While some of the five could be accused of being produced by whites to present a shameful caricature of blacks for ratings and profits, three of them would arguably be blacks shaming blacks for the same ratings and profits.

James writes, the B.E.T. "literally ruined about two-three generations of black children. At the time B.E.T. was the only place black folks could turn to and see images of themselves. It was also the one place artists could get their videos and faces seen on television. And knowing this [B.E.T] allowed the raunchiest, degrading, ignorant, ghetto images of black life to be showcased like never before in the history of America. From sagging pants and gold chains, to the booty-butt cheeks on young teenage girls; nothing was off limits. And anyone who complained was either hatin' or lacked vision and if you worked for him; fired…It was blacks exploiting blacks at its finest…After his grand exploitation of millions of black children…[B.E.T.'s] legacy of teaching consumption, hoochiefied dress and behavior, sagging pants, self-devaluation, and a backwards culture still thrives."

The *Gospel App* proposes the only real solution to black and white humanity's shame is the Gospel—period. Christian blacks of Baltimore, Ferguson, Staten Island, look up into the eyes of Your Creator and see your glorious reflection in His eyes. Your Heavenly Father loves you as much as He loves His own Son; as much as the Son loves the Father, as you are right now. He can't love you any more or any less. You are *right* in His eyes. Ask the Holy Spirit to make His evaluation your own. Policemen of those same cities, look up as well.

The resulting feelings and motivations will be noticeable. Consider the shape on the next page. Look at the horrible list of self-destructive, anti-social

---

40. Xavier James, June 6, 2011, Blog: "Top Five Shows that Shame(d) the Black Community," http://xavierjamesuncensored.blogspot.com/2011/06/top-5-shows-that-shamed-black-community.html.

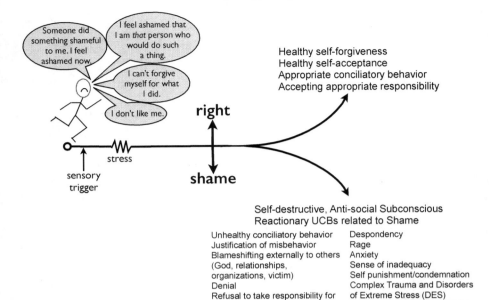

subconscious reactionary UCBs related to core shame. This is not a white or black issue at all. We share this response to shame.

Imagine for a moment the difference in your response to people or situations if Jesus' applied righteousness erupted the healthier OCBs from within you. You would begin to feel a new self-forgiveness and self-acceptance. You may be drawn to appropriate conciliatory behaviors that produce far greater results than riots and looting. You may begin to feel far more capable to accept appropriate responsibility for your own life.

This new freedom from negative anti-social power of shame does not miraculously lift away all of your problems and issues—nor does it wash away the structural problems of the larger society. It does noticeably diminish one of the hidden ever-present powers that is holding you back from experiencing the success, intimacy, and happiness for which you are longing.

The same approach could lead to great forward movement in what some have labeled the "war on women." Couldn't the same approach bear observable fruit in the Israeli-Palestinian conflict? Shame has its ugly tendrils penetrating all levels of society, all races, all people groups, and all families.

I spent some time looking at the top movies of 2013 and 2014 to determine how many of them had major themes related to shame (See next page). There was an overwhelming majority which explored shame.

In a recent Christianity Today cover article, Andy Crouch suggests that

2013-2014 Movies with Significant Shame Theme

Whiplash,
Interstellar,
August: Osage County,
Frozen,
The Hunger Games: Mockingjay Pt 1.,
The Hobbit: The Desolation of Smaug,
The Hunger Games: Catching Fire,
Horrible Bosses 2,
Birdman,
The Expendables 3,
Nightcrawler,
Big Hero 6,
The Internship,
Maleficent,
American Hustle,
Her,
12 Years a Slave,
47 Ronin,
The Invisible Woman,
Divergent,
Saving Mr. Banks,
Dawn of the Planet of the Apes,
Mandela: Long Walk to Freedom,
Unbroken,
Foxcatcher,
Thor: The Dark World,
Prisoners,
St. Vincent,
Transformers: Age of Extinction,
The Fault in our Stars,
Blue Jasmine,
A Most Wanted Man,
Dallas Buyers Club,
Sex Tape,
The Equalizer,
The Immigrant,
The Judge,
Chef,
The Hundred Foot Journey,
Godzilla,
The Secret Life of Walter Mitty,
42,
Philomena,
The Railway Man,
The Great Gatsby,
When the Game Stands Tall,
Elysium,
Noah,
The Other Woman,
Winter's Tale,
Non-Stop,
Robo-Cop,
Rosewater,
Nebraska,
I Frankenstein,
Calvary,
Kill the Messenger,

shame has returned as a dominant issue in the West.[41] "From online bullying to Twitter takedowns, shame is becoming a dominant force in the West." Quoting Kara Powell of the Fuller Youth Institute, "On Facebook, others' perceptions of us are both public and relatively permanent…You post something and everybody comments on it. People tag you, talk about you. And if no one comments, that can be just as much a source of shame." Crouch adds,

> "The personal screen, especially with its attached and always-available camera, invites us to star in our own small spectacle. As our social network chimes, blinks, and buzzes with intermittent approval, we are constantly updated on our success in gaining public affirmation. But having attracted us with the promise of approval and belonging, the personal screen can just as easily herald exclusion and hostility, as the targets of GamerGate found out and as nearly every teenager in the West knows from experience."

Shame is very much a "me too" issue. Any person who testifies that they

---

41. Andy Crouch, "The Return of Shame", Christianity Today, February 2015. Accessed at http://christianitytoday.com/ct/2015/march/andy-crouch-gospel-in-age-of-public-shame.html.

have no shame is in denial. What gaze are you looking into now?

How does shame affect my relationship with God?

That self-assessment of being wrong and the self-condemnation that naturally results is almost always projected upon one's relationship with God.

Since I have concluded that I have fallen short of *my* standards and rightly feel self-condemnation, something deep inside of me fears that God must condemn me as well.

In a recent Christmas Eve service at a western church, participants were asked to anonymously write down their greatest fear. Well over half wrote that they were afraid that God was angry or ashamed of them.

> Fear that I'm not good enough [for God's love],
> Fear that I am not all that God made me to be,
> Fear that I won't hear God say, "Well done, good and faithful servant. Enter into your rest",
> Fear that God is not still pleased with me,
> Fear of not being forgiven anymore because of all the things I have done,
> Fear of God seeing me as a big disappointment,
> Fear that I'm not good enough for God to love me,
> Fear of not measuring up to God because of my lack of intelligence, lack of will power and unbelief,
> Fear that God will not accept me because of my divorce, my depression, my addiction to alcohol,
> Fear that God doesn't love me as I am,
> Fear that the Cross didn't really make me clean enough,
> Fear that when all is said and done, I am not worth anything.

The respondents, to some degree or another for many reasons, conscious and subconscious, were ashamed to boldly look into God's gaze. Like Adam and Eve before them, they could only look down and be swept to and fro by any measuring wind, never willing or able to look up.

There is an epidemic of shame within Christianity today. It does not take a prophet to divine the quality of the prayer lives of the above children of God. Shame causes people to turn away from those they have or feel that they have disappointed or hurt. In this case, they believe that they have disappointed God. They may *not* pray at all. If they do pray, it might end up being blaming, rote, or stiff and ritualistic.

Worship for them will hardly be free and intimate. They may be demanding in worship, consumeristic, expecting the act of worship to give them hits to fill the vacuum left by God's experiential absence in their lives. They may subconsciously erect emotional boundaries to prevent being exposed to God's measuring gaze. They cannot worship *nakedly* before God.

Why would they share their faith? Why risk being rejected? That would be too painful of course. Why would they invite other shamed needy people to look up when they can't? That would be disingenuous of course, painfully obvious hypocrisy.

Gospel App on Shame

Consider the *Gospel App* shape on page 88. Something happened to Stick. Stick is experiencing shame. "Someone did something shameful to me. I feel ashamed now." "I feel ashamed that I am that person who would do such a thing." "I can't forgive myself for what I did." "I don't like me."

Depending upon previous experience and conditioning, he or she will likely subconsciously spiral into self-destructive, anti-social subconscious reactionary behaviors, such as unhealthy conciliatory behaviors (I will make up with you without dealing with core issues), blameshifting externally to others (God, parents, victim, the government, etc.), refusing to take responsibility, self-destructive behaviors (over or under-eating, cutting, drugs, inappropriate sex, or even despondency, rage, abnormal avoidance, and paranoia).

What is needed to break the cycle? What is needed for Stick to have a knee-jerk response to their shame that would lead to healthy self-forgiveness, healthy self-acceptance, appropriate conciliatory behavior, and acceptance of appropriate responsibility? The next chapter will discuss the various modern approaches to dealing with shame, including the path suggested by the *Gospel App*.

The Gospel App Shape

Chapter 7: Dealing with Shame

> *Shame is the fear of disconnection—it's the fear that something we've done or failed to do, an ideal that we've not lived up to or a goal that we've not accomplished makes us unworthy of connection. I'm not worthy or good enough for love or belonging, or connection…shame is the intensely personal feeling or experience of believing that we are flawed and therefore unworthy of love and belonging.*[42]
>
> —Brené Brown

Personal Testimony: Situational Shame

I personally came face to face with the power of *situational* shame—and related guilt—after being caught in an ethical and moral failure during my early twenties. Ultimately the situation led to my salvation, but honestly at the time, it didn't feel very "saving" at all.

      The onslaught of both shame and its related guilt when I was caught red-handed was surprisingly immediate and visceral for me. Only days before I would have denied that I could ever have had such a failure. That was a line that I just wouldn't cross—but then I did. It happened so quickly—so effortlessly. I was *that* person; the one that I thought I would never be. I was shocked, depressed, afraid, and rudderless: in a word, ashamed.

---

[42]. Brené Brown, Daring Greatly, 68-69. Brown offers twelve shame categories: appearance/body image, money and work, motherhood/fatherhood, family, parenting, mental and physical health, addition, sex, aging, religion, surviving trauma, and being stereotyped or labeled.

One of the typical consequences of shame is a subconscious paranoia. I assumed that my family and friends were ashamed of me as well. I only learned later that this was not the truth, only a projection of the feelings that I had about myself—yet at the time, it was functionally true for me.

What did I learn? I learned that I had no on-off switch for either shame or guilt. I had no muscle group to stop their power. I felt very helpless. I even went to visit one of the people that I deeply hurt hoping that he would smack me in the face. I know now that I wasn't thinking too logically, I just wanted subconsciously to get rid of my shame. I figured that any justice meted out would somehow set me free from shame. I can see now—I could not see it in the moment—that I wasn't so interested in *his* feelings as much as in diminishing *my* feelings of shame and self-contempt. I have shared my foolish wrong-headed shame-relief strategy with many others—most of whom understood exactly what I was trying to do. We all get it.

Shame is far worse than guilt. Guilt is about doing wrong or not doing right. Certainly in this case, I realized that what I had done was wrong. I felt guilt for my choices. The problem was that apologizing for my actions was of little help for me. I still carried shame.

In the nagging backwash of my shame, I actively wondered if I did what I did because I was innately *not right:* bad, unethical, self-centered, insensitive, manipulative, or just incapable of acting with responsible and other-directed motives. There was a deep controlling power within me that I could not quiet. It was right after all. I *did* something that I knew was *not right*. And so, my reason concluded, I must be innately *not right* somehow. I sinned. What I did severely affected other people. The only explanation is that I must be, at my core, a selfish, indifferent person. Something is wrong with me that I would do something like that.

I, like most people, want to believe that at my core I am generally a good person who wants to treat others with honor—as I would want to be treated myself. In light of my actions, I suspected that I was not a righteous person at my core. I felt self-condemnation. What could I do to rid myself of this ugly shame?

A Closer Look at the Science Behind Shame

Two *Selves* of Shame. According to some researchers, shame happens when my *Real Self*—the person I see myself to be at this moment; the *self* that I assume that others see—is a far cry from my *Ideal Self*.[43] My *Ideal Self* is shaped by my upbringing and family of origin, the implicit or explicit codes of behavior in my particular culture and people group, and of course, my view of God and His demands upon me and my behavior. From a variety of sources, each of us develops a marshalling expectation of who we *should* be, how we should treat other people,

---

43. See Worthington, E. Jr., Moving Forward: Six Steps to Forgiving Yourself and Breaking Free From the Past, New York: WaterBrook Press, 2013, 56.

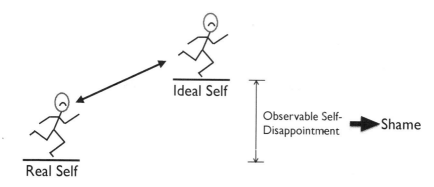

and how we should feel about ourselves related to that. I call this *Ideal Self*, my *Should-of Self*. Shame happens when these two *Selves* are misaligned—when my *Real Self* has fallen short of my *Ideal Self*, my *Should-of Self*.

When the actions of our *Real Self* do not live up to the high standards of our *Ideal Self*, the latter lets us know deep in our psyche. "Look, can't you see you have fallen short—again? You must be flawed—maybe irreparably. Your parent was right about you." Not only does shame happen, it has a very loud inner voice.

Take a look at the above figure. Stick has done something wrong again. He knows it. Perhaps he was caught red-handed in something embarrassing? Or perhaps someone treated him shamefully. Whatever it was, the event triggered Stick's limbic survival system, initiated by a release of a chemical cocktail into his brain. His reason and compassion for others is for all practical purposes, turned off. He now feels shame, guilt, and fear. His subconscious motivation is highly focused and motivated to relieve him of the pain.

Stick subconsciously comes to believe that he has not lived up to his own standards for acceptable behavior; his *should-ofs*. Or perhaps he suspects and fears that others also see him as a failure or a loser per those same standards.

Implicitly Stick's *Real Self* has fallen short of his *Ideal Self* again. The right thing for Stick to do, he thinks, is to internally downgrade his personhood rating from AAA to AA—or worse.

"I am just not the man I think I should be, not the Christian I should be, the husband, father, or the productive provider of house and home that I should be. I am not the son that my parents deserved."

Many things could trigger such a normal reaction. Perhaps Stick has let himself go to pot physically and finally really looked at his uglies in the mirror, or thinks that he overheard people talking about him? Perhaps he has come to see that he is addicted to some substance and has little power to change. Perhaps he had experienced a deep violation decades before that planted roots of darkness. For whatever reason, Stick now contemptuously peers at his *Real Self* with self-loathing. He feels shame.

Shame-Proneness. Psychologists speak of some people being shame-prone. If Stick had come from a critical or abusive family context where he was regularly derided for his ineptitude and imperfections—the failure of his *Real Self* to live up to the ideals of his *Ideal Self* or the *should-ofs* from others—Stick's *Ideal Self* would be over-developed, looming over every thought, word, and decision that he makes. Remember, he may not be aware of the anxiety and tension within. This warfare is generally speaking, subconscious.

As a result, Stick's reactionary largely predictable UCBs would kick in. He may avoid making decisions—over-thinking all variables and options. Certainly he must avoid possibly making a wrong—and therefore criticizable—decision. No decision is better than a wrong one, in Stick's thinking. He may have conditioned knee-jerk strategies for quickly defending himself—all designed to avoid the pain of new shame, and to avoid looking into the negatively assessing eyes of those around him. He may resist admitting any fault or failure, even blind spots.

He might be quite adept at shifting blame to others, "Well I wouldn't have done that if you had told me all the data." He may have learned how to quickly justify his choices, "I wouldn't have made that choice if I knew it would hurt you." Or deny all wrongdoing, "I did not say that, you misunderstood me."

In research studies, proneness to shame is positively correlated with anger, hostility, and the propensity to blame others. This is particularly true for individuals with narcissistic tendencies. It is not uncommon for shamed people, in order to escape the horrific feelings related to their shame to turn the tables, "externalizing blame and anger outward onto a convenient scapegoat...By doing so, the shamed person attempts to regain some sense of control and superiority in their life, but the long term costs can be steep. Friends, co-workers, and loved ones may feel confused and alienated by apparently irrational bursts of anger."[44]

> *"In recent jailhouse studies, higher shame ratings at the outset of incarceration predicted higher recidivism rates, while higher guilt ratings predicted lower recidivism rates."*

He may learn to attack—the best defense is a good offense. "Well, who are you to talk. You did the same thing last week."

Or strategically attempt to change the subject, grasping for some higher ground in the middle of the firestorm. "Do you still love me?"

Proneness to shame is also linked to a broad range of symptoms including low self-esteem, depression, anxiety, eating disorders, post-traumatic stress disorder (PTSD), preoccupation with suicide, and a wide range of substance-related disorders.

In recent jailhouse studies, higher shame ratings at the outset of incarceration predicted higher recidivism rates, while higher guilt ratings predicted lower

---

44. Tangney, "Shame, Guilt, and Remorse," 710-11.

recidivism rates.[45] Shame-prone inmates tended to have more drug and alcohol problems and tended to eschew responsibility and blame others. In contrast, inmate's guilt-proneness related to higher levels of empathy toward others, accepting responsibility and lower hostility. The results were valid across demographic lines.[46]

Shame-proneness can also thrive in some religious contexts where rule-based performance and morality is hyper-prioritized in every aspect of life. In such cases, it is often implied that God is not only harsh and demanding but He is continually leering at you and your performance, ready to "smite" you if you fall out of line. It is taught or implied that God's favor of you—whether God *likes* you or not—is fully dependent upon you doing the right and godly thing—as defined by rules of the community. Such churches, synagogues, and fellowships can be destructive petri dishes of shame and magnets for shame-prone people. Like moths to flames.

Actual orphans and those who have lost parents at a young age may also experience a tendency toward shame-proneness. For them, shame's internal lie might normally sound like this. "If only I was a better child, cuter, smarter, more fun, I would be brought into a real family. I must work hard to be the ideal adoptable child no matter what."

Shame-proneness may devolve further into a shame-prone neurotic pattern.[47] In the minds of some who have been shamed over years or decades, their self-condemnation feels reasonable and appropriate. These shamed ones are difficult to reach with good news. Yet the Gospel can do it.

The shame-prone and the shame-prone neurotic may have explosive hair triggers that can go off with very little provocation launching the persons into severe fight, flight, or freeze defensive under the curve behaviors.

---

45. Tangney, "Shame, Guilt, and Remorse," 715.
46. Ibid, 716. Tangney et al.'s studies of guilt and shame among incarcerated men and women concludes that shame is so powerful that where possible shaming sentences, those designed to shame and humiliate offenders should be avoided altogether. Shaming of any kind "is associated with outcomes directly contrary to the public interest—denial of responsibility, substance abuse, psychological symptoms, predictors of recidivism, and recidivism itself." Rather the courts would find greater success, (i.e., lower recidivism) by enforcing sanctions "designed to foster feelings of guilt by focusing offenders on the negative consequences of their behavior, particularly how their behavior affects their communities, their friends and their families. Community service sentences, for example, may be tailored to the nature of the crime, underscoring the tangible destruction caused by the offense and providing a path to redemption. Drunk drives could be sentence to help clear sites of road accidents and to assists with campaigns to reduce drunk driving. Slumlords could be sentenced to assist with nuts and bolts repairs in low-income housing units. In contrast to shaming sentences that aim to humiliate, the goal of such guilt inducing restorative justice sentences is to prompt offenders to see, first-hand, the potential or actual destructiveness of their infractions to empathize with their victims, to feel behavior-focused guilt, and importantly to actively involve them in constructive solutions."
47. See Fisher, M.L. and Exline, J. (2006) "Self-Forgiveness Versus Excusing: The Roles of Remorse, Effort and Acceptance of Responsibility," Self and Identity, 5, 127-146, and North J. "The Ideal of Forgiveness: A Philosopher's Exploration," in Exploring Forgiveness, ed. R.D. Enright and J. North (Madison WI: University of Wisconsin Press, 1998), 32.

The End of Shame

How is such powerful underlying shame and proneness to shame defeated? For most counselors, the goal is to assist the person to sync their *Ideal* and *Real Selves*.

The current line of thought is that shame is observably diminished when my *Real Self* aligns with my *Ideal Self*. How? Modern therapists suggest that such an alignment happens as participants are invited to find *appropriate* self-forgiveness and self-acceptance.

Self-Forgiveness. Shame interventions that emphasize *self-forgiveness* argue that healing occurs as the person responsibly forgives him or herself for the difference between their *Real* and *Ideal Selves* and to stop judging themselves accordingly. Healing happens as a result of an ongoing, very strange, internal trial where the participant is both Judge, Defendant, and Plaintiff.

I (as Judge):
   Does the Defendant have anything to say?

I (As Defendant):
   I am guilty Judge. I should be a better person. I should be motivated to do good things. I should be more conscientious and caring of others—but I am not. I hurt someone (or myself). I am guilty as charged. I have no reasonable case. Something is wrong with me. I deserve to be punished, exiled, despised, and treated as a condemned person of little value and worth. I do not deserve to be forgiven.

I (As Plaintiff):
   I (As Defendant) did this and have accepted responsibility and so I (As Plaintiff) forgive myself (As Defendant).

I (As Judge):
   I too find the Defendant guilty. I (As Judge) accept their remorse and them taking responsibility for the crime. Justice is satisfied. May this be a deterrent for me (As Defendant) to not do this again.

Such an intervention emphasizes the need for self-forgiveness by inviting the participant to separate (split) their *identity* from their *actions* in hopes of responsibly processing and dealing with the actual *crime* but giving the *self* a break.

I (as Plaintiff and Judge):
   Yes I (as Defendant) see that I did something self-centered, indifferent, immoral, or bad, but I *choose* to not see myself as *innately* bad or not right. I (as Defendant) *choose* instead to accept the responsibility for my crimes and all of

the consequences, and to move into conciliatory behaviors where appropriate. Ultimately I (as Defendant) also *choose* to rationally and emotionally forgive *myself*—but not my *actions*.

Though complicated, this form of therapy has been helpful to some. Therapists are very conscious that care must be taken that any self-forgiveness must *not* be merely a get-out-of-jail-free card for narcissists, cowards, or psychopaths to just do what comes naturally and not admit fault. To be appropriate and not *pseudo*-self-forgiveness, healthy self-forgiveness requires that the person accept appropriate responsibility for their wrongdoing.[48]

"Without these components, self-forgiveness is irrelevant, as there would be nothing to forgive. Where offenders fail to accept responsibility and minimize or excuse the behavior and its consequences, they engage in pseudo self-forgiveness, essentially letting themselves off the hook."[49]

The obvious drawback of such therapy is that shame is highly skilled at hiding to where Stick cannot see it clearly. What shamed Stick likely feels is a powerful subconscious lingering self-condemnation that defies the careful and delicate surgery required to locate the appropriate theoretical divide between self and actions of self. There is an easier way.

Self-Acceptance. Other shame interventions emphasize *self-acceptance*. One popular self-esteem author defines self-acceptance as "my refusal to be in an adversarial relationship with myself." He would advise shamed-ones,

"Self acceptance is the willingness to say of any emotion or behavior, 'This is an expression of me, not necessarily an expression I like or admire, but an expression of me nonetheless, at least at the time it occurred.'…To 'accept' is more than simply to 'acknowledge' or 'admit.' It is to experience, stand in the presence of, contemplate the reality of, absorb into my consciousness."[50]

The super pop-star Lady Gaga concurs. She is arguably the most provocative spokesperson of self-acceptance to shamed-unaware teens and tweens. In

---

48. See Enright, R. D., & the Human Development Study Group. "Counseling Within the Forgiveness Triad: On Forgiving, Receiving Forgiveness, and Self-Forgiveness." Counseling and Values, 40, (1996): 115; J. H. Hall & F.D. Fincham, "Self-Forgiveness: The Stepchild of Forgiveness Research," The Journal of Social and Clinical Psychology, 24 (5) 2005, 621-622; and P. C. Vitz & J. Meade, "Self-Forgiveness in Psychology and Psychotherapy: A Critique." Journal of Religious Health (2011): 250.
49. M. Wenzel, L. Woodyatt, & K. Hedrick, "No Genuine Self-Forgiveness Without Accepting Responsibility: Value Reaffirmation as a Key to Maintaining Positive Self-Regard." European Journal of Social Psychology, 42 (2012), 618; and J. H. Hall, J.H. & F. D. Fincham. "Self-Forgiveness: The Stepchild of Forgiveness Research." Journal of Social and Clinical Psychology, 24 (2005), 621-637.
50. Nathaniel Branden, The Six Pillars of Self-Esteem, Bantam Books, 2005, 92.

every interview and every show, she proclaims her message that you are a rock star. You are a masterpiece, not perfect. We all have ugly aspects, but you are no more or less than anyone else. So don't let others define you, or shame you.

She has her own tale to tell, and does regularly. Gaga provides herself as a living, breathing example of shame's enduring forces. In spite of her phenomenal success as a Superstar, Gaga still openly struggles with insecurities and feeling ugly. Her strategy is to flaunt the *uglies*—to turn her *uglies* into provocative art and expression—and invite others to do the same. If you feel ashamed, glam it. Listen to one of her top of the charts songs, Born That Way.

Born that way!
It doesn't matter if you love him or capital H-I-M
Just put your paws up
'Cause you were born this way, baby

My mama told me when I was young
We are all born superstars
She rolled my hair and put my lipstick on
In the glass of her boudoir
There's nothin' wrong with lovin' who you are
She said, 'cause He made you perfect, babe
So hold your head up, girl and you'll go far
Listen to me when I say

I'm beautiful in my way
'Cause God makes no mistakes
I'm on the right track, baby
I was born this way
Don't hide yourself in regret
Just love yourself and you're set
I'm on the right track, baby
I was born this way, born this way

Whether you're broke or evergreen
You're black, white, beige, chola descent
You're Lebanese, you're orient
Whether life's disabilities
Left you outcast, bullied or teased
Rejoice and love yourself today
'Cause baby, you were born this way.[51]

   51. Lyrics by F. Garibay, P. Blair, S. Germanotta, and B. Jeppe. Published by Lyrics © Warner/Chappell Music, Inc., Sony/ATV Music Publishing LLC.

Dealing with Shame

Per psychologist, Joseph Burgo this approach may indeed offer some immediate limited help to some.

> "[Lady Gaga] has managed to take profound shame and make it into something aesthetic and compelling. By putting her shame on display—she's not afraid to make herself look ugly, or to expose herself in ways that other people might find 'shameless' — she has in a sense triumphed over that shame... For Lady Gaga, the healing of shame doesn't mean some idealized sort of recovery where you completely erase that shame and its effects; instead it involves acceptance of your damage and internal darkness ('marrying the night') and then making the very best of it you can...Being real...actually means realizing that you feel like a loser a lot of the time, that you'll continue to feel that way, and that despite the wish to believe you're beautiful, there's quite a lot about you that's 'ugly.'"[52]

Gaga's shame-acceptance message is resonating with many teens and tweens. I am willing to believe that Gaga, a professing Catholic who prays before all of her concerts, is largely sincere. Her millions of fans sure think so.

You are who you are; a flawed rock star. You were born this way. God doesn't make mistakes. It is normal to feel ashamed, but don't stay there. Fight back, use your flaws to create an artistic expression of the real you, just like I did. Come to my concert, listen to my music and get charged up.

Arguably Gaga's appeal to self-esteem consists of powerful short-term respites from internal self-contempt. It does not appear to represent a legitimate long-term strategy. All the self-talk at Lady Gaga concerts are ultimately powerless to dislodge deeply reinforced shame. Remember, shame is a powerful motivational feeling deeply lodged in our subconscious. There are no real muscle groups to dislodge it even if we thought it was a good idea.

In the end, the goal of modern shame interventions to assist the participant to find authentic congruence between their *Real Self* and their *Ideal Self* through some combination of self-acceptance and self-forgiveness cognitive behavioral therapy techniques is well-meaning and could be observably helpful in

---

52. Teens and tweens that go the path of Gaga's "Little Monsters" may end up merely trading their shame for co-dependency. Often the root of such deeply imprinted shame is early parental criticism, rejection, abuse, lack of compliments or absence of physical or verbal expressions of real love for the person as they were. To argue that they should now just make a heroic choice to accept themselves, choose to honor themselves, to give themselves a break, embrace their uglies can ironically lead to even more self-contempt. They already know that they should do these things. Psychologist Burgo warns of a danger inherent in Lady Gaga's preaching of self-acceptance to those who are immersed in shame. "Telling people riddled with feelings of profound shame that they are "superstars" might make them feel good for a moment — especially if they're listening to your inspirational music and identifying with you in the process. But in the end, such a message only encourages an endless need for more encouragement, in order to keep warding off the underlying bad feelings." Joseph Burgo, "Lady Gaga's 'Born This Way' Music Video and Her Triumph Over Shame," http://blogs.psychcentral.com/movies/2011/06/lady-gaga/.

the short run.[53] The *Gospel App* suggests that shame's power must *first* be diminished by another more powerful entity before self-acceptance and self-forgiveness become truly viable.

The *Gospel App* and the Third Self

The *Gospel App* invites those who are still in denial of their shame to access the power of *right* first, and often, in hopes that the power of this aspect of the Gospel is an effective counter-agent to shame's power. Diminished shame is far easier to deal with.

Right

As presented in the diagram on the next page, we Jesus-Followers have three *Selves* not just two. The third self, my *True Self* is not based upon my perception of myself at all, neither my present assessment of my rightness, or my ideal expectations of my should-of rightness. It is far beyond either, majestically mysterious, an exclusive of the Gospel, and often very counterintuitive.

My *True Self* is how God sees me, based upon the work of Jesus on the Cross alone. The second upward arrow on the *Gospel App*, i.e., *right*, figuratively imagines what a shamed person would feel when they finally look up into the healing measuring gaze of their Heavenly Father. They access and experience *right*.

Jesus did everything perfectly according to the *ideal* requirements of God's Law. In *Gospel App* terminology, Jesus did everything *right*. I did not. My *Real Self* consistently falls far short of any ideal, much less my internal *Ideal Self*.

Good news. We have already seen that my future avoidance of justice's demands was not based upon *my* faithfulness, or *my* rightness. My record of non-right was put on Jesus' shoulders and he took on all of Celestial Justice's demands—perfectly and completely, i.e., *(Sin)*. Then a second miracle happened on the cross.

Mysteriously and wonderfully, not only was my record of sin taken off me and put on the shoulders of Jesus, i.e., *(Sin)*, but His record of perfect faithfulness was taken out of his portfolio and put into my resume, i.e., *right*.

Jesus' resume of perfection and faithfulness was put into *my* biography. It was accomplished mysteriously two thousand years ago. I recall experiencing it as true for me when I was 35 years old—years after my conversion at 21.

When I was 21, I remember experiencing the first of the *Gospel App's* four arrows, *(Sin):* the saving grace of Jesus' judicial substitution for me. I

---

53. See Tangney, et al., 717.

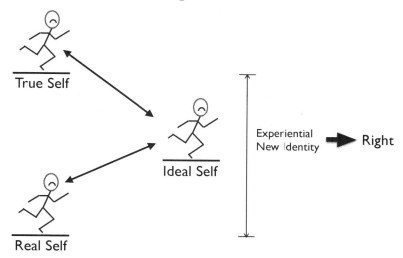

believed that God's criticism and judgment toward me and my crimes were gone—not just waved away, but perfectly and totally dealt with. I envisioned Jesus on the Cross lifting my guilt—like a huge backpack—off of my weary guilty shoulders and placing it on His own. I got it—that I would never ever be judged again for my transgressions.

Though both events happened at the same time, based upon the same single work of Jesus on the Cross, this second grace of the singular Gospel, *right*, became clearer to me some fourteen years later. I had no doubt heard about this grace before. If asked the question, I could have described this action of Jesus on my behalf. But for some reason, my personal present experience of it had been lacking.

It was a stark moment of deep personal need when I finally knew that two thousand years ago, Jesus' righteousness was imputed into my account. I have the righteousness that Jesus had—and all that such righteousness brings with it. Don't get me wrong, I am still attempting to grasp the vast ramifications of this huge grace. Yet in that moment—and many moments since, I was dynamically assured deep in my soul that God actually loved me as I was. In that moment my shame was dealt a death-blow—not gone completely—but drastically de-fanged.

The upshot of the transaction of this imputation? Everything that Jesus' perfect record perfectly earned is now perfectly mine. To receive this exchange is to receive all of the love and favor that such perfect faithfulness deserves. Now God *must* love me to the very same degree that the Father loves the Son and the Son loves the Father. This is true no matter what I have done or not done, what has been done to me, or not, and whether I feel that it is true in the moment. God cannot ever love me any more or any less than He does right now. His love for me can never waver. None of this is due to anything that I have done. It is all a function of what Jesus has done on my behalf, and that record *"imputed"* to my resume.

What did I need to do in order to earn the transaction? Nothing. There is no way that I could ever earn such a magnanimous gesture. Ever. All I need is need. All I can do is open up helpless and empty shamed hands and passively receive all of God's indiminishable favor toward me as I am right now. He proclaims me right and now treats me as if my *True Self* and *Real Self* were one and the same.

How Do I Get that Sense of *"Right"* again?

Full disclosure is appropriate here. I must admit I still go through most of my week living as if I do not really believe this to be true about me. My bent is to keep trying to earn such a feeling of "rightness" from any and all other sources— functionally denying that I am already made right in Christ.

It should be clear how this would begin to affect a person of shame who has not been able to accept themselves or forgive themselves? One can see how this powerful Gospel would be the enemy of such shame. As displayed by the figure below, shame is ultimately agreeing with your very subjective messed-up gaze at your own reflection and concluding that you are not right somehow. Your *Real Self* has fallen disappointingly short of the constant critical demands of that perfectionistic *Ideal Self* within you—again.

The *Right* spoken of in the *Gospel App* shape is a powerful capacity to

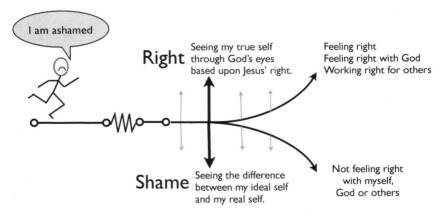

look up into the gaze of God and confidently trust His assessment of your rightness (your significance, security, and belonging) in and through Christ alone. In His eye's assessing reflection, you can see, by faith, that He has counter-intuitively aligned Jesus' *Real Self* with your *Real Self*. In his epistle to the Romans, Paul says this,

This *right*eousness from God comes through faith in Jesus Christ to all who believe. There is no difference. (Rom 3:22 NIV)

Biblically, this confidence of being *right* can be creatively envisioned as a "stuff" that comes *from* God through faith. I became not-right by something that I did, or something that was done to me. The *right*-gap can be made up significantly by going to God with my need and asking Him to make me *right-with-Him* (or better, to make me feel the *right-with-Him* already purchased for me by Jesus). My present sense of being *right* comes from God through faith, not by my own effort.

Again Paul says,

> For if, by the trespass of the one man, death reigned through that one man, how much more will those who receive God's abundant provision of grace and of the gift of *right*eousness reign in life through the one man, Jesus Christ. (Rom 5:17 NIV)

My present experience of being *right* is a gift from God, not something that I have to work hard to earn and protect. There is *right* in overabundance in the hands of God for those in need. All shamed Jesus-followers need is need. That is hard for shamed people.

This concept is apparently very important to Paul. At least three other times he describes the nature of this present sense of being *right* with God.[54]

> "Christ is the end of the law so that there may be *right*eousness for everyone who believes." (Rom 10:4 NIV)

> "I do not set aside the grace of God, for if *right*eousness could be gained through the law, Christ died for nothing!" (Gal 2:21 NIV)

> "What is more, I consider everything a loss compared to the surpassing greatness of knowing Christ Jesus my Lord, for whose sake I have lost all things. I consider them rubbish, that I may gain Christ and be found in him, not having a righteousness of my own that comes from the law, but that which is through faith in Christ — the *right*eousness that comes from God and is by faith." (Phil 3:8-9 NIV)

When Paul speaks of righteousness that comes from the Law, he is referring to any and all actions designed to earn God's favor by keeping the law. In 1st ct. Judaism, the *Ideal Self* was informed strictly by the Torah. If one

---

54. For more discussion on the Hebrew and Greek concepts of right and righteousness, see Appendix 1.

did Torah perfectly, they should feel right with God. There should be no guilt or shame. Unfortunately, God's Law is far more demanding than anyone could pull off (Gen 18:13, Dt. 17:1; 28:1-2, 14-15; Matt 5:48; Rom 3:10; 6:23). The Law is by nature a perfectionist. Inevitably, no one could truly feel favored (Heb. 10:2-22).

It turns out that this *right* only comes from the Holy Spirit in me accessed by means of faith (Rom 10:4). It cannot be earned by anything that I do, even it if my behavior tracks the Law (Gal 2:21).

Faith and Being Right

We will speak more about specific Biblical *faith* in a later chapter. Suffice it to say here that this narrow *faith* is the present work of the Holy Spirit where He makes me assured that the Gospel's promises are true for me right now. One moment, I am having a hard time seeing myself right. I can only see my *uglies*, my failures, the gap between my *Ideal* and *Real Self*. I can only hear the oppressive voice of the rule standard bearer criticizing me of being a loser. I can only feel the darkness of the abuse forced upon me.

Then the next moment, I feel something different. It is not from within me, like a choice to see only good in the universe. It is more than just a choice to accept my *uglies*, to be more vulnerable, or to forgive myself. It is a sense, a deep powerful, and some ways unreasonable confidence that I am good. This goodness is never based upon my actions. By faith, through the work of Christ on my behalf, I can be made aware that God looks at me and assesses me *right*. Over all of my flesh's shame-objections, I begin to shift to God's assessment and to some degree embrace as valid the *True Self* proclaimed by the Holy Spirit in me.

Remember the all too familiar parable of the Prodigal Son. He knew shame. He had to suspect that when he got home, he would see that terrible look in his father's eyes. He just knew that his father would be ashamed of him. It was due him. He had earned it. But the punch line of the parable is that he was wrong. His father loved him, and without a moment's hesitancy privately and publicly proclaimed the full restoration of the son to former glory. The father treated the son as if he had been faithful all the time.

All well and good. How did the son fare in the welcome home party? We are not told. Was he able to embrace the shocking turn of events? Or was it still awkward at best, or deeply uncomfortable at worse. To put it in shame language, the Father was not ashamed of the son. Was the son ashamed of the son?

There is a work of the Holy Spirit that opens the eyes of shamed sons (and shamed daughters) to feel adored again, to feel honor again, to actually feel loved again. How? By being assured that God's feelings toward them are based upon their *True Selves*, based upon Christ's imputed record of faithfulness and *right*. This is not achievable through cognitive behavioral therapy. It is a miraculous work of the Holy Spirit through faith. He alone can make the shamed feel *right* again.

It is definitely counter-intuitive. When I feel shame, when I cannot forgive myself, when I don't feel right, my first reaction is to hide from God. Honestly, I don't recall that strategy working very well. Good news. Biblically, my shame has a predator—a supernatural enemy, the righteousness of Christ along with all that earns me. This right is a function of faith.

> "In you, O Lord, I have taken refuge; let me never be put to shame; deliver me in your *right*eousness." (Psalm 31:1 NIV)

Good news for those who are shamed. How can you make a dent in your shame? By faith, hold up empty hands to be filled with the *right*ness of Christ. *Right* (being right and feeling right) actually only comes from God.

> ***"It turns out that this right only comes from the Holy Spirit in me accessed by means of faith (Rom 10:4). It cannot be earned by anything that I do, even it if it largely tracks the Law." (Gal 2:21)***

Lady Gaga's Little Monsters, isn't this better than just trying so hard to "glam" your uglies over and over again. By the way, there is absolutely nothing wrong with "glamming" the uglies. First access a sense of being right with God as your measurement. Then glam away.

You who have been abused, dishonored, mistreated, dissed and so feel less than "right" about yourself and/or in the eyes of others, how do you get rid of shame and guilt and begin to feel right about yourself and relationships again?

I invite you to get this sense of being *right* from God not by trying harder. How do you get this right? Answer? By faith through the Holy Spirit. Ask.

You messed up, did something stupid or irresponsible, something that you know God doesn't approve of—How do you get rid of shame and guilt and begin to feel right about yourself and relationships again? Answer? From God, not by your hard works or faithfulness. How do you get it? Answer? By faith through the Holy Spirit. Ask.

Either you attempt to fix it and attempt to regain your *right* by your own effort, which hasn't really worked to-date, or you run to God and ask for Jesus' *right*eousness, over and over until you get it.

God, Make me feel right!

To the extent that I actually, by faith, embrace that I am presently loved by God as much as the Father loves the Son and the Son loves the Father, my flawed *Real Self* becomes fully reconciled with my *True Self*. According to God, strictly due to

Jesus' efforts not mine, my *True Self* has been declared to be lovable, good, worthy, and right. I have the righteousness of Jesus. That can never change.

Others may measure me differently, yet the true measurement is already done. God says to me "Well done, good and faithful servant." By faith, I can experience this powerfully as true, no matter how I was raised, whether I was abused or not, whether I was raised in a moralistic angry-God context, no matter what I have done, or what was done to me, this is still true of me.

God's verdict of me is in.

The Verdict is In

Tim Keller provocatively puts it this way, "The verdict is in."[55] What is the ultimate opposing power to your shame and guilt? It is the power of God's verdict about you.

> "Why are some of you as concerned as you are about how you look? Some of you spend quite a bit of time and quite a bit of thought and quite a bit of money on how you look. And I want you to know that even those of us who seem not to care, actually do. And the reason that we all do is because you know there are people passing verdicts. People are walking around there looking at you. You are doing the same thing. You are looking at people's appearances and passing verdicts. You are saying 'Wow,' or 'Hmm,' or you are saying "Yuck" or your saying 'Another one of those.' Verdicts!"

We find verdicts about us everywhere, in everyone's eyes. It is not just about our appearance, it is how we live.

> "All of us in everything we do [are] trying to please our parents, we are trying to get the opposite sex to like us, trying to get peers to think we are good. We desperately need verdicts. We need people from the outside to come and say 'great well done.' Every elementary school teacher told you and every Made-in-America TV movie has told you it shouldn't matter what others think. All that matters is what you think…That is bunk. Because you know that if I just think that I am fine and everybody else is telling me how awful I am—that just doesn't work. I need someone from the outside to tell me, 'You're great, well done, best I have ever seen!' Those verdicts are like breath of life. Why are we so desperate?…We are always proving ourselves. [Why?]. Because we feel like we are in a courtroom…We are desperate for verdicts."

The verdict is in. It was in 2000 years ago. If you are a follower of Jesus

---

55. Keller, Tim. "The Ascension of Jesus." Sermon, Acts: The Gospel in the City from Redeemer Presbyterian Church, New York, NY., November 18, 2012.

and you have the Holy Spirit dwelling in you, you can hear that same verdict every day.

"You are beautiful, you are gorgeous, you are successful, you are great, you are in him--in the eyes of the only person in the world who matters, the only court of opinion that matters. [Now] you don't have to be driven anymore. You don't have to be afraid anymore."

The Holy Spirit will make this verdict real to you today, tomorrow, and the next day. Until He applies this verdict to your heart, you have to look for lesser verdicts from lesser sources. Here is the real good news. The more that you accept and believe God's verdict upon you, the less you will need the verdict of others.

> *"You are beautiful, you are gorgeous, you are successful, you are great, you are in him--in the eyes of the only person in the world who matters, the only court of opinion that matters. [Now] you don't have to be driven anymore. You don't have to be afraid anymore."*
> *Tim Keller*

"[Now] you don't have to worry what other people say. You don't have to tear your clothes off anymore in order to get a sense of self worth because somebody likes you, You don't have to work and burn-out. Your identity isn't how much money you make and it's not your dress size. It is none of that anymore. And when the Holy Spirit comes into your life it makes it so real to you."

Does this actually work? Does embracing by faith, through the Holy Spirit in me actually diminish the power of shame and self-contempt within me? According to recent scientific studies, it does. A 2012 study by McConnell and Dixon[56] confirmed that a person's ability to self-forgive was scientifically related to their perceived personal experience of God's forgiveness toward them. Interestingly, it was also determined that a generic broad theological confession of God's attributes of love and forgiveness did *not* correlate with higher rates of self-forgiveness. Only those with a personal relationship to God and a personal experience of God's love and forgiveness for them as they are, experienced higher levels of self-forgiveness.

---

56. McConnell, J. M., & Dixon, D.N. (2012). "Perceived Forgiveness from God and Self- Forgiveness." Journal of Psychology and Christianity 31 (1), 31-39. See also Hall and Fincham 2005.

Make Me Want to do Right Toward Others: The Dual Function of the "right" of Christ

Someone at this point of exploration of the mysterious work of Jesus on our behalf on the Cross may be tempted to decry, "Wait a minute. If you tell people that God loves them no matter what they do or do not do, they may just go crazy and party their brains out. If you remove the restraining power of shame and guilt, what will keep people in line? What will make people do good things for others?"

Biblically, this miraculous second grace of the singular Gospel has two functions, 1) to make you *feel* right and 2) to empower you to want to *do* right for others (See Appendix 1). First it is a powerful counter-agent to the forces of shame in you. Second, it reshapes and empowers your motivations to be other-oriented—to lead you to loving and conciliatory actions.

Martin Luther agrees. In the preface to his Commentary on the Galatians he writes:

> "But," you ask, 'Shouldn't we do good works? Or do we just go and do whatever we want to do because Jesus' righteousness is in our account and can never be diminished?' Absurd of course. If the truth were known, a person who is immersed in the received righteousness of Christ is the only one who truly is doing good works. When I have this received righteousness reigning in my heart, I descend from heaven as the rain making fruitful the earth, that is to say, I do good works, all the time, no matter what occasion. If I am a minister of the Word, I preach, I comfort the brokenhearted, I administer the Sacraments. If I am a householder, I govern my house and my family, I bring up my children in the knowledge and fear of God. If I am a magistrate, the charge that is given me from above I diligently execute. If I am a servant, I do my employer's business faithfully. To conclude: whoever is persuaded that Christ is his or her righteousness, not only cheerfully and gladly works well in his or her vocation, but also submits himself or herself through love to the government leaders and to their laws, even though they are severe, sharp and cruel, and if need be, to any and all manner of burdens and dangers of this present life, because he or she knows that this is the will of God, and that this obedience pleases Him."[57]

It turns out that this "right" of Christ is more than just feeling right about oneself. At the very core of the Greek and Hebrew words for right and righteousness is the notion of relationally caring for others over yourself. When I access by

---

57. I took the liberty to modernized and abridge this portion of Luther's Preface from St. Paul's Epistle to the Galatians, http://www.1517legacy.com/1517legacy/2014/02/martin-luthers-commentary-on-galatians/.

faith this second grace of the singular Gospel I feel right and I also miraculously want to do right to others.

Conclusion

> "There is no fear in love. But perfect love drives out fear, because fear has to do with punishment. The one who fears is not made perfect in love." (1 John 4:18 NIV)

It was only days after I was caught in my moral failure that I heard a preacher inviting shamed people, like me, to the foot of the Cross, to envision Jesus, the dying Jesus on the cross gazing down at us. I was raised in church. I mistakenly understood God to be a very critical, demanding, perfectionist who favors those who are successfully right, not people like me who turned out to be such a disappointment to Him.

> "Do you feel ashamed?" The talking head on the huge overhead screen said. "Imagine your shame to be a knapsack on your back, weighing you down, robbing you of joy and life."

So far so good. I did resonate with his words. It seemed that he was speaking to me.

> "Now imagine looking up into the eyes of Jesus. Do you see them? Do they love you? As you are?"

This was a bit harder for me. Shamed people can be a bit paranoid, assuming that everyone is ashamed of them too. I did.

> "Do you want to get rid of your shame?"

Yes, I did.

> "Then ask Jesus from the Cross to take your vile dehumanizing knapsack off your shoulders and to put it on his own."

"Seriously," I thought to myself. "That's it? That's all it takes? Will he do it? He must be disappointed in me too, right?"

> "Just ask Jesus to do it? Envision Him saying, 'Of course, silly. That is why I am up here on this Cross. I am here to carry your shame. Give it to me without delay.'"

And so I did. My next experience is difficult to describe. All I can say is that my shame was gone. In a moment. Gone. I felt joy, peace and even the very favor of God. I felt God smile at me—as I was—the failure.

Is it that easy? Of course it is. And for shamed people, it is that hard. We are often too ashamed to imagine a God who is not ashamed of us. In that scenario, He's the very last person that I would run to for help. I fear looking up into His eyes and seeing disappointment, judgment or despise.

Fear had been ignited by my brain chemicals and I was acting out of the realm of my State Memory, not reason but survival: flight, freeze, or fight. In that moment, I was not looking up.

Why would God do that for me? No one else has served me like that? No one else saw me as an object of honor. Why would I even imagine that He would? The risk was too great.

Then I heard the Gospel's answer to my shame's why questions. God does His very best work with failed people. That is His nature. He loves shamed people. He loves people who have done shameful things and those who have been shamed by others.

> *"All we need to do is to look up into the loving gaze of our heavenly Father. This is as easy as can be—and equally as hard."*

All we need to do is to look up into the loving gaze of our heavenly Father. This is as easy as can be, and equally as hard.

Whose gaze am I looking into to see who I am? How valuable am I? In the assessing eyes of God? Or others? My feelings, some metric of success (beauty, age, health, wealth, popularity)? Yet even now, I will far too often first run to my go-to idols to find righteousness, to feel right. It's habitual, largely subconscious, and very powerful, rather than to run to my Lover-King-God to gaze into His eyes and see once again who I am, to find myself, to align my *Real* and *True Self* in his powerful gaze, to have my deepest wounds healed, to find power to forgive, and to experience justice for crimes against me.

Some of these lovers are good—not evil. Yet they do not see me the way God sees me, ever. In the *Gospel App* shape, Stick can either find his or her identity from things and be left feeling fearful, unloved, not measuring up, addictive, grabby, or can run to God, look into His eyes by faith and feel loved, adored, a vessel of honor and rest.

My go-to habitual behavior is to run to anything other than God's gaze. Luther provocatively calls this bent "evil."

"There is something twisted in us that runs back to our original flaw. Humanity's reason cannot restrain itself from active or working righteousness, that is to say, his/her own righteousness: nor lift up his/her eyes to the beholding of the received righteousness, but runs back to the path of active righteousness: so deeply is this evil rooted in us."[58]

It is our independent survivalist flesh that will always struggle with this thing called *faith*. It's foolish, shameful, and outrageous when you think about it rationally. Why would we run to those "things" that can't really satisfy, more than hits here and there? Yet we do. Over and over again. They are highly conditioned habits.

Last Word on Shame

Dan Allender works with some of the most extreme cases of shamed men and women, those who have been sexually abused. He asks this question to these deeply wounded people.

> "Who will be your shame bearer? Every one of us knows sexual brokenness. Every one of us knows what it is to desire and to know harm. Every one of us knows that we have spoken words that have done harm to others…Who will hold that shame for you? Who will cover that shame for you? The Gospel does not make sense unless you have a heart to enter your own shame. And you will not have the work of the Kingdom of God guiding your mind and heart unless you have the courage to enter even into your own simple, broken stories of shame. Who will pursue you? Who will tap you on the shoulder, and who will offer you the eyes of delight that invite you back to the table, after something in your own heart says no one could hear me. No one could understand me, I am alone, I am an exile, I at the very core am an ugly man or woman. May we have both the courage to name our stories, a heart open to ask for the hands and eyes of Jesus."[59]

In the *Gospel App* discipleship program, such people are invited to not only tell their stories in a safe place, but to hear hope of a miraculous external power already purchased for them by Christ that can noticeably engulf them with a sense of being made *right* again.

The change may only be partial this side of heaven, nevertheless, it is a foretaste and a reminder that no matter who you are, how you feel, what you have or haven't done, or what has or hasn't been done to you, a restoration to being whole and right is in the cards for you. God has underwritten it. The Son has already paid for it. The Holy Spirit has the present capacity and power to begin to open your eyes to its power. He can give you a deep beyond-comprehension assurance that you are indeed right.

How? Get on your knees (if you physically can). Hold up your empty

---

58. Ibid.
59. Allender, Dan (2014). On Shame: Jubilee 2014 Main Session [Video] Retrieved March 15, 2015, from https://youtu.be/6QiHzlwqeOE.

shamed hands. Ask God to give you a powerful present assurance that He loves you as much as the Father loves the Son and the Son loves the Father. Pray over and over,

> "Make me feel right, God. Right with You. Right with myself. Right with others who have been affected by my shame and the consequences."

Keep asking until you feel the power of the Holy Spirit, even if it takes days or weeks.

> "God, right now I feel ashamed, dirty, lost, ugly, despised, alone, like a tragic character in a bad TV soap opera. I do not feel that I can look up into Your gaze. I am afraid of what I will see. I do not feel that I should be forgiven, or redeemed based upon what I did, or didn't do. I do not feel that I could ever be loved again, appreciated again, adored again, ever. Having said all of that, God you can give me a powerful gift of righteousness. You alone can make me feel right again. I realize that I have no other hope than You working a huge miracle in me now. Give me that sense of being right. Make me know that I am right beyond my normal human ability to figure this out. Make me feel right."

As you are praying to God for His external assurance of being right, be conscious of changes in your inner-being. Are you in this moment, truly feeling better about yourself? Less self-loathing? Less fear of being rejected? Less darkness for the shame brought upon you? More willing to be vulnerable? More willing to accept your uglies? More hopeful? Make note of any change.

As you lean into the promises of God, remember Paul's model prayer for the Ephesians.

> "For this reason I kneel before the Father, from whom his whole family in heaven and on earth derives its name. I pray that out of his glorious riches he may strengthen you with power through his Spirit in your inner being, so that Christ may dwell in your hearts through faith. And I pray that you, being rooted and established in love, may have power, together with all the saints, to grasp how wide and long and high and deep is the love of Christ, and to know this love that surpasses knowledge—that you may be filled to the measure of all the fullness of God. Now to him who is able to do immeasurably more than all we ask or imagine, according to his power that is at work within us, to him be glory in the church and in Christ Jesus throughout all generations, for ever and ever! Amen." (Eph 3:14-21 NIV)

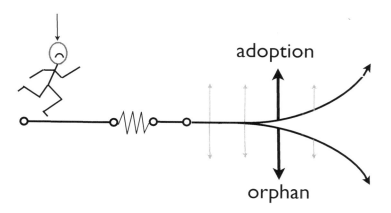

Chapter 8: Orphan Behavior Versus Adoption

"Because our age is characterized by bigotry, loneliness, and insecurity, we who live in it need the unity of the family of God, the fellowship of a heavenly Father, and the security that comes from knowing the Son of God."
—Robert A. Peterson

According to the Scriptures, pardon, acceptance, and adoption are distinct privileges, the one rising above the other in the order in which they have been stated.... while the first two properly belong to (the sinner's) justification, as being both founded on the same relation [with God] as a Ruler-and-Subject, the third is radically distinct from them. as being founded on a nearer, more tender, more endearing relation [with God] as Father-and-Child... The privilege of adoption presupposes pardon and acceptance, but is higher than either."
—James Buchanan

Adoption is an act of God's free grace, whereby we are received into the number, and have a right to all the privileges of the sons of God
—Westminster Shorter Catechism Question #34

Here is the truth, Jesus-follower. Not only were you rescued from the consequences of your body of crimes against God, creation and humanity, i.e., (*sin*), invested with Jesus perfect record of faithfulness which earned for you all of the love in the universe, i.e., *right;* you have also been adopted to be the very son or daughter of God Himself.

The *Gospel App* vector (*sin*) extends to you an eternal assurance that no matter what you do, or do not do, God can never ever judge you, be critical of you, or be contemptuous toward you. He was all of those toward Jesus in your place.

The *Gospel App* vector *right* assures you of the undying love of God, no matter what others may or may not think of you.

The *Gospel App* vector *Adoption* assures you of an unending intimate and honorable relationship with your benevolent Father. This aspect of the Gospel affords to the sons and daughters of God infinite unchanging significance, belonging and security beyond anything that this world affords. No matter how hard you try, where you look, how good or bad your relationships are, you can't get there from here on your own.

Biblical *adoption* is miraculous and inscrutable, far beyond our capabilities to earn or gain.

Orphanness

How relevant is this concept of adoption on a day-to-day basis? The 2014 Academy Award winning film, Birdman: Or (The Unexpected Virtue of Ignorance) is about a washed-up former super hero film star whose career has cratered. In hopes of resurrecting his career and life, he has written and stars in a very tepid Broadway play, which it turns out has very little hope of succeeding.

Societally speaking, he is insignificant, an all-too brief Wikipedia footnote of someone who once was memorable—but that was years ago. His recently out-of-rehab wreck of a daughter decries, "You are doing this in order to feel relevant again....You're the one who doesn't exist. You're doing this because you are scared to death like the rest of us. You don't matter; and you know what? You're right. You don't! It's not important. OK, you're not important, get used to it." Not only is he aware of his lack of significance, he is obsessed by it.

Before opening night he happens upon "the" theater critic who holds his future in her hands. She tells him that she has already written the review and it is bad. Any hope that he had of regaining glory is DOA. As the opening night of the play slides into the dark abyss of hundreds of other unmemorable theater failures, he figures that he has one card left to play—if he has any shot at significance. He replaces a prop gun with a real one and actually shoots himself on stage.

Two surprising things happen. First, he survives, barely. Second, he, and what he did, goes viral. He is at last noticed and *significant* again. Viewers get it that such social media awareness, much less "virility," is very flimsy and fleeting and disturbingly overvalued.

In my conversations with other movie goers about Birdman, most resonated with Birdman's plight—his searching and longing for notoriety, for recognition, to be in a place where "everyone knows your name." Whether we admit it or not, consciously or subconsciously, we are in a lifelong search for such *significance*. We look for it in our successes, our attachment to others, reviews, and even trace *significance* projected by our own feelings and emotions. The absence of such significance, security and belonging can be encapsulated in a single state: the state of being an orphan.

What do we mean by the concepts of "orphan" or "orphanness?" Imagine a wily self-sufficient boy or girl who has adapted to survive day-to-day on the cold sidewalks of an urban ghetto, all alone. He or she has no family, no father or mother to love, protect, or to be a mentor to them. The orphan's sense of significance, security, and belonging at the end of the day is solely based upon his or her efforts—no one else's, every day, every month and every year. On the streets, life is a zero sum game where all orphans must compete for the shreds of value and belonging that the streets afford. Be careful who you trust. Be careful what you say and how you say it. The bottom-line for orphans? You must prioritize survival over thriving.

No matter who you are, or how healthy your particular nuclear family might have been, we are all born spiritual orphans in this fallen place. Metaphorically, Paul imagines all creation groaning (Rom 8:22)—somehow aware at a deep identity level that it is lacking something important. This is to one degree or another true for all of us. We are planted feet-first in this chaotic zero-sum game of Life—with award winners and losers being announced multiple times a day.

Like the Birdman, my present experience of significance, security and belonging may go viral for an all-too fleeting moment and then crash the next. Some make the Red Carpet this year, but get no such invitation next time around. Then the banal award cycle continues. It is notable that even though Birdman won Best Picture Oscar, Michael Keaton (The Birdman) did not get the acknowledgment of being Best Actor? Irony abounds.

Biblically, there is a powerful cure for such creation groaning. Hear this, fellow functional orphans. Orphans can be adopted into a life-producing relationship as legit adored sons and daughters of the King of Kings.

"By adoption the redeemed become sons and daughters of the Lord God Almighty; they are introduced into and given the privileges of God's family. Neither justification nor regeneration expresses precisely that. Adoption is, like justification, a judicial act. In other words, it is the bestowal of a status, or standing, not the generating within us of a new nature or character…Adoption, as the term clearly implies, is an act of transfer from an alien family into the family of God himself. This is surely the apex of grace and privilege. It staggers imagination because of its amazing condescension and love."[60]

60. John Murray, Redemption Accomplished and Applied (Michigan: Wm. B. Eerdmans Publishing, 1955), 132-133.

Adoption crosses cultural, gender, and socio-economic lines. All of us—including atheists, Buddhists, Muslims, Methodists, Baptists, Republicans, Democrats, wealthy blue-bloods, or the structurally impoverished—everyone—groans for this same grace, a single once for all time proffer of significance, belonging, and security which can never be lost.

If the truth were known, we desperately long to be in such a relationship in which we are valued, outlandishly valued, as we are, not for what we do—not our successes, not our track record—us.

What is wrong with me that I need something so much? Answer? My flesh has a powerful intrinsic sense of *orphanness* that could technically be unpacked into the three elements that absent make one a functional orphan: significance, belonging, and security. This *orphanness* is a power that virulently shapes me, motivates me, and drives me to one degree or another 24/7. This powerful incessant longing is part of being human post-Fall.

My only real hope to become the "me" that I was supposed to be is to by faith through the Holy Spirit in me access *orphanness*' counter-power, *adoption*—not merely the one-time event, but an ongoing present awareness deep in my psyche that I have significance, belonging and security now as a necessary part of my having been adopted as a child of my benevolent Heavenly Father.

This adoption is miraculous, inscrutable and permanent. Adoption means that God is forever my beloved unhesitant Father no matter what I do, or should have done, or how others have treated me. My benevolent position is strictly due to the adoption declared over me by God the Father, purchased for me by Jesus my Lord on the Cross and both sealed once for all time and continually a topic of testimony to my doubting fearful spirit by the Holy Spirit.

> "Because you are sons, God sent the Spirit of his Son into our hearts, the Spirit who calls out, '*Abba*, Father.'" (Gal 4:6 NIV)

It is unbelievable that we can be given significance, security, and belonging that lasts beyond the next award show. Needless to say, orphans have great difficulty processing such a gift. It is way too unlikely. There has been absolutely no precedent for such a handout without strings. Zero.

Paul on the Adoption of Natural Orphans

> "For if you live according to the sinful nature, you will die; but if by the Spirit you put to death the misdeeds of the body, you will live, because those who are led by the Spirit of God are sons of God. For you did not receive a Spirit that makes you a slave again to fear, but you received the Spirit of sonship. And by him we cry, 'Abba, Father.' The Spirit himself testifies with our spirit that we are God's children. Now if we are children, then we are heirs—heirs

of God and co-heirs with Christ, if indeed we share in his sufferings in order that we may also share in his glory." (Romans 8:13-17 NIV)

Notice that the Apostle juxtaposes two "spirits." The first "spirit" enslaves me to fear. This is a horrifying image. The second "spirit," no doubt the Holy Spirit, seals me to God as His beloved child.

How are "fear" and "adoption" functional opposites in any context? One would expect Paul to speak of fear's usual antonyms: bravery, confidence, fearlessness, or contentment. Perhaps we can posit an answer by unpacking "adoption" to its normal trifold fruit: the actualization or experience of personal significance, belonging and security. Fear then would be the fear of finding out that, when all is said and done, when the last chapter of my life is finally written, I realize that I am not and have never been really significant, I belong to no lasting community, and I have no safety net that is any more trustworthy than Social Security.

> *Biblical adoption is a significant and unbelievable change in relational status where the Holy Spirit finds me stuck in fear regarding my lack of experiential significance, wondering whether I have any place where I really belong and am adored and appreciated, and I am innately worried at some level that I don't have relational security anywhere, with anyone. And He, out of His own motivations and reasons, makes me His kid, a full card-carrying inheritor of all the glory in the celestials (Eph 1:3).*

Biblical *adoption* is a significant and unbelievable change in relational status where the Holy Spirit finds me stuck in fear regarding my lack of experiential significance, wondering whether I have any place where I really belong and am adored and appreciated, and I am innately worried at some level that I don't have relational security anywhere, with anyone. And He, out of His own motivations and reasons, makes me His kid, a full card-carrying inheritor of all the glory in the celestials (Eph 1:3).

I remember the Cheer's theme song, "Don't you want go where everyone knows your name?" Here are the original lyrics by Gary Protnoy and Judy Hart Angelo.

> Making your way in the world today
> Takes everything you've got;
> Taking a break from all your worries
> Sure would help a lot.
> Wouldn't you like to get away?

Sometimes you want to go
Where everybody knows your name,
And they're always glad you came;
You want to be where you can see,
Our troubles are all the same;
You want to be where everybody knows your name.

It was the familiar theme song for the successful comedy "Cheers," yet it could easily be the theme song for all of our innate *orphanness*. Adoption happens when God finds us in our own Cheers bar, still unfulfilled, still underachievers and He unilaterally gives us a home and a family that we can't imagine with our shriveled orphan brains.

The Science of Orphanness: Anxiety and Avoidance

Orphanness is a fierce predator to our hope of ever experiencing significance, security, or belonging. It proclaims a vicious anti-Gospel to us—that if the truth were known, we don't actually matter to anyone, that we have little or no significance or purpose, that we have no place to belong, no relationship that can last beyond the next argument or breakdown.

Attachment Theory

Are there telltale evidences of a soul who struggles in their orphanness? According to Attachment Theory research, there are identifying behaviors.

The Attachment Theory was originally developed by British psychoanalyst John Bowlby who observed the distress which infants seem to experience when separated from their parents.

> "Attachment is an emotional bond or tie to somebody or something. Attachment is a necessary process for survival; an infant is totally dependent upon parents or caregivers for everything pertaining to life and death. Infants lack any ability to care for or nurture themselves. When an infant has a need, food, soiled diaper, fatigue, he or she expresses that need through crying or throwing an infant tantrum. In a healthy normative situation a parent or caregiver responds to that need. The infant cognitively realizes that the need will be met and they can relax and trust in the ability of their caregiver to provide for them. It is in this repetitive process that bonding, trust, security and attachment is nurtured."

For children, a "healthy normative situation" only comes from regular and consistent processes of attachment.

Orphan vs. Adoption

"This process of bonding occurs through eye contact, holding, feeding and it occurs hundred's of thousands of times during the first three years of life."[61]

"For the healthy person, reared in a functional environment, normal attachment and bonding occurs as needs are met. A child's first 18-36 months are critical for the process of bonding. It is during this time that the infant is exposed in a healthy situation to love, nurturing, and life sustaining care. The child learns that if he has needs someone will gratify that need, and the gratification leads to the development of his trust in others."[62]

Unfortunately, in the case of many orphans (and non-orphans), the regular hits of significance, security, and belonging are starkly absent.

"When crying goes unmet or a diaper unchanged, fear and insecurity get rooted in the individual and deep survival mechanisms are instilled that potentially hinder and paralyze them in their ability to bond and form connectivity or attachment with other individuals."[63]

God finds us all as orphans.

"When this initial attachment is lacking, children lack the ability to form and maintain loving, intimate relationships. They grow up with an impaired ability to trust that the world is a safe place and that others will take good care of them."[64]

Now it makes more sense that Paul would observe all creation groaning (Rom 8:22). To merely survive, since significance, belonging, and security are in limited supply, the orphan will find, humanly speaking *must* find, counterfeits wherever they can, or finally resolve to stop trying.

"Without this sense of trust, children believe that they must be hyper vigilant about their own safety. Unfortunately, their idea about safety prevents them from allowing others to take care of them in a loving, nurturing manner. They become extremely demanding and controlling in response to their fear. Emotionally they believe that if they do not control their world then they will die."[65]

---

61. Nancy Thomas, "What is Attachment Disorder/Reactive Attachment Disorder (RAD)?" Families by Design, September 17, 2005, http://nancythomasparenting.com/rad/html.
62. Senna, G. "The Doctrine of Adoption." (MA Thesis, Reformed Theological Seminary, 2006), 68.
63. Senna, Adoption, 68.
64. Nancy Thomas in Senna, Adoption, 68-69.
65. Senna, Adoption, 69.

Could this help us understand the normal struggles that occur within all relationships (including marriages, families, gangs, business and even faith based communities), struggles that may include demandingness, desire for control, fear of failure, and competitiveness? This describes my own heart most days of the week. According to researchers Fraley and Shaver,

> "When a child perceives an attachment figure to be nearby and responsive, he or she feels safe, secure, and confident and behaves in a generally playful, exploration-oriented, and sociable manner. When the child perceives a threat to the relationship or to the self (e.g., illness, fear, or separation), however, he or she feels anxious or frightened and seeks the attention and support of the primary caregiver. Depending on the severity of the threat, these attachment behaviors may range from simple visual searching to intense emotional displays and vigorous activity (e.g., crying and insistent clinging). Attachment behavior is "terminated" by conditions indicative of safety, comfort, and security, such as reestablishing proximity to the caregiver."[66]

Separated infants will cry out, squirm, and frantically look around to find their missing parent. These crying and searching reactions are labeled "attachment behaviors."

Think with me. How much of our adult behaviors are actually subconscious attachment behaviors justified with a thin veneer of normality? Researchers speak of the attachment behaviors common to traumatized children, but certainly it could describe much of the way that I react to life, to others, and to God. This is humanity's core operating system.

> "The attachment system essentially "asks" the following fundamental question: Is the attachment figure nearby, accessible, and attentive? If the child perceives the answer to this question to be "yes," he or she feels loved, secure, and confident, and, behaviorally, is likely to explore his or her environment, play with others, and be sociable. If, however, the child perceives the answer to this question to be "no," the child experiences anxiety and, behaviorally, is likely to exhibit attachment behaviors ranging from simple visual searching on the low extreme to active following and vocal signaling on the other... These behaviors continue until either the child is able to reestablish a desirable level of physical or psychological proximity to the attachment figure, or until the child "wears down," as may happen in the context of a prolonged separation or loss. In such cases, Bowlby believed that young children experienced profound despair and depression."[67]

---

66. Fraley, R. C., & Shaver, P. R. (2000). "Adult Romantic Attachment: Theoretical Developments, Emerging Controversies, and Unanswered Questions." Review of General Psychology, 4(2), 133.
67. R. Chris Fraley, 2010, "A Brief Overview of Adult Attachment Theory and Research," http://internal.psychology.illinois.edu/~rcfraley/attachment.htm, 1.

The absences of early cues related to significance, security and belonging can have life-long ramifications. After scores of failure to be able to reestablish connection with their caretaker, the child will often stop looking for their significance, security and belonging in that direction.

Doesn't this begin to explain the reactionary behavior of your spouse? Your teenager? If you could be severely honest for a moment, doesn't this at least begin to partially describe your reactions to them? Aren't both of you ultimately groaning for the security, significance, and belonging that your relationship is not providing you? Your relationship was never designed to provide such things.

Further, isn't this a helpful picture of fallen humanity's all-too-often reactionary behavior exhibited against our Creator?

> "If significant others are cold, rejecting, unpredictable, frightening, or insensitive, however, the child learns that others cannot be counted on for support and comfort, and this knowledge is embodied in insecure or anxious working models of attachment. The insecure child is likely to regulate his or her behavior accordingly, either by excessively demanding attention and care or by withdrawing from others and attempting to achieve a high degree of self-sufficiency."[68]

As an exercise, replace "others" above with "God." It would read something like this.

> "If [God] seems cold, rejecting, unpredictable, frightening, or insensitive, however, the [Christian] learns that [God] cannot be counted on for support and comfort, and this knowledge is embodied in insecure or anxious working models of attachment. The insecure [Christian] is likely to regulate his or her behavior accordingly, either by excessively demanding attention and care or by withdrawing from [God] and attempting to achieve a high degree of self-sufficiency."

Now replace "God" with "my church." Honestly, haven't we all felt this at one time or another?

Three Categories of Infant Attachment Behaviors

Researchers have identified three categories of infant attachment related behaviors, 1) secure, 2) anxious-resistant, and 3) avoidant.[69]

The *secure* child becomes upset once they are aware that they are separated from their parent, and is quickly comforted and returns to normal behavior

---

68. Fraley & Shaver (2000), 136.
69. Fraley, 2010, "A Brief Overview", 3-4.

when the parent returns. According to research this represents about 60% of the studied population.

The *anxious-resistant* child is "ill-at-ease initially, and, upon separation, becomes extremely distressed. Importantly, when reunited with their parents, these children have a difficult time being soothed, and often exhibit conflicting behaviors that suggest they want to be comforted, but that they also want to 'punish' the parent for leaving."[70] Close to 20% of the children studied reflected this attachment behavior.

The last category is the *avoidant* child. "Avoidant children (about 20%) don't appear too distressed by the separation, and, upon reunion, actively avoid seeking contact with their parent, sometimes turning their attention to play objects on the laboratory floor."[71]

The *secure* child has learned that in the arms of their caregiver they have significance, security, and belonging. They can rest. They develop with more confidence, freedom, and creativity than the other two categories of children. The *avoidant* and *anxious* child also learns, but learns that he or she cannot rely upon their caregiver to provide significance, a sense of security and belonging. They develop definable UCBs (attachment behaviors) such as anger, indifference toward their caregiver, demandingness, avoidance of vulnerability, and desperate unwillingness to give up control to anyone else.

Orphan (RAD)

Recent research among actual orphans has validated the observations of the Attachment Theory. Orphans have had to learn subconsciously that their parent will not return, no matter how hard they cry or complain. Unlike other children, the significant caregivers never attempted to regain the trust of the infant through eye contact or touch. In many cases the orphaned infant never knew such significance, belonging, or security. They were conditioned early on to suspect that others will not be a trustworthy reliable source of significance, security and belonging. Adoptees are 100 times more likely than non-adoptees to present a range of serious emotional problems.[72]

Bascom and McKelvey highlight one of the consequences of such a vacuum among orphans: "reactive attachment disorder" (RAD).

> "RAD is the failure of a child to make emotional attachments to parental figures, usually due to neglect or abuse during the first two years of life or from repeated bonding breaks with caregivers, such as multiple moves within

---

70. Fraley, 2010, "A Brief Overview," 3-4.
71. Fraley, 2010, "A Brief Overview," 3-4.
72. Marshall D. Schechter, "Observations on Adopted Children," The Adoption History Project, 1960 [online; available from http://darkwing.uoregon.edu/~adoption/studies/SchechterOAC.htm; Internet] accessed 5 October 2006.

the foster-care home system."[73]

So how are such children to adapt? To diminish their RAD? According to the secular research literature, the mainstream answer is to place the child in a context where he or she will consistently receive unconditional yet tough love. Yet, Senna rightly observes that very often "love" of an adoptive parent is unfortunately *not* enough to heal the adoptee. Often, it is such love that is the most frightening thing.

"The challenge for adoptive parents is that raising a traumatized child is so often counter intuitive. They may think that love is enough to heal. While noble, it is naïve. Hurt children are often so frightened by intimacy they will go to any lengths to avoid it. They are afraid to love because people in their past, those who should have loved and protected them, instead, hurt and abused them. Their deep assumption is that their adoptive parents, like everyone in their past, will hurt them and leave them too. When that happens, it will be much easier to be left by people they hate. In adoptions, a loss of control early on in the life of the adoptee results in the person reliving the deep-seated emotions they felt when they were abandoned. The byproduct of this loss of control is a hyper-vigilant need to control all of life around them. The world becomes safe for them if they are in control of all of life. The person does not have the ability to develop nor connect in normal healthy relationships, which results in the formation of an attachment or bonding issue. Their inability to connect in a meaningful manner to those that are reaching out and extending love to them is thwarted and stunted."[74]

Stop for a moment and wonder if there may be signs of spiritual RAD in your relationship history with others, with a church, or with God. If you too had become cynical and burned in core relationships with significant others who betrayed you, let you down, or didn't come when you cried out, could it be possible that you have carried that dysfunction into your relationship with your heavenly Father unaware?

"Stop for a moment and wonder if there may be signs of spiritual RAD in your relationship history with others, with a church, or with God."

What if your story is that institutions betrayed you? They were supposed to nourish and protect you, teach you, mentor you, sustain justice for you. Yet such institutions,

---

73. Barbara Bascom, and Carol McKelvey. The Complete Guide to Foreign Adoption. New York: Pocket Books, 1997, 6-7, 21. Though other likely disorders could include Oppositional Defiant Disorder (ODD), Conduct Disorder, and Attention Deficit Hyperactivity Disorder (ADHD), Mood Disorders, Depression or Bipolar Disorder, Posttraumatic Stress Disorder (PTSD), Attachment Disorder (AD), and Reactive Attachment Disorder (RAD)."
74. Senna, "Adoption," 73-4.

e.g., family, government, judicial, religious, business, disappointed you again and again. Haven't you, orphan, earned the right to suspect institutions?

If previous intimate relationships have deeply scored your soul, you may fear making yourself vulnerable to a far more potentially dangerous relationship with God.

Adult/Romantic Attachment

More recent research has found a similar triad of attachment behaviors in adult relationship styles.[75] Adult romantic partners can be "secure," "attachment related-anxiety" or "attachment related-avoidance."

People who, conditioned by experience in past relationships, score high on *attachment related-anxiety* tend to worry whether their partner is available, responsive, or attentive. Hazan and Shaver (2000)[76] describe such anxiety in a series of self-descriptive sentences. "I find that others are reluctant to get as close as I would like. I often worry that my partner doesn't really love me or won't want to stay with me. I want to get very close to my partner, and this sometimes scares people away."

What would this sound like related to my relationship with God? "I would like it if God really came close to me—but I cannot say that I always feel that He has. Sometimes I feel that I have messed up the relationship. That God has pulled back."

People who, conditioned by experience in past relationships, score high on *attachment related-avoidance* prefer not to rely on others or open up to others. "I am somewhat uncomfortable being close to others; I find it difficult to trust them completely, difficult to allow myself to depend on them. I am nervous when anyone gets too close, and often, others want me to be more intimate than I feel comfortable being."

What would this sound like related to my relationship with others and God? "I am somewhat uncomfortable thinking about God being too close to me. I am not sure if I trust Him all that much. I can accept that God really loves the church, but I get a bit uncomfortable to say that God intimately loves me."

Secure partners may testify, "I find it relatively easy to get close to others and am comfortable depending on them and having them depend on me. I don't worry about being abandoned or about someone getting too close to me."

In the garden pre-Fall, Adam and Eve were *secure* partners with God. There was a singular trusted assessor of their significance, security, and belonging. To what other gaze would they turn? What could possibly motivate them to look

---

75. Fraley, R. C., Waller, N. G., & Brennan, K. G. (2000). An Item Response Theory Analysis of Self-Report Measures of Adult Attachment. Journal of Personality and Social Psychology, 78, 350-365.
76. Fraley, R. C., & Shaver, P. R. (2000). Adult Romantic Attachment: Theoretical Developments, Emerging Controversies, and Unanswered Questions. Review of General Psychology, 4(2),135.

elsewhere? They were created children of God and knew nothing else. Deprivation was not a word in their dictionary.

Attachment Theory and the Bible

God loved Adam and Eve, with all of the love in the Universe. There is no recorded hesitancy from God. Everyone was naked in the relationship—what you see is what you get. Admittedly, it is unnerving to think of such an audience with God. Yet that is how insecure I am in this or any other relationship. We are so far from such a wondrous and frightening thing.

Adam and Eve, pre-Fall were in Attachment Theory terminology, *secure*. They were able to accept, receive, enjoy, and process God's love for them without the questions and doubts. They would never have asked:

> "Does God really love me? As much as Adam? As much as Eve? Would he love me still if I let Him down? What if God gets tired of me and looks for a more exciting relationship, or a daughter/son who is more faithful, talented, better looking, more pious?"

Since there were no attachment behavior related doubts and fears, there were also no attachment behavior empowered barriers required to protect them from God's gaze. They swam in the pool of infinite unwavering intimate belonging. They only knew this endless source of significance, security and belonging.

Not so for us. We are born post-Fall, with a flesh, our sinful nature, that regularly manufactures fears, hesitancies and unresolved doubts. I wonder if that is what happened at the Fall. Adam and Eve, relatively speaking, *died*. It was if they had been exiled somehow from their only real source of higher humanity. Now any possible dignity had to be fought for and clung to as only an anxious or avoidant infant separated from their parent would. It is not evil—rather normal human attachment related anxiety and avoidance.

Could this be what the Serpent meant when he said: "You will be like God?" Adam and Eve became less like Yahweh and in fact, more like the gods of the nations—individualistic deities who regularly divided into warring factions, struggled with hurt feelings and anxiety of their place in the Pantheon. In the pagan court, there was no *one* assessor of glory, worth, dignity or honor. Zeus was the King of the Hill but had limited authority and power. It turned out Zeus had his own relationship insecurities—hardly a secure child.

The Code of the Street

In *Code of the Street: Decency, Violence, and the Moral Life of the Inner City*, sociologist Dr.

Elijah Anderson studied a hyper-ghetto near Philadelphia.[77] Though he did not use attachment theory language or terms, his observations were nonetheless of a culture that was deeply conditioned to extreme attachment behaviors.

It is a tragic snapshot of what a community might look like that has remained stuck in unending *orphanness*. Instead of the terminology secure and avoidant/anxious, Anderson employs similar concepts, decent and street respectively.

The "decent" majority are those individuals and families who are to one degree or another committed to middle class values. In Attachment terms, they are more or less secure. However, the reality is that there is an oppositional culture, "the street," whose "norms are often consciously opposed to those of mainstream society."[78]

> "These two orientations—decent and street—organize the community socially, and the way they coexist and interact has important consequences for its residents, particularly for children growing up in the inner city. Above all, this environment means that even youngsters whose home lives reflect mainstream values—and most of the homes in the community do—must be able to handle themselves in a street-oriented environment. This is because the street culture has evolved a "code of the street," which amounts to a set of informal rules governing interpersonal public behavior, particularly violence. The rules prescribe both proper comportment and the proper way to respond if challenged. They regulate the use of violence and so supply a rationale allowing those who are inclined to aggression to precipitate violent encounters in an approved way. The rules have been established and are enforced mainly by the street-oriented; but on the streets the distinction between street and decent is often irrelevant."[79]

In such extreme *orphanness*, the higher concepts of significance, belonging and security has been displaced by a single concept, respect, "loosely defined as being treated 'right' or being granted one's 'props' (or proper due) or the deference one deserves."[80]

> "In the street culture, especially among young people, *respect* is viewed as almost an external entity, one that is hard-won but easily lost—and so must constantly be guarded. The rules of the code in fact provide a framework for negotiating respect. With the right amount of respect, individuals can avoid being bothered in public. This security is important, for if they are bothered, not only may they face physical danger, but they will have been disgraced or

---

77. Elijah Anderson. Code of the Street: Decency, Violence, and the Moral Life of the Inner City. W. Norton Company, 1999.
78. Ibid, 33.
79. Ibid, 33.
80. Ibid, 33.

"dissed" (disrespected). Many of the forms dissing can take may seem petty to middle-class people (maintaining eye contact for too long, for example), but to those invested in the street code, these actions, a virtual slap in the face, become serious indications of the other person's intentions. Consequently, such people become very sensitive to advances and slights, which could well serve as a warning of imminent physical attack or confrontation."[81]

Wouldn't this begin to explain recent events in such urban areas as St Louis, New York and Baltimore? To the *decent* majority (in Code of the Street language), the riots might seem over reactionary. To the *street*, the riots may be urgent attempts to regain precious lost respect. I am not arguing whether the behavior is intrinsically right or wrong at this point. I am attempting to change the dialogue to address the *why* question.

Gospel to the Street?

What if by faith through the Holy Spirit you could access a higher *respect*—without doing anything—only receiving what another earned? What if there was a Deity who is trustworthy, just, and fair; a God who will truly love you as you are, more than anyone has ever loved you? What if this Deity has promised to underwrite all of the injustices that have occurred to you—every single one of them. This God promises to make right—to restore you to wholeness. There is hope for you by faith in God, but there is no lasting hope through the Code of the Street.

"The code of the street is actually a cultural adaptation to a profound lack of faith in the police and the judicial system—and in others who would champion one's personal security. The police, for instance, are most often viewed as representing the dominant white society and as not caring to protect inner-city residents. When called, they may not respond, which is one reason many residents feel they must be prepared to take extraordinary measures to defend themselves and their loved ones against those who are inclined to aggression. Lack of police accountability has in fact been incorporated into the local status system: the person who is believed capable of "taking care of himself" is accorded a certain deference and regard, which translates into a sense of physical and psychological control. The code of the street thus emerges where the influence of the police ends and where personal responsibility for one's safety is felt to begin."[82]

Perhaps a helpful way of looking at this is that each of us is made up of both *decent* and *street* powers. The *street* within each of us erupts when we forget that there is ultimately one Judge, one executive for us, one good and fair Father.

81. Ibid, 34.
82. Ibid, 34.

He has promised to resolve all injustices, restore all losses, and props: to pay all our debts.

The final grace to humanity is God as Judge resolving *all* injustices for *all* people. The Biblical High Court promises perfect justice (trial, verdict and punishment) and restoration to wholeness of all losses (payments of all debts). No one goes into the afterlife non-whole. This good news can defang most of the street's power. If lack of objective and trusted justice is the genesis of the street, then the Gospel of a just God who freely distributes significance, belonging, and security to all who come to Him is a powerful reparative.

Delayed Justice

To be clear, this *delayed* justice may sound irrelevant to one who has endured many injustices, experienced horrors of crimes and losses in the here and now. I understand and can relate to that. The Gospel involves a significant amount of delayed justice.

Delayed justice is maddening to us. It is beyond our ability to comprehend what purpose might justice and restoration delayed entail when a loved one has been murdered, or cancer has been found in a family member, or terrorists slaughter innocents to achieve their evil goals. Or one race, sex or socio-economic group is treated with chronic prejudice and bigotry.

Inner city street-empowered orphans, and we are all such to a large degree functionally, have adapted to a corruption of the Golden Rule.[83] If someone hurts me, I must hurt them back. The Golden Rule was never meant to cover godless communities.

If there were no God, no ultimate Judge, no ultimate trial with *expected* perfect judicial outcomes, then there is only the aberration of "eye for an eye" which in practice normally devolves into survival of the fittest—never a resolution that satisfies or is life-giving. There is no significance restored, belonging re-established, or ultimate security gained by godless justice, whether vigilante or secularist courts.

"Given its value and its practical implications, *respect* is fought for and held and challenged as much as honor was in the age of chivalry. *Respect* becomes critical for staying out of harm's way...Much of the code has to do with

---

83. "As the problems of the inner city have become ever more acute, as the public authorities have seemingly abdicated their responsibilities, many of those residing in such communities feel that they are on their own, that especially in matters of personal defense, they must assume the primary responsibility. The criminal justice system is widely perceived as beset with a double standard: one for blacks and one for whites, resulting in a profound distrust in this institution. In the most socially isolated pockets of the inner city, this situation has given rise to a kind of people's law based on a peculiar form of social exchange that is perhaps best understood as a perversion of the Golden Rule, whose by-product in this case is respect and whose caveat is vengeance, or payback." Anderson, Code, 66.

achieving and holding *respect*. And children learn its rules early."[84]

The street cannot sustain respect and props. Having said that, one of the true benefits of the active voice of the Holy Spirit in us is to empower us beyond our ability to imagine and comprehend (Eph 3:20-21) that such justice *is* coming and that it *will* indeed satisfy all. There will be no need for appeal by any defendant or perpetrator. Only Heaven-sourced faith can make the street get this. One author puts it this way.

"For some, and probably for more than are ready to admit it, faith appears like a dead surface of a frozen river. And what I want to say is that below the dead-looking surface is a living river too—a glorious dark. What appears to be dead is really alive, alive like the wind. Faith, as I've been told, is the story of things unseen. That's the story of the frozen river. A primal flow secretly gushes on whether it's seen or not—below the surface, that is. Underneath every story of death and darkness and doubt is a hidden flow of God's resurrection and power and glory, which almost nobody chooses to see."[85]

We are not suggesting that you just accept this imagery and rhetoric as proof of the validity of God's resolution of any and all injustices. We are proposing that you ask for powerful faith, from the Holy Spirit in you that alone can make you be assured of God's promises. This is the nature of Biblical faith.

Apart from this mysterious final, though future, justice accessed by faith through the Holy Spirit, now, we will be driven to take matters into our own orphan hands and we will end up acting like, feeling like, orphans on the street.

Apart from this living conduit to the heavens where I can continually be doused with deep significance, belonging and security, my flesh will drive me ten times out of ten to find respect, props, security in other places, lesser gazes that will never ultimately satisfy.

> *"We are proposing that you ask for powerful faith, from the Holy Spirit in you that alone can make you be assured of God's promises. This is the nature of Biblical faith."*

Cain the Prodigal Orphan

"Adam lay with his wife Eve, and she became pregnant and gave birth to Cain. She said, 'With the help of the Lord I have brought forth a man.' Later she gave birth to his brother Abel. Now Abel kept flocks, and Cain worked the soil. In the course of time Cain brought some of the fruits of the soil as

---

84. Ibid, 67.
85. A.J. Swoboda, A Glorious Dark: Finding Hope in the Tension Between Belief and Experience, Grand Rapids: Baker Books, 2014, 1-2.

an offering to the Lord. But Abel brought fat portions from some of the firstborn of his flock. The Lord looked with favor on Abel and his offering, but on Cain and his offering he did not look with favor. So Cain was very angry, and his face was downcast. Then the Lord said to Cain, 'Why are you angry? Why is your face downcast? If you do what is right, will you not be accepted? But if you do not do what is right, sin is crouching at your door; it desires to have you, but you must master it.' Now Cain said to his brother Abel, "Let's go out to the field." And while they were in the field, Cain attacked his brother Abel and killed him. Then the Lord said to Cain, 'Where is your brother Abel?' 'I don't know,' he replied. 'Am I my brother's keeper?' The Lord said, 'What have you done? Listen! Your brother's blood cries out to me from the ground. Now you are under a curse and driven from the ground, which opened its mouth to receive your brother's blood from your hand. When you work the ground, it will no longer yield its crops for you. You will be a restless wanderer on the earth.' Cain said to the Lord, 'My punishment is more than I can bear. Today you are driving me from the land, and I will be hidden from your presence; I will be a restless wanderer on the earth, and whoever finds me will kill me.' But the Lord said to him, 'Not so; if anyone kills Cain, he will suffer vengeance seven times over.' Then the Lord put a mark on Cain so that no one who found him would kill him. So Cain went out from the Lord's presence and lived in the land of Nod, east of Eden. (Gen 4:1-16 **NIV**)

In Gen 4, we read of the first two recorded sacrifices made to Yahweh. We are not told of any previously given guidelines given by God, any specifications regarding good or bad offerings. Were such clear directions given? Perhaps. We cannot be sure. Based upon later directions both offerings were *kosher* on their face (See Leviticus 1-2).

Why would someone make such a sacrifice to deity? One brings an offering to God in order to experience His favor. Perhaps this sense of favor has been lost due to sin? Perhaps the person is recognizing that there is nothing more important than the favor of the Deity and is being proactive. Either way, at the heart of the matter is that the supplicant feels the need to do something to regain that present experience of the Deity's favor. Personal significance, security, and belonging is a function of such Heavenly favor.

Unfortunately, as a result of the first recorded offering, only one supplicant was left experiencing the favor of Yah, Abel. Genesis tells us that God gazed with favor (Hebrew: *sha'a*) only upon Abel and Abel's offering. Upon Cain's offering? No favorable gaze.

As a result, Cain was dissed publicly and certainly left with questions regarding his relationship with Yahweh. His response? He was angry and looked at the ground (face downcast) initiating the negative turn in the narrative.

Why does Yahweh publicly show favor toward the younger son Abel and not Cain? The author of the New Testament Epistle to the Hebrews, with a couple of thousand years of hindsight, proclaims Abel's offering was more favorable because it was energized by *faith*; whereas Cain's was lacking such faith.

> "By faith Abel offered God a greater sacrifice than Cain, and through his faith he was commended as righteous, because God commended him for his offerings." (Heb 11:4 NIV)

We will be discussing the nature of such *faith* in the next chapter. Important to the current topic is that, as a result, the rightful firstborn heir of Yahweh's blessings, Cain, would have walked away feeling to one degree or another discarded, insignificant, insecure, and like an outsider related to God. In a word, he would have felt like an orphan instead of feeling like the first-born, heir to the largest portion of the familial blessing. With the code of the street violated—or so Cain would have thought—maybe his deceptive inner voice was goading him:

> "Why did God disregard my offering? Doesn't He know that I am the firstborn? Wasn't the sacrifice according to the accepted guidelines? Why did He choose to publicly embarrass me for no obvious reason at all? And in front of everyone? What is it about little brother that makes God prefer Him to me? I have to do something about this."

We are told two things about Cain, post-sacrifice. He is angry and he refuses to look into the face of God. The phrase for the latter is "his face was downcast." It is mentioned twice in short order, the second time from the very mouth of God Himself. "Why are you angry? Why is your face downcast?" Cain, why won't you look into my face? Why won't you look up into my gaze?

Here's the question for we the readers of the account. Are we to understand that God *disliked* Cain so much that this was a public disinheriting? Is God signaling "Cain, I am done with you. I pick for all eternity, Abel!"? Is that the moral of the story? Or is there some other plot afoot?

Clearly there is something else in the mind of Yahweh. For He tells the recalcitrant, arguably anxious, and avoidant Cain this,

> "If you do what is right, will you not be accepted?" (Gen 4:7 NIV)

A difficult verse to translate, but perhaps rightly expanded: "Cain, if you only do right, will you not experience a lifting up, be restored to your place of favor and forgiven for your lack of faith?"

God is inviting Cain to restoration, not exile. What is the basis of restoration? In context, Cain's experience of favor with God would have been a result of him choosing to look up into God's loving downward gaze. God's favor is never earned by sacrifice (Heb 10).

With his orphanness in full eruption, Cain chose to take matters into his own hands in an attempt to fix his situation by his own wiles and might. There were two paths available to him. Either he could hold up empty needy hands and by faith receive God's favor, or Cain, the functional orphan, could attempt to find some substitute for that favor by some other means.

Wouldn't it make sense that this is the overarching point of this early narrative? Cain was expecting God's favor on the basis of a sacrifice. "If I do this duty, then God owes me the favor due me." Could it be that God is using this opportunity to teach Cain—and us—that His favor is not gained by any sacrifice?

Cain chooses the latter path. Acting like an orphan, he pursues significance, security, and belonging by another path—any other path, other than the one that requires looking up into the gaze of God. Shame is that debilitating to the Cains of the world.

Do we see evidence of attachment behavior in Cain? The publicly shamed anxious-resistant child who is distressed will have a "difficult time being soothed, and often exhibit[s] conflicting behaviors that suggest they want to be comforted, and that they also want to "punish" the parent for leaving."[86] In this case Cain probably subconsciously wants to punish God for giving preference to Abel. Cain refuses to confess even in the light of overwhelming evidence (not to mention that the all-knowing Yahweh doesn't need physical evidence to qualify truth). Cain rudely blames God for the consequences of his crime.

The avoidant child upon reunion with the parent figure may "actively avoid seeking contact with their parent, sometimes turning their attention to play objects on the laboratory floor."[87] Cain why is your face downcast?

What might a *secure* Cain look like? Arguably, if trust in God was still a viable option in his mind, he might look up and take account of God's loving and adoring measuring gaze. Does God still see him as His beloved son? If so, Cain just might repent, throw himself upon God for repair and redemption. But Cain will not, he cannot.

Yahweh has one last card to play to reclaim His prodigal son. Cain in his paranoia has concluded that others will find him and kill him because he is unprotected. He no doubt assumes that he has given up his right for a protector.

"You are driving me off the land today…whoever finds me will kill me." (Gen 4:14 NIV)

Perhaps the world was a dangerous place? We are not told. However, it is hardly uncommon for street-wise orphans to feel that others feel toward them the same way they feel toward themselves. If they despise themselves for what they did, they will often assume that others feel the same way. Could this be a keyhole look into Cain's hatred of himself for what he has done?

God stoops down to Cain and promises to his self-orphaned son some-

---

86. Fraley, Overview, 2.
87. Fraley, Overview, 2.

thing that is beyond belief.

> "All right then, if anyone kills Cain, Cain will be avenged seven times as much." Then the Lord put a special mark on Cain so that no one who found him would strike him down. So Cain went out from the presence of the Lord and lived in the land of Nod, east of Eden." (Gen 4:15-16 NIV)

Here's the image. After murdering his younger brother, Cain did accomplish much to seal his fate. His father Adam and mother Eve had to have been very distraught and angry. It would have normally been Adam's role to be the "blood avenger" of his family. Though the specifics of the role of blood avenger are not catalogued for decades, the role would have no doubt been established long before in human cultures. It is typically the role of the family, of the tribe, to protect their own. If one from another tribe takes out one of your tribe, there must be retaliation—a justice. Someone of each family would, explicitly or implicitly, take on the responsibility of being the blood avenger. In Cain's case, it is God Himself who personally takes on this family role *for* Cain.

God reminds the convicted criminal Cain that though he is a tragic excuse for a human being, nevertheless he still has a blood avenger. Though his family may not avenge his death, God will. Nothing will ever change that. God is the blood avenger for even the scum of the world.

This is not a God who has given up, turned His back, sent a son to perpetual judgment; though no court in the celestials would have questioned such a response in this case. This God remains the blood avenger for a cold-blooded murderer. God's love is undeterred, undiminished for the likes of Cain. Yet Cain's orphanness was so powerful, so blinding, so overwhelming that he could not, would not, look up. The author of Hebrews would no doubt concur that Cain still lacks faith.

The Gospel-Adoption

The third aspect of the Gospel reflected in the *Gospel App* is a powerful counter-agent to our innate post-Fall orphanness. It is unfortunate that the theology of *adoption* has become the stuff of dusty theology books—something that is true for me, but frankly has no real effect on my life. If the truth were known, adoption to sons/daughters of God is the pinnacle of my identity and life now. Are you groaning for more significance, security, and belonging than you have achieved here. You have hope in one path: *adoption*.

This *Adoption* is both declaratory and experiential.

First, adoption is a declarative matter, an alteration of our legal status. Two thousand years ago, on the Cross—and this is true for all who are Jesus followers—I was formally and legally adopted as God's child. All paperwork completed and approved, all interviews done, the adoption is filed in Heaven's celestial vaults. It is finished. This act, accomplished apart from my actions, was initiated and finalized solely by the works and will of God the Father. It is the greatest glory that I can *never* earn.

This change in familial status is mine due to nothing that I ever have or ever could do. It was earned by Jesus on my behalf and miraculously and mysteriously given to me by the Father. I am a child of God with all rights and privileges intact. I am a son of God as much as Jesus is a Son of the Father. I am heir of all heavenly blessings (Eph 1:3).

That is the first aspect of my adoption. I have been (past tense) declared to be the son of God. It is irreversible and perfect. There are no phases of adoption. No trial runs or probationary period. No hesitancy. I am now a child of God.

God says over me, "This is my son with whom I am well pleased." In the eyes of the heavenlies and of the tragic inhabitants and vile rulers of Hell, I am irrevocably adopted as God's beloved kid. There is no greater award. I did nothing to gain it.

Back to our metaphor of awards. In entertainment, there are many award shows. There are the Golden Globes, the People's Choice, even the Razzies. But there is only one Academy Award. I received the Best Son award, two millennia ago, based upon Jesus' amazing performance as the perfectly faithful child of the King. There are no more award shows for me to add to my mantel. I have been acknowledged by all creation to be a Son of God.

It has been declared over us by the only one who can define and proclaim our true identities, our names (Eph 3:14-5). We legally and irreversibly become God's children. Through adoption, the Christian has the inalienable right to look affectionately and trustingly upon God as Father, rather than as a slave driver and taskmaster.

There is a second aspect of my adoption to Sonship. Strangely enough, I confess that I rarely experience such celestial significance on a day-to-day, event-by-event basis. I "forget." I live my life as if I was only a celestial orphan disaffected by a series of attachment behaviors. My stubborn flesh is committed to it.

There is continuous, though constantly shifting conscious and subconscious groaning inside my gut that still needs to gain more awards, even lesser awards to add to my experience of significance, security, and belonging. I must be noticed more, or I will quickly become anxious and discouraged.

I will even attempt to squeeze significance out of my day-to-day relationships with others who are attempting to accomplish the same ends. I find myself regularly attempting to find significance and intimacy in my successes, or to dodge insignificance in my failures. It is a destructive tragic cycle, like a hard to watch Greek tragedy where the rightful King suffers unaware of their rightful yet forgotten title and glory.

Orphan vs. Adoption

When I experience my declared adoption in the moment, I mysteriously do feel all three aspects of a secure relationship.

Significance. "I can truly get it that my true value, worth, and relationship is a function of the singular assessment by God and willingly submit to that assessment. "God, I accept what you say about my worthiness in this relationship. Your gaze towards me is favorable, in spite of what I have done in the past, strictly because of Jesus' record imputed to me, I rest in that. I look to no other measurers. I feel it."

Belonging. "God—through the finished work of Jesus on the Cross You love me perfectly, unhesitatingly, as I am right now without any hesitancy.

Security. "I can feel God's engaged love for me right now. It is as if He has picked me up in His vast arms and is hugging and kissing me. Miraculously, my fears, paranoia, hesitancies, knee-jerk boundaries are not popping up. I can at last rest in God's love, at least for a moment or two. I have accessed power to grasp the height, width, length, and depth of the love of Christ for me right now (Eph 3:17-18). The stranglehold of my fears and doubts are for the moment diminished, their lying voices silenced."

Don't mistake this. My innate orphanness, my doubts, fears, paranoia, my inner anxious and avoidant child remains in my flesh like an ugly toxic lump. It will never stop trying to rob me of my real value in Christ. I need regular power from God to counter its deceptive tactics. God gives me His Spirit whose job is largely to 1) *make* me get the benevolence of our Father now and 2) to make me feel toward God in part how a loving child feels toward a benevolent loving parent.

In the Bible, when people are brought into the presence of God, they most often feel great fear, unbearable exposure, vulnerability, guilt (Isa 6)—anything but joyful childlike tenderness and openness toward God. It boggles the mind to try to imagine anyone actually comfortable and transparent, resting in the arms of the Holy God. It would take a miracle, requiring the Spirit's ongoing work in us generating previously absent "filial love" toward God that is larger than my trepidation and fear. Theologian John Murray says about the Holy Spirit,

> "He is called the Spirit of Adoption, not because he is the agent of adoption but because it is he who creates in the children of God the filial love and confidence by which they are able to cry, 'Abba, Father" and exercise the rights and privileges of God's children…the repetition indicates the warmth as well as the confidence with which the Holy Spirit emboldens the people of God to draw nigh as children to a father able and ready to help them. … It is to be noted that it is by or in the Holy Spirit that this approach is made.

Without the filial reverence and tenderness fostered by the Spirit, the address is presumptuous and arrogance."[88]

Apart from the regular and ongoing "adoptive" working of the Holy Spirit, I will not ever be comfortable in the embrace of God this side of Heaven. Have you ever attempted to have a relationship with a perfectionist? Or felt warmly at ease toward a Judge who holds your fate in his hand? Imagine approaching God without first being filled by this miraculous adoptive power? Looking into the eyes of the one, the only one who knows everything that you did and why and at the same time feeling safe, adored and secure.

This is the co-witness of the Holy Spirit within us. According to John Calvin, the Spirit "testifies to us, that we are the children of God, he at the same time pours into our hearts such confidence, that we venture to call God our Father."[89]

Conclusion

Just for the sake of argument, let's make a projection based upon the previously mentioned research on adult romantic relationships[90] of similar attachment related behaviors among Christianity.

If so, then we can estimate that perhaps as many as 60% of Christians are *secure* in their relationship with God. As in any relationship, there are times when God feels absent, when each of us feels alone, orphaned. A little under two-thirds are confident somehow that God has not really left them. It may feel like it sometimes, but it is not true. They remain the beloved of God. They are miraculously confident somehow that His return is imminent and the adoption relationship is unharmed. All injustices will be made right. All mysteries and doubts will be resolved.

Then we can also estimate that perhaps 20% of the Christian population at any given time might feel anxious in their relationship with God. They are God's beloved children because of the work of Christ, but on a day-to-day basis feel "ill-at-ease" and when they feel that God is absent, they will quickly "become extremely distressed." When God "returns" they are still anxious and have a "difficult time being soothed, and often exhibit conflicting behaviors that suggest they want to be comforted, but that they also want to "punish" the parent for leaving." I definitely know such people. On any given day, this could be me.

Then there would be the last 20% who would be described as *avoidant* children of God. In those times when their feelings tell them that God is absent, gone again, not available, not responding to their cries, they bivouac behind

---

88. John Murray, The Epistle to the Romans, Grand Rapids, Wm. B. Eerdmans Publishing, 1977, 296-297.
89. John Calvin, Commentary on Romans, 19:299.
90. Fraley, 2010.

subconscious walls, careful to not "appear too distressed by the separation" for that would be to give God too much power over them. When God at last returns in their lives, they would have trouble really allowing themselves to be happy, have great difficulty dancing with their heavenly Father. Rather, as a conditioned attachment behavior they would—largely subconsciously—"avoid seeking contact" with God, turning their attention to other lesser gazes that they feel are more trustworthy than God. I know each of these remain children of God.

If you are a Christian and are experiencing either of these last two states, anxious or avoidance, please hear this. Your reactions are not necessarily evil; they are very human. None of your reactions in any way affect your adoption as God's beloved child, though admittedly it feels like it.

Honestly, in a 24 hour day, I probably exhibit all three states. Perhaps a better way of processing this data is to suspect that 60% of my day I am secure in Christ. The other 40% of the time I swing from being anxious to avoidant.

May I invite you to fall to your knees, as you are, with or without any attachment behavioral defenses in place and plead with God for power that comes from Him in order to really know your sonship and daughtership is intact?

"God, make me know that I am your beloved son or daughter, right now. I do not feel it. I am anxious. I am avoidant. I don't seem to be able to help it. So I need. I need your intervention again. So give me faith, through your Spirit in me to know beyond knowledge how we are doing. I feel like I can relate to Cain. Looking to the ground is a safety thing for me—but not satisfying whatsoever. God make me see your gaze now, please before I do something stupid."

The Gospel App Shape

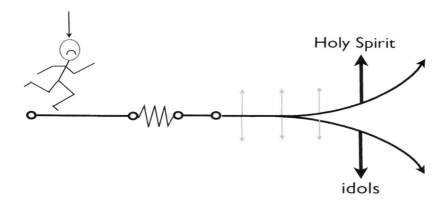

Chapter 9: Idolatry versus the Holy Spirit

"Once as I rode out into the woods for my health in 1737 for divine contemplation and prayer. I had a view that was extraordinary of the glory of the Son of God as mediator between God and man and of his wonderful grateful pure and sweet grace and love. This grace appeared so calm and sweet that the person of Christ appeared with an excellency great enough to swallow up all of my thought and conception which continued as near as I can judge about an hour and kept me the greater part of the time in a flood of tears and weeping aloud. I have several other times had views very much of the same nature which have had the same effects."
—Jonathan Edwards

"So deeply rooted in our hearts is unbelief, so prone are we to it, that while all confess with the lips that God is faithful, no man ever believes it without an arduous struggle."
— John Calvin

Idolatry is baked into fallen humanity—all humanity. Placing *idols* as one of the four key *power* vectors that drive and accelerate UCBs is to say that we fallen humans, including redeemed-fallen humans, have an unconscious destructive bent toward idolatry.

What are idols? Idols are anything or anyone that you or I run to, lean on, or count on to make us feel right about ourselves, our relationships, our accomplishments, our worth, value or identity—other than God. They are anything that I trust, implicitly or explicitly to save me from my guilt, shame, and orphan bent other than God. Anything other than God that gives me significance, security and belonging. Idols may be perceived as good and helpful. Or they may be bad and destructive. Needless to say, they are everywhere.

Anything, and in particular good things can be and most often are idols. Tim Keller is helpful.

> "We think that idols are bad things, but that is almost never the case. The greater the good, the more likely we are to expect that it can satisfy our deepest needs and hopes. Anything can serve as a counterfeit god, especially the very best things in life. What is an idol? It is anything more important to you than God, anything that absorbs your heart and imagination more than God, anything you seek to give you what only God can give. A counterfeit god is anything so central and essential to your life that, should you lose it, your life would feel hardly worth living. An idol has such a controlling position in your heart that you can spend most of your passion and energy, your emotional and financial resources, on it without a second thought."[91]

"[Idols] are anything that I trust, implicitly or explicitly to save me from my guilt, shame, and orphan bent other than God. Anything other than God that gives me significance, security and belonging."

Idols are everywhere. The most normal of human wants can be idolized. Approval from others can be an idol. What's wrong with approval? Our drive to be efficient can be an idol. So can independence, dependence, my comfort, my discomfort, how attractive or unattractive I consider myself, my religion, or irreligion, my politics, or my disinterest in any specific ideology. Even my family and relationships can be sources of culturally acceptable idols. Even that last piece of pizza can be an idol. Whatever we use as an idol, we become its slave.

"Such false gods create false laws, false definitions of success and failure of value and stigma. Idols promise blessing and warn of curses for those who succeed or fail against the law: If you get a large enough IRA, you will be secure. If I can get certain people to like and respect me, then my life is   valid."[92]

Into whose eyes do you gaze?

"As a human being, I am "finished" by others; I have no independent identi-

---

91. Tim Keller, Counterfeit Gods: The Empty Promises of Money, Sex, and Power, and the Only Hope That Matters. Penguin Group, 2009.
92. Powlison, D. "Idols of the Heart and 'Vanity Fair.'" Journal of Biblical Counseling, 13(2) 1995, 35.

ty apart from the "gaze" of others."[93]

If, because of Christ alone, God adores me as I am right now, then it follows that my true identity and being is ultimately drawn by His gaze upon me. The Cross and Resurrection purchased that for me from God.

No other person has ever felt that way toward me, even on my very best day. Not even the love of my mother achieved such heights.

I stand before God in a position of perfect favor and glory. If I could look directly into His eyes, I would see in His eye's reflection that He actually likes me. He loves me. He is delighted in me. He is crazy about me, as I am right now, whether or not I have been good this week or not so good. He sees me, now and continuously into the future, as His child of infinite glory and honor, not due to anything that I have done or accomplished.

To repeat, not one iota of His measuring gaze is a result of my efforts. His gaze is upon me favorably 24/7 no matter what I have done or not done, said or not said, whether I feel it or not. I know this is true by the power of faith. Jesus alone accomplished this.

True worth and identity comes from God's reflective gaze alone. Idolatry, then, is looking into the lesser measuring gaze of other people or things, other than God, in order to glean one's significance, security, and belonging. All idolatry is a lesser "finishing."

Yet I still go to hundreds of other lesser sources a day to see how I am doing. A surprising myriad of "Mirror, mirror on the wall, who's the fairest of them all." My problem, and humanity's bent, is that we regularly look into multiple non-God gazes throughout the day and week. Further, we will even *proactively* invite others, or other things to measure our success, value and worth for us. This behavior is to one degree or another destructive in the long term.

Why do we do it? Three reasons. First, idolatry is a deeply ingrained and conditioned habitual behavior. I do it because I have done it that way for weeks, months, and decades.

Second, gazing in God's eyes requires a lot of the specific *faith* that uniquely comes from the Holy Spirit. To employ such faith, I have to be willing to humbly admit that I don't innately have it and that I need God to fill me with such a faith first. Simply put, my pride and self-sufficiency gets in the way. I don't like depending upon anyone. I would truly like to believe that dependence is for the spiritually immature alone. I prefer the notion that when we earn our stripes we can achieve Jesus on our own from that point on.

Unfortunately, contrary to my preferred way of thinking, this faith that is rooted in the Holy Spirit is an exercise immersed in mystery and never-ending dependency, part of my "daily bread" that I need from God (Matt 6:11).

In contrast, gazing into the eyes of physical people and things requires *little* faith. I can choose to look into a myriad of lesser gazes on my own—and

93. Mandolfo, 12.

typically do.

Lastly, we have a residual fear that if we dare to wholeheartedly look into the perfect eyes of the Holy, Holy, Holy God, we will not see His favor. We fear that He will finally see us and all of our messiness and faults and turn away in contempt. Why? Because we would despise us if we were Him. Per John Calvin,

> "The believer finds within himself two principles: the one filling him with delight in recognizing the divine goodness, the other filling him with bitterness under a sense of his fallen state; the one leading him to recline on the promise of the Gospel, the other alarming him by the conviction of his iniquity; the one making him exult with the anticipation of life, the other making him tremble with the fear of death. This diversity is owing to imperfection of faith, since we are never so well in the course of the present life as to be entirely cured of the disease of distrust, and completely replenished and engrossed by faith. Hence those conflicts: the distrust cleaving to the remains of the flesh rising up to assail the faith enlisting in our hearts."[94]

Remember the Groucho Marx quip? "I don't care to belong to any club that will have me as a member." It is in some ways easier, more intuitive, and safer to gaze into the eyes of our myriad of false gods.

On any given day, in multiple situations and interactions, choices are required. Do I gaze into the eyes of innumerable very accessible idols to feel significance, security, and belonging; or do I humbly admit my lack again, and access faith through the Holy Spirit in me in order to gaze into the eyes of God?

Benefits of Idols?

People consciously or subconsciously make decisions based upon perceived beneficial outcomes. So the right question is this. "What are the perceived benefits of idols and idol worship?"

Why did the ancients go to temples to worship statues? In their minds, the perceived benefits of serving an idol (and the gods or goddesses they represented) included such things as hope, security, blessings, promise of abundance and fruitfulness (i.e., children), power, identity and even community.

> "The old pagans were not fanciful when they depicted virtually everything as a god. They had sex gods, work gods, war gods, money gods, nation gods—for the simple fact that anything can be a god that rules and serves as a deity in the heart of a person or in the life of a people. For example, physical beauty is a pleasant thing, but if you deify it, if you make it the most important thing in a person's life or a culture's life, then you have Aphrodite, not just beauty. You have people, and an entire culture, constantly agonizing

---

94. John Calvin. Institutes, 564.

over appearance, spending inordinate amounts of time and money on it, and foolishly evaluating character on the basis of it. If anything becomes more fundamental than God to your happiness, meaning in life, and identity, then it is an idol."[95]

When the ancient Spartans made sacrifices to the goddess Artemis before a military campaign, they hoped that she would bring them victory—or negatively that she would not cause defeat because of a lack of devotion. Others worshipped the very same goddess in hopes of her providing children and the security that a family brings.

The goddess presumably offered the worshippers something that was important and valuable to them. It was a contract of sorts. In response to the dedicated *gaze* (obedience, worship, participation in the temple) of the worshippers, the idolized deities would make the supplicant happy, secure, or blessed. To join with an idol gave one a sense of the rightness that they lacked, or so they hoped.

Bible Study: Idols

The New Testament radically expands the concept of idolatry far beyond the physical worship of a physical made-by-human-hands statue. Paul observes that idolatry encompasses every bent of our sinful nature. In his letter to the Colossians, Paul lumps five major sin categories under the overarching rubric of idolatry.

"Put to death, therefore, whatever belongs to your earthly nature: sexual immorality, impurity, lust, evil desires and greed, which is idolatry." (Col 3:5)

If you were filing each of the above sins in your office file cabinet, you would put them in the larger folder labeled "Idols". Sexual immorality, impurity, lust, evil desires and greed don't come from outside of you. They come from inside. If you rolled them all together into a grotesque awkward ball—that is idolatry—or perhaps more precise, your ravenous subconscious bent toward idols to measure you and give you a sense of significance, security, and belonging.

Counselor David Powlison observes that it is very significant that the Apostle John wraps up his short epistle with the succinct uncomfortably out-of-place warning, "Dear children, keep yourselves from idols" (1 John 5:21 NIV). "In a 105-verse treatise on living in vital fellowship with Jesus, the Son of God, how on earth does that unexpected command merit being the final word?"

Powlison's answer?

---

95. Tim Keller, Counterfeit Gods: The Empty Promises of Money, Sex, and Power, and the Only Hope That Matters. Penguin Group, 2009.

"John's last line properly leaves us with that most basic question which God continually poses to each human heart. Has something or someone besides Jesus the Christ, taken title to your heart's trust, preoccupation, loyalty, service, fear, and delight? It is a question bearing on the immediate motivation for one's behavior, thoughts and feelings…The alternative to Jesus, the swarm of alternatives, whether approached through the lens of flesh, word or the Evil One, is idolatry."[96]

Idolatry, per Richard Keyes, is the main category to describe unbelief. "The Bible does not allow us to marginalize idolatry to the fringes of life…it is found on center stage."[97]

Perhaps what John has in mind is to present to Christians, then and today, two opposite approaches available to Jesus-followers. On the one hand, we can just fall-back on the innate subconscious bent of the flesh, exacerbated by the world and Satan. Or there is the supernaturally empowered alternative. We can access a new Heaven-sourced power and motivation by faith through the Holy Spirit and find our significance, security, and belonging in the gaze of God alone.

In the *Gospel App*, our bent toward idols is portrayed as being in conflict with our desire to depend upon and be filled with the Holy Spirit. The war rages on until we go to Heaven.

Let's go back to Chapter 2 in John's first epistle where he begins to lay out his arguments of the pervasive dangers of idols.

> "Do not love the world or anything in the world. If anyone loves the world, the love of the Father is not in him. For everything in the world—the cravings (Gr: *epithumia*) of sinful man, the lust (Gr: *epithumia*) of his eyes and the boasting (pretentious pride—meaning a foolish boasting not based upon substance or reality) of what he has and does—comes not from the Father but from the world. The world and its desires (Gr: *epithumia*) pass away, but the man who does the will of God lives forever." (1 John 2:15-17 NIV)

In 1 John 2:15-17, idols are not even mentioned of course, yet he does refer to the deep, innate, normal, conscious and subconscious power that drives the pursuit of idols (i.e., *epithumia*).

John begins with a command, an imperative. We are a people who love imperatives. Just tell me what I need to *do* in order to feel right, to feel less wrong, to feel that God and I are good, to feel that I am successful and on the right track. What do I need to do?

"Do not love the world or anything in the world…"

---

96. Powlison, D. "Idols of the Heart and 'Vanity Fair.'" Journal of Biblical Counseling, 13(2) 1995, 35.
97. Richard Keyes, "The Idol Factory" in Os Guiness and John Seel (eds), No God But God: Breaking with the Idols of Our Age, Chicago: Moody Press (1992), 31.

John, honestly, this doesn't help me much. How am I to *not* love the world? Of course it is arguably easy to *not* love evil things, bad things, ugly things. It might be easy to *not* love bigotry, hatred, oppression, slavery, addictions, or evil men and women who abuse others.

John does not narrow the field to *not* loving *unlovable* things. He says, "Don't love the world," which necessarily includes both lovable and unlovable things, good and bad things, constructive and destructive things.

How do I *not* love a New York strip steak, cooked medium rare sizzling on a plate right in front of me? *Not* love the fall colors of the Aspens in Colorado? Or an incredible sunrise? A new born baby?

Even those distinctions are a bit too clean. How do I not love ice cream, and even a lot of ice cream, even though I know that there might be significant negative effects to my health? How do I not love the NFL playoffs—especially when my team is in them, even though it perhaps takes me away from community and service to others? How do I not love so many other things that can become destructive or addictive?

I don't know about you, but I do not have an identifiable muscle group to *love* or *not love* the world or anything else for that matter. If there was such an emotional muscle group, someone would divine exercises to make me successful. That would certainly make relationships more straightforward. If we are honest, we do not know how to turn love *on* or *off*. Whoever said that love is a choice is well-meaning yet largely mistaken.

Certainly John knew that. If so, at face value, then his charge to us is pretty maddening—on the surface unhelpful. If Biblically, I am supposed to *choose* to not love the world and I can't accomplish the task at hand, then I am in for a frustrating ride. I will fail.

Maybe there is another way to read verse 15. For the sake of argument, let's just say that John knew exactly what he was doing. He was commanding you and I to do something that if we were bluntly honest, we cannot do. My expected reaction?

Me: "What? I can't do that!"

John: "Exactly. You can't. You lack the ability to love or to not love good or bad things."

Me: "Still not helpful John!"

John: "Now you are beginning to see that you have a deep seated ongoing need in this area, my child. You are right. You can't choose to love or choose to stop loving. What you can do is to by faith ask God to give you His love (Eph 3). Admitting your need and looking to the only source for love is a game changer."

The principle that John is teaching, now that he has our attention is this:

> "If you were presently filled with the love of the Father, the height, width, length and depth of the love of Jesus, then you would notice something stunning happening right before your helpless eyes. You would notice, and others would as well, that you love the world and the things of the world (good and bad) *less*. You can't, but He, and specifically His love in you, can satisfy the deep innate longing that was subconsciously driving you to idols."

Do you find yourself worried about your reputation and so work hard to keep it unsullied? Sounds reasonable. Yet do you lose sleep when there is a possibility that your reputation can be diminished? Work late and weekends to guard your reputation in the eyes of your boss, your co-workers, your employees or your clients? This sounds so very right and normal.

Yet John would say, "Quick, run to God by faith, through the Holy Spirit in you, and access 1) your reputation in Christ (that is *His* right reputation) and 2) receive God's love for you and for others. To the extent that you receive and apply these two things, you will feel the need to guard your reputation *less*. To the extent that you receive and apply these two things, you will find yourself being more motivated to further the reputation of *others* more. You may need to win (i.e., to beat others) *less*. You may be happier when others win.

Is all hard work idolatry? This side of heaven, it is safe to say that all of my hard work will be laced with a poisonous desire to succeed and to further my own reputation. Laziness is likewise laced with the poison of self-centeredness.

What is John's principle that gives us a new life-strategy? If the love of the Father is in me, I will *not* love the world as much.

The call to action? Go and by faith get the love of the Father (Eph 3:14-21). If the miraculous love of the Father is *not* rushing into you and overflowing to your motivation and decision processes, you *will* naturally love material things and worldly reputations. You will humanly speaking *have* to. You must do one or the other. You can't just try hard to *not* love the things of the world. So stop it!

In a very sophisticated section, John unveils our deeper problem. It turns out that what you and I have most often imagined as love is in reality something far more damaging and out of our control. Upon closer inspection the "love of the world" in verse 15 (Gr: *agape*) is now revealed to be a powerful unmanageable *passion* (Gr: *epithumia*). To be overly simplistic, if *agape* speaks of a love that is the fruit of an appreciation of the innate beauty and value of an object, its selfish step-sister-on-steroids *epithumia* might be described as a largely subconscious demanding desire to devour, consume and use said object for my own pleasure.

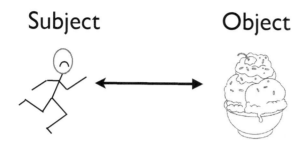

Consider the illustration above of a familiar subject-object interaction. If motivated purely by *epithumia*, the *subject's* sole interest in the *object*, a bowl of ice cream, would be to devour it. He or she might see the decorative bowl, the sharp presentation of the dessert, may even wonder about the impressive technology that is used these days to manufacture ice cream, but most likely would only be interested in eating up the icy taste-filled wonder.

Epithumia sees the object, the bowl of ice cream. In fact, the more that *epithumia* thinks about it, the more that it can't think of anything else. *Epithumia* craves its object, longs for it, and may even dream about it. It has little concern about the calories, the cholesterol, sugar and fat, or other long-term consequences. Its concern is to *consume*.

The *subject* feels that need to satisfy those internal *"epithumia-ic"* longings, passions and desires without a lot of concern about consequences or the well-being of the object of his or her lust.

In contrast, if motivated by *agape*, the *subject* may not only see the *object*, but would also appreciate it—its beauty, its value, its context, and even its flavor.

In Colorado there are majestic mountain peaks. Imagine arriving at the peak of a great mountain only to see laid out before you a stunning vista, perhaps an indescribable sunset. What surges out of you is probably *agape*-esque. You cannot own the view. You cannot use or abuse the view. You cannot consume it. You can only appreciate it and its beauty.

Epithumia is best understood as a powerful subconscious motivator that largely bypasses our cognitive functions. Your brain may not really kick in until your fourth bowl of *Cherry Garcia*. Or your fifth 60-hour week at your job, or after the affair has been discovered. John puts it this way.

> For everything in the world—the cravings (*epithumia*) of sinful man, the lust (*epithumia*) of his eyes and the boasting of what he has and does, comes not from the Father but from the world. (1 Jn 2:15-16 NIV)

So not only can you *not* stop *loving* the world (double negatives intentional), it turns out that your most natural love is better identified as a lustful, self-focused, demanding subconscious craving that is very capable of bypassing your brain's impotent warning flags.

John uses *epithumia* twice: that of the "flesh" (Gr: *sarkos*) and of the "eye" (Gr: *ophthalamos*). *Epithumia* is reflected in both craving and sight. Not only is something inside of you *making* you want something incessantly, You can't get it out of your mind's eye. You just keep on seeing it, over and over. It seems that the only way to stop seeing it and wanting it is to go and take it.

Then there is the boasting, or better, the pretentious pride. Maybe what John has in mind is the folly of boasting that "I could choose at any time to *not* consume the object again. After all, I am in control of my yearnings and lustings." The boasting is foolish because it denies the subconscious power of our flesh and its cravings that bypass our will over and over again. I think of a number of alcoholics who have told me that they could stop anytime.

Hope of Agape

Don't mistake this. John gives us real hope, but not in our own efforts, not in our locating a previously hidden muscle group that can stop *epithumia*, but rather in our becoming in-sync with the will of God.

> The world and its desires pass away, but the man who does the will of God lives forever. (1 John 2:17)

What is the "will of God" in this context? God desires that your deepest desires, preferences, and wants would be totally in-sync with His. Then you will be motivated by a whole new power—the only one given to humanity that can overwhelm the *epithumia* of the flesh and pride.

Consider such a miracle for a moment. What would your relationships look like if your *wants* were in alignment with God's?

Consider a recent irritation caused by someone. What would it have looked like, or felt like, to the one who irritated you, if in this moment you were in-sync with God? Imagine.

What if your *epithumia* to get justice or vindication had been diminished? And you were filled with a surprising compassion for the other? Paul agrees with John. In his letter to the Galatians, he writes,

> So I say, live by the Spirit, and you will not gratify the desires (*epithumia*) of the

sinful nature. For the sinful nature desires (*epithumia*) what is contrary to the Spirit, and the Spirit what is contrary to the sinful nature. They are in conflict with each other, so that you do not do what you want. (Gal 5:16-17 NIV)

James and Peter offer similar warnings about our *epithumia*.[98]

> Dear friends, I urge you, as aliens and strangers in the world, to abstain from sinful desires *[Gr: epithumia]*, which war against your soul. (1Pet 2:11 NIV)

> As a result, he does not live the rest of his earthly life for evil human desires *[Gr: epithumia]*, but rather for the will of God. (1Pet 4:2 NIV)

> When tempted, no one should say, "God is tempting me." For God cannot be tempted by evil, nor does he tempt anyone; but each one is tempted when, by his own evil desire *[Gr: epithumia]*, he is dragged away and enticed. Then, after desire *[Gr: epithumia]* has conceived, it gives birth to sin; and sin, when it is full-grown, gives birth to death. (James 1:13-15 NIV)

Look at how our *epithumia* is starkly portrayed. It wages war against our soul. It is in continual conflict with the will of God. It initiates temptation within each of us. Very little of our *epithumia* is cognitive. It is largely subconscious. I never have conversations like this. "OK my strategy is to obsess over this until I get it. Yep, good plan."

How do you break free from the subconscious control of idols, of addictions? Biblically, it is impossible to truly diminish your addictive behaviors, your go-to idols, until you are able to diminish the power that is driving your addictive behavior: your largely subconscious *epithumia*. How do you do that?

You can't. Not in your own power. Fortunately there is a Plan B. Paul says that if you "live by the Spirit" (Gal 5:16), you will not live by your *epithumia*. In the *Gospel App*, the opposite power to *idols* is the *Holy Spirit* Himself in our inner-being. The effective counter agent to your subconscious *epithumia* is the power that you can regularly access from the Holy Spirit in you.

To put it in familiar *Gospel App* terminology: if *idols* are anything, anyone, any institution, or any measuring gaze that you run to in order to find your significance, belonging, and security other than God, then it seems obvious that the better option would be to run to God, look up into His measuring gaze alone, and experience the significance, security, and belonging that Christ has already purchased for you two thousand years ago. You can regularly access the benefits of being a child of God. Sounds too easy, right? The question remains, how do you do it?

---

98. Powlison, Idols, 36.

The Gospel App Shape

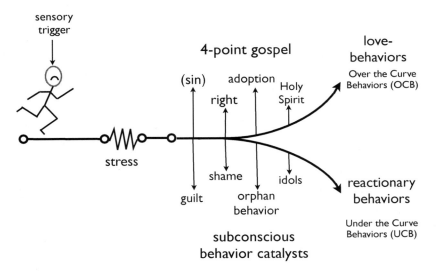

So How do We Receive the Spirit's Benefits?

Theologian John Calvin was so concerned about the above question, he dedicated Book Three of his Institutes to the issue: "The Way in Which We Receive the Grace of Christ: What Benefits Come to Us From It, and What Effects Follow." Chapter 1 is titled "The Things Spoken Concerning Christ Profits Us By The Secret Working of the Spirit." Calvin writes,

> "We must now examine this question. How do we receive those benefits which the Father bestowed on his only begotten Son—not for Christ's own private use, but that he might enrich poor and needy men? First, we must understand that as long as Christ remains outside of us, and we are separated from him, all that he has suffered and done for the salvation of the human race remains useless and of no value for us. Therefore to share with us what he has received from the Father, he had to become ours and to dwell within us."[99]

It is by Him, the Spirit of Christ who indwells all believers, and his "*secret working*" that we Christians can even begin to presently "enjoy Christ and all his benefits", including a deep abiding present awareness of the above mentioned three aspects of the Gospel. Calvin continues, "The Holy Spirit is the bond by which Christ effectually unites us to himself."[100]

The Holy Spirit's efforts do not stop at salvation. He continues as the "root and the seed of heavenly life in us...By the grace and power of the same Spirit we

99. John Calvin, Institutes, 537.
100. Ibid, 537.

are made his members, to keep us under himself and in turn to possess him."[101]

To be clear, you can be a saved Jesus-follower, heaven-bound and yet still live on a day-to-day basis as if you were all alone in the universe, a functional deist.

Or you can by faith through the Holy Spirit's *"secret workings"* access a deep awareness of your current beloved standing with God—your intimate relationship with your Father in Heaven. This union with Christ is yours experientially only through the ongoing power and work of the Holy Spirit. As the Spirit manifests this miraculous assurance to your inner-being, you will actually believe that God does love you as you are right now. This will affect everything you do, you want, and even how you treat everyone around you.

Your part in this transaction? First, all you need is need. Second, you must ask for the Holy Spirit to shower you with His spiritual faith, one of the Spirit's fruit mentioned in Gal 5:22-23). Neil Williams writes about this powerful and accessible-upon-the-request "Spirit/faith dynamic":

> "We are grafted into Christ by faith and we continue to receive the blessings of that union by faith. The Spirit brings to us everything that belongs to Christ through the instrument of faith. This Spirit/faith dynamic helps us answer such related questions as: How are we justified? By faith in Christ through the Spirit who justifies (1 Cor 6:11). How are we adopted? By faith in Christ through the Spirit of Sonship (Rom 8:15). How do we persevere? By faith in Christ through the work and power of the Spirit (Phil 1:19; Heb 12:1 – 2). How are we sanctified? By faith in Christ through the sanctifying Spirit (1 Cor 6:11; 2 Thess 2:13; Titus 3:5; 1 Pet 1:2). So we are justified by faith, we are adopted by faith, we persevere by faith—and we are sanctified by faith."[102]

This specific type of spiritual faith from the Holy Spirit alone is the active, empowering, and ongoing bond that immediately and presently unites you to Christ and all that He purchased for you two thousand years ago. As the Spirit of Adoption, the Holy Spirit alone can give you a powerful *present* experience of your adoption in good standing through His faith. "To live by faith is to live by the Spirit. Sanctification by faith is about the Spirit's power transforming our hearts

---

101. Ibid, 538-541.
102. Just to be clear, Williams adds, "By grounding sanctification in our union with Christ, we are not saying that justification and sanctification are the same thing. What we are saying is that they come through the same means. Christ is our justification and sanctification, and we receive Christ and his blessings, including justification and sanctification, through the Spirit and by faith." Neil H. Williams, The Theology of Sonship, World Harvest Mission, 2002. Theologian John Owen writes, "This, I suppose, will be granted, that if we receive any thing from Christ, it must be by faith, it must be in the exercise of it, or in a way of believing; nor is there any one word in the Scripture that gives the least encouragement to expect either grace or mercy from him in any other way, or by any other means (John Owen, The Glory of Christ, ed. William H. Goold, The Works of John Owen, vol. One (Edinburgh: Banner of Truth, 1965), 459. Quoted in Williams, The Theology of Sonship, 6)

and behavior."[103]

> *"Faith is the principal work of the Holy Spirit...Faith itself has no other source than the Spirit."*

No matter how you may feel right now, you can access a present awareness of God looking upon you as a loving benevolent Father. By faith, you can access the power to know this grace, right now. The Spirit is the present guarantee and seal of your inheritance. Through Him you will want to cry out Abba Father! John Calvin suggests that no work is more important to the Holy Spirit in you.

> "Faith is the principal work of the Holy Spirit...The Spirit is the inner teacher by whose effort the promise of salvation penetrates into our minds, a promise that otherwise would only strike the air or beat upon our ears...Faith itself has no other source than the Spirit... Perfect salvation is found in the person of Christ...We may become partakers of it as he baptizes us in the Holy Spirit and fire."[104]

What is this specific Faith that accesses the Holy Spirit in me?

We use the word faith in many ways. We can speak of "faith" as a composite of religious confession or religion. "What faith are you?" "I am Baptist, Catholic, etc." We can speak of a faith as some hoped for occurrence. I have faith that it will not rain this weekend. Both are reasonable modern usages of the word faith. While appropriate these are not what Paul had in mind when he spoke of the specific faith that is a fruit of the Spirit.[105] J. Gresham Machen is helpful in his book, *What is Faith?*

> "When we come to see that what Paul calls the flesh is a mighty power, which is dragging us resistlessly down into an abyss of evil that has no bottom, then we feel our guilt and misery, then we look about for something stronger to help us than our own weak will. Such a power is found by the Apostle Paul in faith; it is faith, he says, that produces or works itself out in the life of love."[106]

Such faith is a specific and intentional fruit of the Spirit, i.e., an aspect of God's DNA—*not* ours—the ongoing power from God that alone makes the Jesus-follower really know in the present moment that

---

103. Neil H. Williams, The Theology of Sonship, 10.
104.. John Calvin, Institutes, 541.
105. In his letter to the Galatians, Paul uses the Greek word pistis 20 times. Only once do our modern versions translate pistis 'faithfulness.' Nineteen times, pistis is translated faith. Once it is faithfulness. Faithfulness has a different connotation. It implies that it is a result of my own effort and choice. On the other hand "faith" is something that originates from God's hands. Very different. It is better to see faith as a fruit of the Spirit.
106. J. Gresham Machen, What is Faith?, The Banner of Truth Trust, 2012, 216.

Idolatry vs. Holy Spirit

God is not judging me—no matter what I have done or haven't done,

God loves me as I am, no matter how I have been loved here,

God feels only honor toward me—no matter what my current circumstances are—no matter what my current feelings say.[107]

Bible Study: Faith

Shortly after Paul left the newly planted Galatian churches, certain theologians arrived from Jerusalem to "clarify" some points for the new Christian churches there. Their pitch would have gone something like this:

> "Well no wonder you are not jazzed by your relationship with God right now—or maybe you're feeling like Christian failures, or huge disappointments to God, or feel guilty about your recent backsliding? What you did to get into faith was OK. Now, you need to move further in toward God by good old hard work and clean living. Didn't Paul tell you what you should be *doing* in order to feel God's pleasure and love for you? What are those things? Well two things for sure. First, you need to get circumcised. Second, you need to start following all of the food and dietary laws that God Himself gave us. If you do those things, then your spiritual life will just take off. Then you will feel your shame and guilt diminished. Then you will really feel God's love for you."

Paul viscerally disagrees and is clearly incensed that these so-called Jerusalem theologians are unraveling what the Holy Spirit's *faith* began.

> You foolish Galatians! Who has bewitched you? Before your very eyes Jesus Christ was clearly portrayed as crucified. I would like to learn just one thing from you: Did you receive the Spirit by observing the law, or by believing what you heard? Are you so foolish? After beginning with the Spirit, are you now trying to attain your goal by human effort? (Gal 3:1-3 NIV)

He urgently writes to the young baby Christians in Galatia:

---

107. "The experience of the Spirit is expressed in words quite distinct from those describing creation and God's 'works' in history. The words used for the Spirit are 'outpouring,' 'flowing,' and so forth. The Spirit is 'poured out' on all flesh in the Last Days (Joel 2:28ff; Acts 2.16ff.), and then old and young, men and women, all alike, will have dreams and visions. Through the Holy Spirit the love of God is poured out into our hearts..(Rom 5.5). ...These are the divine energies which already quicken life now, in the present, because they are the energies of the new creation of all things. (Jurgen Moltmann, The Trinity and the Kingdom of God: The Doctrine of God, SCM Press Ltd.19981, 104).

> For in Christ Jesus neither circumcision nor uncircumcision has any value. The only thing that counts is faith expressing itself through love. (Gal 5:6 NIV)

Here is a more expanded translation that remains faithful to the text:

> For in Christ, neither circumcision nor uncircumcision has any power to accomplish anything. On the contrary, it is *faith* that makes love happen.

This is a shocking verse. Certainly Paul would know who commanded the Jews to be circumcised in the first place? God Himself commanded the practice. How could Paul now say that being circumcised is of little import to the Christian walk?

Modern Jews list 613 distinct laws, some more important than others. Circumcision was among the many such commands of God to His people. To what end? The implication is that if one was *not* feeling the favor of Yahweh, was not receiving an assurance of their significance, security, and belonging with his or her Heavenly Father, all that was needed is to work harder: doing even more of what God commanded them to do.

It might be an implicit or explicit precept of Judaism and much of modern Evangelicalism that one's present experience of his or her relationship with Yahweh as merciful and loving Heavenly Father would just take off if only he or she would do _____ (fill in the blank).

Biblically, if you would take all of the verses into account, such Godly favor requires *absolute faithfulness, all the time*.

> "If you *fully* obey the Lord your God and *carefully* follow *all* his commands I give you today, the Lord your God will set you high above all the nations on earth. All these blessings will come upon you and accompany you *if* you obey the Lord your God...Do not turn aside from *any* of the commands I give you today, to the *right* or to the *left*, following other gods and serving them. However, *if* you do not obey the Lord your God and do not *carefully* follow *all* his commands and decrees I am giving you today, all these curses will come upon you and overtake you." (Dt 28:1-15 NIV, emphases mine)

So the Jerusalem theologians were partly correct. If you want to presently experience Yahweh's loving devotion toward you, one of the paths is to do *everything* exactly according to the Law your entire life. For those who didn't live up to that standard (and nobody comes anywhere near it) there is a single other path: Jesus' record of perfect faithfulness can be imputed to your account. Then God's favor is yours as if you had been perfect—even though you were not.

Modern day Galatians hear this: if you would experience the godly devotion and love that Jesus' record has already purchased for you, it is not *more* work that makes that happen. God's favor toward you cannot be diminished even if you do less Torah.

Paul says that the key to experiencing the significance, security, and belonging that is yours by Christ is faith. *Faith makes love happen.* If you are not feeling that God likes you, it is not because you are a screw-up in your actions. You have a "faith" problem.

So if you are jonesing for significance, belonging, and security that is your inheritance in Christ, it doesn't matter whether you are circumcised or not. This is true for any and all modern "circumcisions."

> Whether you read your Bible 30 minutes a day or don't read it 30 minutes a day, neither has any power to accomplish anything—on the contrary faith makes love happen.

> Whether you go to church regularly or not, neither has any power to accomplish anything—on the contrary faith makes love happen.

> Whether you pray consistently or not, neither has any power to accomplish anything—on the contrary faith makes love happen.

> Whether you love your neighbor or not, neither has any power to accomplish anything—on the contrary faith makes love happen.

> Whether you tithe 10% consistently or don't give anything at all—on the contrary it is only the power of spiritual faith that can ever make you feel that God likes you.

None of these broad ranging "circumcisions" can result in your feeling more like a child of God with all privileges. None have the power to draw God closer. None of them change who you are or your identity as a child of God. None of them, no matter how good you are at them have the capacity to make you feel that God loves you one additional iota more. Your spiritual life will not take off if only you would do these more consistently. Only the specific *faith* that comes from God has the capacity to make you feel the love and devotion of your Heavenly Father (Eph 3:14-21).

In fact, these "good" things can end in undesired and unintended consequences. If you are one of those who are consistent at doing these good things, your flesh may blossom a spirit of arrogance and self-righteous judgment toward those who aren't as *right*.

On the other hand, if you fail to live up to your standards for any or all of the above, you may feel shame or guilt erupting from your flesh.

To be clear, there is nothing inherent in "doing" those things that can make you really feel honored by God, loved by God, validated and approved by

God. Nothing.

If you rely on doing things in hopes of gaining even a tiny bit of God's favor, you can never know where you stand. You can have no lasting assurance derived from your efforts.

So important is this specific dynamic working of the Holy Spirit in us, that Paul uses *faith* as a *synechdoche* (using a part to represent the whole) for all that the Spirit does in us.

> "What does Paul mean when he says that "faith works"? Certainly he does not mean what the modern pragmatist skeptic means when he uses the same words; certainly he does not mean that it is merely faith, considered as a psychological phenomenon, and independent of the truth or falsehood of its object, that does the work. What he does mean is made abundantly clear in the last section of this same Epistle to the Galatians, where the life of love is presented in some detail. In that section nothing whatever is said about faith; it is not faith that is there represented as producing the life of love but the Spirit of God; the Spirit is there represented as doing exactly what, in the phrase "faith working through love," is ascribed to faith."[108]

In Gal 5:6 it is *faith* that alone can produce love—nothing that we do or choose to do. But starting in Gal 5:14, it is the Holy Spirit that produces love.

Faith's Deep Confidence

Do you wonder at times if God really loves you? Or likes you at all? Calvin argues that there is knowledge of God's love for individual Christians and then there is *knowledge* that is far beyond the former. A husband may have faith that his wife loves him—she made a public vow at their wedding—she has been committed to the relationship—she is living in the same house. He could rightly in a sense say that he has faith that she loves him.

Yet there is available to the husband even more: a greater *knowledge* of love without which the relationship is greatly lacking. This *knowledge* occurs in her physical and passionate embrace, a fruit of his being lavished with passionate kisses. It is then that he gets this greater love which doesn't discount the former, but is certainly better and richer in so many ways. In this sense, he really has *faith* that she loves him, though the two are quite different. The Greek word of choice for Paul to reflect such a confident assurance is *pleroforia*.

> "Very different is that feeling of full assurance (*pleroforia*) which the Scriptures uniformly attributes to faith—an assurance which leaves no doubt that

---

108. Machen, Faith?, 216-7. His logic goes like this. In Gal 5:6, Paul teaches that faith makes love happen (Gal 5:6). But later in the same chapter, it is the Spirit that produces love. The Holy Spirit making love happen and faith making love happen represents the same phenomenon. This Biblical faith is solely of the Spirit, not humanity.

Idolatry vs. Holy Spirit

the goodness of God is clearly offered to us. This assurance we cannot have without truly perceiving its sweetness, and experiencing it in ourselves. Hence from faith the Apostle deduces confidence, and from confidence boldness. His words are, "In whom (Christ) we have boldness and access with confidence by the faith of him," (Eph. 3: 12:) thus undoubtedly showing that our faith is not true unless it enables us to appear calmly in the presence of God. Such boldness springs only from confidence in the divine favor and salvation. So true is this, that the term faith is often used as equivalent to confidence."[109]

This higher *knowledge* that we speak of related to the Holy Spirit's power alone is more than mere human comprehension, says Calvin.

"The word is not received in faith when it merely flutters in the brain, but when it has taken deep root in the heart, and become an invincible bulwark to withstand and repel all the assaults of temptation…Hence the Spirit performs the part of a seal, sealing upon our hearts the very promises, the certainty of which was previously impressed upon our minds. It also serves as an earnest in establishing and confirming these promises. Thus the Apostle says, 'In whom also, after that ye believed, ye were sealed with that Holy Spirit of promise, which is the earnest of our inheritance' (Eph. 1:13, 14). You see how he teaches that the hearts of believers are stamped with the Spirit as with a seal, and calls it the Spirit of promise, because it ratifies the gospel to us.[110]

God's accessible knowledge is superior to our intellect.

"[This greater] knowledge is so much superior, that the human mind must far surpass and go beyond itself in order to reach it. Nor even when it has reached it does it comprehend what it feels, but persuaded of what it comprehends not, it understands more from mere certainty of persuasion than it could discern of any human matter by its own capacity. Hence it is elegantly described by Paul as ability 'to comprehend with all saints what is the breadth, and length, and depth, and height; and to know the love of Christ, which passeth knowledge' (Eph. 3: 18, 19)."[111]

---

109. Calvin, Institutes, 561. Calvin continues, "My purpose is that they may be encouraged in heart and united in love, so that they may have the full riches of complete (plerophorias) understanding, in order that they may know the mystery of God, namely, Christ." (Col 2:2) "…Because our gospel came to you not simply with words, but also with power, with the Holy Spirit and with deep (plerophorias) conviction." (1 Th 1:5 NIV). "We want each of you to show this same diligence to the very end, in order to make your hope sure (plerophorias)." (Heb 6:11 NIV) "Let us draw near to God with a sincere heart in full assurance (plerophorias) of faith, having our hearts sprinkled to cleanse us from a guilty conscience and having our bodies washed with pure water." (Heb 10:22 NIV)
110. Calvin, Institutes, 583-4
111. Calvin, Institutes ,559-560.

How do I receive such faith?

> "Let it suffice to observe, that the spirit of faith is used by Paul as synonymous with the very faith which we receive from the Spirit, but which we have not naturally (2 Cor. 4: 13). Accordingly, he prays for the Thessalonians, 'that our God would count you worthy of this calling, and fulfill all the good pleasure of his goodness, and the work of faith with power' (2 Thess. 1: 2). Here, by designating faith the work of God...he declares that it is not of man's own nature; and not contented with this, he adds, that it is an illustration of divine power. In addressing the Corinthians, when he tells them that faith stands not 'in the wisdom of man, but in the power of God' (1 Cor. 2: 4)."[112]

This *true faith* is not part of my nature. I don't have a faith/trust/belief muscle group that I can exercise to do this miraculous faith. I can "choose to believe" but that is very different. The good news is that God has piles of "faith-power" that is mine upon the asking. Like Jesus says, "You have not because you ask not" (James 4:2, John 16:24).

Most of us have never been told that we can ask for *faith* from God. We need this "stuff," this faith-power from God before we can do anything above the curve. It is appropriate to say that Jesus lived perfectly by this faith. It is equally right to say that He perfectly lived by the Spirit. Same thing.

It is almost too easy. If I really want to love more, I need to stop doing what I am doing and run to God with empty needy hands and ask for His power, His faith, in order to love, and in order to feel love.

I am invited to daily receive *faith* from above. This *faith* is a *fruit* of the Spirit.[113] I should regularly ask for it. To feel God's love for you and others, stop trying so hard to "believe." Rather, run to God and receive. *Faith* is not "done," it is received. It is a fruit of God that can be regularly and daily received.

> "True faith, strictly speaking, does not do anything; it does not give, but receives. So when one says that we do something by faith that is just another way of saying that we do nothing—at least that we do nothing of ourselves. It is of the very nature of faith, strictly speaking, to do nothing...instead of doing something ourselves we allow someone else to help us. That force which enters our life at the beginning through faith, before we could do anything at all to please God, and which then strengthens and supports us in the battle that it has enabled us to begin, is the power of the Spirit of God."[114]

---

112. Calvin, Institutes, 582-3.
113. Paul uses the Greek root for faith (pistis) 20 times in his letter to the Galatians. Only once do the translators ever translate it "faithfulness." Only in the list of the fruit of the Spirit in Gal 5 is pistis translated "faithfulness." Faith and faithfulness are two very different words. One refers to what I do, the other, what I receive from God.
114. Machen, Faith, 217.

What then does it mean to live by spiritual *faith*? To live by this *faith* is to live with an ongoing awareness that I am lacking such *faith* all the time and to enter into a posture where I constantly go to God asking for my fill of His *faith*. Run and ask for the Holy Spirit to fill you right now.

The Gospel App Shape

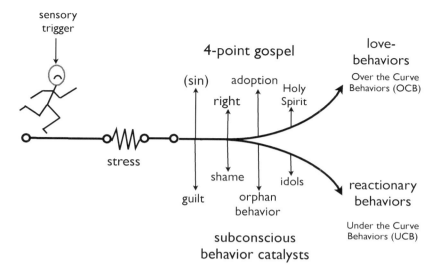

Conclusion

> *"You have not because you ask not."*
> —James 4:2

Jesus-follower, may I have the privilege to remind you of the singular Gospel of Christ one last time?

#1- (Sin)

First, two thousand years ago, Jesus died for all of your crimes against God, humanity, and creation, every single one of them (i.e., (sin)). There was a trial for everyone of your crimes. You were declared guilty for each. No point in objecting at all to the findings of the Judge.

For each guilty verdict, the celestial objective punishment was death. There is no point in objecting to the punishment either. The wages of sin are death (Rom 6:23).

In the great and wonderful mystery of the Gospel, Jesus willingly and intentionally took your place. He took the penalty rightly due you upon His shoulders. The upshot of His actions is this. Now, God can never be critical toward you again—much less judge you. Jesus has already been judged and criticized perfectly for every single iota of your faulty record.

Having said that, you may often still find it quite difficult to really believe this is true. You may struggle daily, longing for a real heart-level experience amidst easier to find rational confessions of faith. If you are like me, you may often feel guilt for actions and thoughts that just seem to roll out of your brain. Your guilt may even be pervasive and debilitating at times. Preach this Gospel over and over again to yourself. Ask for present spiritual faith from God.

#2- Right

The second aspect of the Gospel is the *imputation* of Jesus' righteousness to your account. In layman's terms, Jesus' record of perfect faithfulness related to the Father's wishes is irrevocably put into your biography. It is official and perfectly legal.

According to your dramatically adjusted record, there is only evidence of perfect faithfulness to the Father—not by *your* faithfulness of course. It is of Jesus' efforts alone, an undeserved gift. It is as yours as it is His.

The upshot? Now you are to be afforded everything that His perfect faithfulness earns. Included in that is the absolute love and devotion of God toward you without hesitancy, probation, or any other imaginable cause for diminishment. In other words, God *must* love you as much as the Father loves the Son and the Son loves the Father. This is true no matter how good a week you have had. Whether you were loved by others, or loved others yourself, or even loved yourself much. Whether you have sinned greatly or not. Either way, you are *due* (humanly speaking) unimaginable devotion from God.

Even so, you can still largely go through your week not experiencing this stunning grace. You can be driven by shame. You can fall back to relying on the lesser measurements of your still-too-many idols. Your *epithumia* (over-the-top desires) can rage on seemingly unchallenged. Preach this Gospel over and over again to yourself. Ask for heavenly-sourced faith.

#3- Adoption

The third aspect of the singular Gospel reflected in the *Gospel App* shape is that you have been irrevocably adopted to be a son or daughter of the Living God. The greatest honor that you can *never* earn is now yours: perfect, irreversible, and eternal. When you, at times, truly experience your spiritual adoption, you will finally feel the significance, belonging, and security for which you have so deeply longed. Preach this Gospel over and over to yourself. Ask for faith.

#4- Holy Spirit

Fourth, you have been given access to the Holy Spirit Himself, His fruit, the fullness of the Father (Eph 3), spiritual gifts as He distributes, and perhaps the most important of all the fruit, faith: the heavenly power to believe with supernatural confidence that all of the above is indeed true about you, now. All you need is need. Ask child of God. Ask now. Ask regularly.

Posture of the Ground Prayer (POG)

A simple activity may help hammer this into our thick heads. It is a four part prayer that matches the four part Gospel. I recommend that it become a twice per day regular exercise.

Here is how the great reformer Martin Luther imagined such a prayer. Consider the spiritual and emotional posture of the scorched dry ground on its metaphorical knees looking up to the water-filled skies above, far out of its reach. It knows that it needs the rain to grow anything. It has no Plan B. It is dependent upon something over which it has no control, the rain. If and when it receives the rain—which comes from some timetable beyond the thirsty ground's pay grade—life will be produced. So metaphorically speaking, it falls to its knees and holds its cracked, dry, and yet desperate opened-to-receive-hands skyward. It is less a plan and more of a humble posture of faith. "God rain upon me the stuff that makes life happen" (Gal 5:6-7). Here is how Luther puts it.

> "Here is a helpful image. Wouldn't it be absurd and enormous hubris for the thirsty dry ground to even think about demanding rain from the clouds? Picture the ground holding up its empty dry and cracked hands skyward believing that it if only did it right, held its hands up at 10 and 2 o'clock or 11 and 1 o'clock—or better waved them up and down frantically in some liturgical exercise believing that if it only did it right, the clouds would open up in a torrent of life-giving rain. No, hardly. The ground knows its place and humbly can only hold-up empty dry hands to receive the rain that God ordains to fall upon it. It is the same with righteousness. There is nothing that we can do that moves God to shift his original plan to rain righteousness down upon us. We must get it into our thick heads that we are not able to do anything by our own strength and works to win this heavenly and eternal righteousness; and therefore we shall never be able to get it, unless God himself by mere imputation and by his unspeakable gift gives it to us."[115]

Let this simple exercise, the *Posture of the Ground Prayer* (POG Prayer), repeated two or more times a day be the beginning of your path to learning how to receive and apply the Gospel to the real lives of real people who have to live in this real world, beginning with you. This is a way, a powerful way, to begin to appropriate such received righteousness into your life today.

---

115. I took the liberty to paraphrase and abridge this portion of Luther's Preface from St. Paul's Epistle to the Galatians, http://www.1517legacy.com/1517legacy/2014/02/martin-luthers-commentary-on-galatians/.

The Gospel App Shape

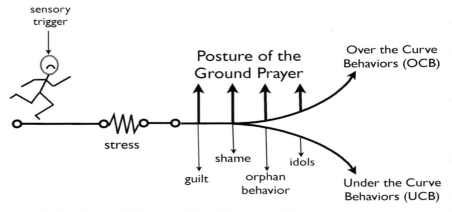

Posture of the Ground Prayer #1- (Sin) vs. guilt

Are you feeling *guilt* for something that you did or didn't do? Said or didn't say? Then get down on your knees, throw up your empty and needy hands to the sky in a posture of submission and need. Boldly pray to God to make you feel the 2000 year old death of Jesus specifically for your crime. Pray something like this in your own words.

> I feel guilt. Jesus, I need to know. Did you die for that sin too? I am afraid that if I looked into God's eyes right now, I would only see His disgust with what I did. I know I acted selfishly, indifferently, even unlovingly—again. Make me feel that You really did die for what I did and will eventually pay all of my victims back in full somehow. Make me know that God is not in Heaven crossing His arms and shaking His head critically at me. Remove my guilt, now please.[116]

Posture of the Ground Prayer #2- Right vs. Shame

Are you feeling *shame*? You wonder if something is wrong with you? Some *ugly* that you see when you look in the mirror or in the reflected gazes of those around you? Then pray:

> Jesus, what's wrong with me? I am ashamed to be the kind of person who would act this way; ashamed to be that person whom others would treat that way. I don't like what I see in the mirror. I should be a better person. Can You really love me as I am? But You do! It's the Gospel. Your record of doing everything right has been shoved into my bio. So the Father must love me—as I am—as much as He loves You and as much as You love Him. He can't love

---

116. Rom 8:1, Heb 10:19-22.

me any more even if I were different. He can't love me any less—ever. This is true no matter what I have done, or what's been done to me—whether I feel it or not right now. I confess that I am not feeling that amazing love right now. So make me feel right—now please, before I do something else stupid and harmful.[117]

Posture of the Ground Prayer #3- Adoption vs. Orphan

Are you feeling like an orphan right now: disenfranchised, disrespected, or overlooked? Do you feel like a failure, a person of dishonor, a loser? Do you feel lonely, that no one has your back? Then pray:

> I am not feeling honored or honorable right now. In fact I feel dishonored by others. When I look in the mirror, I don't feel honor toward myself either. I have tried to be honorable, but nothing has worked. I am tired and feel alone in the universe. But the Gospel says that I am an adopted son/daughter of Yours—right now—a person of great honor and value. The greatest honor I can *never* earn is irrevocably mine. I can't add to it. It is mine strictly through Your work on my behalf. Make me believe it now—before I do more damage—using others and things to gain honor on my own. Make me hear You say, "Well done, good and faithful servant!"[118]

Posture of the Ground Prayer #4- Holy Spirit vs. Idols

Have you found yourself looking to a myriad of idols to determine your significance, security, and belonging? Do you feel that you are disconnected from God's love and embrace? Do you wonder what might happen when you finally look into the eyes of God? Maybe He just hasn't forgiven you for what you did or didn't do? Have you looked into the gazes of things or others and felt less than appreciated? Then pray:

> I have felt so powerless lately. I can't do it anymore. The places where I run to find my value, identity, and honor have measured me badly. I just keep falling short of expectations. I am far too worried about what others think of me. My flesh is so dominant. Holy Spirit, make me look up into the measuring gaze of God to be reminded who I really am in Christ. Give me the powerful faith to believe that the other aspects of the Gospel are really true for me—right now. Fill me with Your fruit, so much so that it is noticeable by others around me. Now please.[119]

---

117. 2 Cor 5:21, Eph 3:14-21.
118. Gal 4:4-7.
119. Gal 5:16-23, Isa 42:17.

Pray all four prayers, in your own words, words that express the deepest cry of your soul. Do it twice a day, or more, for a month. Note changes in your prayers, in your feelings. Note comments that others are making about you. Changes are inevitable and should be noticeable. You are accessing power from God.

Remember, the flesh is with us until that grand Holy operation as we enter Heaven. Our hope, though is that its present and daily power over us will be noticeably diminished. Imagine if your shame and guilt has been diminished by 10%, or 20%. Don't kid yourself that it wouldn't be noticed by you and others. What if it could be regularly diminished by 20% for the rest of your life? Imagine the improvements to your heart and relations, your sense of being a person of honor and worth, your feeling more lovable by God. Why, you might even smile more. If you feel that coming on, don't fight it.

In Closing

We will let one of history's greatest reformers and revivalists have the last word. In the preface of his masterful *Commentary on the Galatians*, Martin Luther laid out a philosophy of *sanctification* that is both simple and revolutionary. Remember his context. He was serving in an era where there was one massive church that was riddled with corruption, heresies, and confusion. If any organization could be described as institutionalized Christendom, it was the Roman Catholic Church of the 16th century. I am not at all casting dispersions upon Catholics or the entire history of the Catholic Church. This particular period in the church was observably shady and nefarious.

Luther's hope was to reform the church so that the Gospel could be heard again. What resulted from the efforts of Luther, Calvin and others? Revival. Below is an imaginary interview between the *Gospel App* and Martin Luther, incorporating a paraphrase of the preface of his masterful Commentary on the Galatians.

Gospel App:

Dr. Luther, you have stated that the most critical element to a present revival within the Church of Jesus Christ is the doctrine that you have labeled as *passive, Christian* or *received* righteousness. Could you expound for our readers?

Luther:

We are under constant danger and fear that Satan will up and take from us this pure doctrine of faith, and bring into the Church again the impure doctrine of works and men's traditions. Therefore it is very necessary, that this doctrine be kept in continual practice and public exercise; read and heard over and over again. And no matter how well we think that we know it, or have learned it, the devil, our adversary, continually wanders about seeking to devour us. He is not dead. Likewise, our flesh and old man is still very much alive. To make our situation even more dangerous, we are aggravated and oppressed on every side by all kinds of temptations. So you see why I say again that this doctrine of *passive* or *received righteousness* can never be taught, urged, and repeated enough. If this doctrine is lost, then the whole knowledge of truth, life and salvation is also lost and gone. On the other hand, if this doctrine flourishes, then all good things flourish: religion, the true service of God, the glory of God, the right knowledge of all things and states of life.

Gospel App:

So what you are saying is that if we majored on this one specific doctrine there would be revival, and if we got distracted even to other *good* doctrines, we would end up with almost nothing to show for it?

Luther:

Yes, that is true. Paul speaks of first things first. It is the very core argument of the Epistle to the Galatians. Paul sees this received righteousness to be of utmost importance to the young Christians in Galatia and to us today. Clearly, Paul is jumping through every possible hoop to be clear to his readers about Christian *received* righteousness in specific: the singular doctrine of faith, grace, and forgiveness of sins. Nothing is more important to Paul than that we have a clear knowledge of Christian righteousness and have the ability and discernment to perceive the differences between that singular miraculous righteousness and all other kinds of righteousnesses.

Gospel App:

For our readers could you define received righteousness?

Luther:

Let us be clear, there are different sorts of righteousness. First, there is a "legal righteousness," which legislators, courts and law officers deal with. Second, there is what I have labeled as "manners righteousness," guidelines that define acceptable right behavior; different to every culture and people group. No one in their right minds believes that these rules have any power to satisfy for sin, to placate God, or to deserve grace: but they are good and helpful for living together. Besides these, there is a third category of active righteousness, the "righteousness of the law," or of the Ten Commandments, which Moses teaches. This is good, but it is of a second priority to the Christian after the doctrine of faith and Christian righteousness.

There is a fourth righteousness which is above all these: the righteousness of faith, or Christian righteousness, which we must not only understand but discern the difference between it and the other three. Let us be clear, the other three are quite contrary to this righteousness.

Gospel App:

Are you being provocative here? With all due respect, you have a bit of a reputation for using over-the-top rhetoric to make a point. Why do you say that what you call received righteousness is contrary to the 10 Commandments for instance?

Luther:

Why do I say that? Two reasons. First, the former three righteousnesses flow out of the laws of governments, the traditions of institutionalized religion, and the commandments of God. Second, they consist in our works; anyone can do them out of their own determination and strength with or without God. Don't get me wrong; I am not disparaging the first three righteousnesses. They are good, in fact they are gifts from God, like so many other things God has given to us. They are good to the extent that we don't misuse them, or mistake their roles.

But the fourth righteousness is far beyond the other three. It is not of our efforts, but is strictly accessed by faith that God through Christ, without us doing or not doing anything, imputes unto us. It is neither legal nor related to manners. It is not a function of God's law, nor consists in our ability or determination to do good things, but is radically different. In one narrow sense it could be described as mere passive righteousness, as the other above are active. For in this we work nothing, we render nothing unto God, but only we receive what another has accomplished for us, and God Himself works within us. Therefore it seems right to call this righteousness of faith, Christian righteousness, or received righteousness.

This received righteousness is a righteousness hidden in a mystery, which the world does not know. In fact, Christians themselves do not thoroughly understand it, and can hardly take hold of it in their day-to-day struggles. Therefore it must be diligently taught and continually practiced.

And whoever does not understand or apprehend this righteousness in afflictions and terrors of conscience, will be overthrown, will fall away, will get caught up into consumerism, will become discouraged in their Christian walk, will not find intimacy and purpose and joy. For there is no comfort of conscience so firm and so sure, as this *received righteousness*.

Gospel App:

This is quite similar to what the *Gospel App* is hoping to (to use your phrase) hammer into our heads. We have parsed received righteousness into four redemptive powers that we can and must access by faith, through the Holy Spirit in us, in order to have any chance of counteracting shame, guilt, our bent towards works righteousness which we have described as orphanness, and idolatry. We say, 'All we need is need, and most of the time we don't even have that."

Luther:

Yes, of course. Here is the huge fallacy of our normal human thinking, Christian and non-Christian alike. No matter what we do right, or how we attempt to measure our status with God, the Law's perfect demands eventually crush us. Then in our misery, terrified consciences and fears of death, we see how much we have failed God—not to mention all of our past failures that are unaddressed. Then the poor soul with great anguish of spirit groans, and thinks to himself: "Alas! I now see so clearly how badly I have messed up my whole life. But all I need is a little longer and I will fix everything. I'll get it right this time."

There is something twisted in us that runs back to our original flaw. Humanity's reason cannot restrain itself from active or working righteousness, that is to say, his/her own righteousness: nor lift up his/her eyes to the beholding of received righteousness, but runs back to the path of active righteousness: so deeply is this evil rooted in us.

Gospel App:

To be clear, you are not equating doing good things with evil, right? Aren't you arguing that our relying on any good work—no matter how good—in order to earn anymore of God's blessings and favor is wrongheaded, foolish and arguably described as evil? This is a wake-up call to our modern Christian culture that puts such great emphasis on what we are supposed to be doing. Our modern discipleship programs don't involve indulgences, as were prevalent in your time, but we do seem to imply that if a person only gets their act together and leans into spiritual formation exercises, or missional activities that then they would feel Gods pleasure and then their spiritual life would finally really take off.

You seem to be suggesting that such active righteousness—by which we mean anything that I do that I expect would earn more of God's favor than I already have in Christ—is a deep evil bent rooted in the flesh of all humans, including Christians.

On the one hand, it seems to me technically akin to the essence of paganism. If I do this or that, then God is more pleased with me and vice versa.

Martin Luther:

Exactly. On the other hand, all Satan has to do to abuse this tragic flaw in our nature is to make us ruminate on our failings and our deep innate desire to fix it again. In the end, our poor consciences always end up troubled, terrified and confounded.

It is humanly impossible for us to see that our real comfort comes from looking up to grace only. Instead in the throes of the horror of our sin and failures, we just can't imagine that our real problem is our desire to do righteous works. Humanly speaking, receiving God's righteousness is too hard for us, far harder than trying to do the Law better.

So we must be very skilled at making clear the difference between these two kinds of righteousness, active and received: to the end that none of the other righteousnesses are ever used by those in our care to repair their daily shame and guilt.

That's the whole point of the letter to the Galatians. We must be aware of our ongoing tendency to go back to works righteousness, and to hold on to this received righteousness. For if this article of justification be once lost, then is all true Christian doctrine lost. Tragically, we are surrounded by those that preach active righteousness, both in institutional Christendom, institutional religions of some other sort, even unbelievers. "Do this or that practice and you will finally feel God's blessing for you. Do this list over and over and your spiritual life will just take off. No wonder you are feeling like God is distant. Here are some things that will take care of that." We love such teaching—but it does not work.

We must keep saying, at every opportunity that there is no compromise between the righteousness of the law and the received righteousness of Christ. He who strays from this received righteousness must fall into active righteousness; that is to say, when a person has turned away from the received righteousness of Christ alone, he must fall into the confidence of his own works—and it doesn't work.

So we must passionately repeat this doctrine of faith or Christian righteousness, often and always, so that our charges will be able to discern received righteousness from active righteousness. For only by this doctrine the Church is built, and in this it consists. Otherwise we shall never be able to hold the true faith, but by and by we shall either become legalists, mere lifeless observers of ceremonies, institutionalized Christians—so darkened and lifeless that we will be no earthly good to anyone in the church.

If we will be teachers and leaders of others, it behooves us to have great care of these matters, and to mark well this distinction between the righteousness of the law and the received righteousness of Christ. And this distinction is easy to be uttered in words, yet in use and experience it is very hard. It is harder still to draw a distinction when guilt, shame or fear is involved. Then these two righteousnesses look more alike than anyone would wish or desire. But one of the paths is to life, the other to death.

Gospel App:

But, aren't we then supposed to do good works? You aren't suggesting that it doesn't matter then what we do, are you?

Luther:

It is a good question of course. "Shouldn't we do good works? Or do we just go and do whatever we want to do because Jesus' righteousness is in our account and can never be diminished?"

The question is absurd even on its face of course. If the truth were known, a person who is immersed in the received righteousness of Christ is the only one who truly is doing good works. When I have this received righteousness reigning in my heart, I descend from heaven as the rain making fruitful the earth, that is to say, I do good works, all the time, no matter what occasion. If I am a minister of the Word, I preach, I comfort the brokenhearted, I administer the Sacraments. If I am a householder, I govern my house and my family, I bring up my children in the knowledge and fear of God. If I am a magistrate, the charge that is given me from above I diligently execute. If I am a servant, I do my employer's business faithfully.

To conclude: whoever is persuaded that Christ is his or her righteousness, not only cheerfully and gladly works well in his or her vocation, but also submits himself or herself through love to the government leaders and to their laws, even though they are severe, sharp and cruel, and if need be, to any and all manner of burdens and dangers of this present life, because he or she knows that this is the will of God, and that this obedience empowered by God's righteousness blossoming in the actions and motivations of His children pleases Him.

Gospel App:

Thanks for your time, Dr. Luther.

Wrap-Up

In the introduction I used an illustration from C.S. Lewis' *The Great Divorce*. I want to repeat it now for I imagine that it has even more relevance to the reader at the end of this book. There is great hope for Jesus-followers who remain on Planet Earth for a time. There is no wonder why you are lonely, dissatisfied, riddled by that endless nagging murmur of discontent, looking for significance, security, and belonging in all the wrong places and never really finding what you desire. Lewis puts this in perspective related to the good news of the new life Jesus has purchased for people like me.

> "And yet all loneliness, angers, hatreds, envies and itchings that it contains, if rolled into one single experience and put into the scale against the least moment of the joy that is felt by the least in Heaven, would have no weight that could be registered at all. Bad cannot succeed even in being bad as truly as good is good. If all Hell's miseries together entered the consciousness of yon wee yellow bird on the bough there, they would be swallowed up without trace, as if one drop of ink had been dropped into that Great Ocean to which your terrestrial Pacific itself is only a molecule."[120]

Have you come to believe again, for perhaps just a moment that there is such a mind-bending joy that is accessible by you now for the asking? You have not because you ask not, James wrote (4:2). It's simple. Per Lewis again:

> "But what of the poor Ghosts who never get into the omnibus at all?"

> "Everyone who wishes it does. Never fear. There are only two kinds of people in the end: those who say to God, 'Thy will be done,' and those to whom God says, in the end, 'Thy will be done.' All that are in Hell, choose it. Without that self-choice there could be no Hell. No soul that seriously and constantly desires joy will ever miss it. Those who seek find. To those who knock it is opened."[121]

The Gospel App Discipleship Course

What is the next step in receiving and applying the Gospel to the real lives of real people in the real world, beginning with me? In the companion discipleship workbook, The *Gospel App*, participants are taught specifically how to use the shape to receive and apply the Gospel to themselves and their own lives and struggles *first* and to others *second*. By the end of the ten weeks discipleship class, participants should be able to both receive and apply the four aspects of the Gospel to such issues as the following:

120. Lewis, Great Divorce, 139.
121. Lewis, Great Divorce, 75.

How do you make a real dent in your entrenched addictions?

How do you really say that you are sorry (i.e., repentance)?

How do you positively deal with conflict?

How can you "fairly" forgive a person who has deeply hurt or wounded you?

How can you kick-start your desire to witness to your neighbors?

How can you fix your lackluster prayer life?

These are beyond the scope of this book. Here we want to merely initiate a new journey for the reader, a new bent and direction.

If you are like me, or many others that I have spoken to, you were likely told that when you were a baby Christian you could depend upon God a lot. But as you matured you should be able to walk more and more on your own strength of spirituality and Christ-likeness. Discipleship then is working hard to become more like Jesus. If you have heard anything from the previous chapters it is this. That approach was well-meaning but largely destructive.

Christian discipleship is the path to become more *dependent* upon Christ and His Spirit as you mature in your faith—and in fact, to more and more see independence as a core agenda of your flesh and Satan himself.

So how do you access such power from God that can act as a counter-agent against your knee-jerk heavily conditioned flesh? By now you have picked up on an oft-repeated phrase—the living drum beat—of the *Gospel App*. "All you need is need." If you are aware of your need, present or ongoing, run to God, throw up empty needy hands and plead with your Heavenly Father to give you that power. Remember Jesus said, "You have not because you ask not."

Welcome to the *Gospel App*.

Appendix 1: Biblical Righteousness
(From The *Gospel App* discipleship manual, p. 41-43)

The Biblical concept of right and righteous are a bit confusing to moderns, particularly those of us in the West. There are few more important subjects. The Hebrew root *tsdq* is used over 660 times in the OT. The parallel Greek *dikaio/dikaoisune* is evident 333 times. Together they are used almost 1000 times in the Bible. They are very important concepts.

How do Bible versions translate the word? It is very difficult to land on a single word. Depending upon the context, translators may choose right, righteous, just, justified, or vindicate. It can also pick up a sense of hospitality, victory, just decree, integrity, uprightness, fair judgment, to put things right, to be right, to do right, to declare right, salvation and even prosperity. Obviously, some of these English words have very different connotations.

To make it worse for Western readers, few ever mention the word, and then hardly in a Biblical way. One may hear of:

> self-*righteousness*—a negative posture of being overly confident of one's own being right or being in the right, typified by a certain smugness and intolerance of the opinions and behavior of others.
> *righteous* indignation-that reactionary anger over perceived mistreatment.
> *righteous* shoot- police lingo for a justified by-the-book firing of weapon.
> street/slang *righteous* referring to anything that contains the best possible attributable qualities ("Man, that car is righteous!"), or as an interjection of excitement or pleasure, "*Righteous!*"

None of these are very faithful to its Biblical meaning. So it is no wonder when the typical Westerner reads the Bible that such words as this are misunderstood and often misappropriated.

If a group is asked to define Biblical righteousness, the overwhelming answer would have something to do with conforming to the law, God's or other. A righteous person, then, is someone who lives according to the accepted rules and laws: God's, governmental, or moral (i.e., the Golden Rule).

"The righteous man leads a blameless life; blessed are his children after him." (Prov 20:7)

"And if we are careful to obey all this law before the LORD our God, as he has commanded us, that will be our righteousness." (Dt 6:25 NIV)

According to this narrow understanding, the righteous person lives their life in accord with the law. The wicked do not. When the righteous are tried in God's court, they will be declared innocent—i.e., declared to be right and so subject to all rights of a citizen in good standing. So to be righteous—in the individual ethical sense—is to live your life according to a certain code of ethics, the Ten Commandments, the Golden Rule, etc. Right?

It is true. Both the Hebrew and Greek words can reflect ethical, legal and moral behavior, or can speak of a legal declaration of being on the right side of the Law—i.e., justified.

But, for both *tsdq* and *dikaioo*, these legal and ethical understandings are valid but are secondary derived meanings of the word. At its core, right, righteousness, just, righteous, are relational.

Tsdq and *dikaioo* are, at their core "the fulfillment of the demands of a relationship." OT scholar, Olley observes that the "righteous" king necessarily does right for his people. Righteousness is not primarily individualistic, it is focused upon the community. The nature of the righteous King's right is that he

> "...is one who brings a good and a happy life for all his subjects. One featured means is through edicts at the time of accession which include remission of debts, freeing of slaves and release of the land. Thus, there is close association with ideas of 'generosity,' 'mercy,' and setting free'...Unfortunately the English word "righteousness" never suggests such actions, which are far from mere legal or moral rectitude. Semitic emphasis is upon actions which bring about prosperity, benefit, equal rights for all subjects, including freedom from external oppression and deliverance from enemies... [Such righteousness] is not only a royal attribute but is to characterize all of God's people, with a similar concern for the well-being of one's fellows...In a broad sense then [*tsdq*] signifies actions that bring about what is right and good for all or the state where this is so."[122]

So it is far better to understand Biblical "right" as to be right with others, God and community, and to want to do right for the well-being of those same others. The adjective form "describes a person rightly related to God and concerned for the well-being of others."[123]

Perhaps a better and more dynamic rendering of "right/righteous/righteousness" then is to do "what is right for others," or to "bring about what is right." The end of righteousness and the desire of a righteous person is to do those things that bring about the good of the community, including such things as punishment of evil-doers, restoration and vindication of the victims.

Israel's "right" is integrally related to God's *tsdq*. There is a clear link

---

122 J. W. Olley,"'Righteousness'-Some Issues in Old Testament Translation Into English," The Bible Translator 38(3) (July 1987), 309.
123 Olley, Righteousness, 312.

"between the promise that Yahweh will bring about what is right and beneficial (deliverance, vindication, prosperity, with judgment upon oppressors) and Israel's responsibility to do what is right toward Yahweh and toward others (actions within the covenant community)."[124]

In Psalm 72, Solomon requests that God give him God's justice and righteousness. Only then (implied) can the King do right for the people.

> "Endow the king with your justice, O God, the royal son with your righteousness. He will judge your people in righteousness, your afflicted ones with justice." (Ps 72:1-2)

So Solomon understood that God's right, His desire to do good things for others can be received and applied by the King. In fact, it was critical that the King receives and applies God's desire to do right for others. Otherwise, the King could not be a right King. The same can be true for us. It is not enough that the King not get a speeding ticket, or break some other law himself. The heart of Biblical right is to honor, care for, and rescue others.

How does this understanding of righteousness relate to the forensic notion of being legally justified by Christ? Doesn't the Bible teach that you are justified, made righteous by the means of Jesus death on the Cross for your crimes? Your unrighteousness is taken upon His righteous shoulders and the Law is satisfied by His corporal punishment? You are made right, treated as if you were in fact innocent of all charges by Jesus' efforts alone?

Yes, but that understanding, as important as it is, still remains limited. The core essential meaning of righteous presses beyond that limited use. You who are under the blood of Jesus are not only legally declared innocent and acquitted, but are now freed to be agents of God's righteousness for others, accessible by faith through the Holy Spirit in you. A person who has been made or declared right by an authority of the court has been restored to their community with all the rights and privileges of a citizen; to enjoy the full benefits of life in the community without shame, guilt or fears from the court. You can now return to being right with others and doing right for others. You are right with the Judge.

So how do you bring the two aspects of righteousness together? Is there a common thread to obedience to the law and caring for the well-being of others? Of course. Jesus summed up the entire requirements of the law in four short verses.

> "'Love the Lord your God with all your heart and with all your soul and with all your mind.' This is the first and greatest commandment. The second is like it: 'Love your neighbor as yourself.' The Law and the Prophets hang on these two commandments." (Matt 22:37-40 NIV)

---

124 Olley, Righteousness, 312.

If your motivation is to be and do right then you necessarily desire the well-being of others. Your motivation then, is in-sync with good and right laws. If you are driven by a desire to do right for others, why would you rob? Steal? Have an affair? Why would you justify the use of pornography?

Upshot? Since God has made you right, declared you right, justified you, etc., that is the same as saying that now His intentions toward you are fully loving. He and you are "right." This relational rightness is beyond merely legal. It is irreversible. It is not a function of your doing or being right. It is a function of Jesus already accomplishing all of that for you. Now God declares you and Him right, as you are.

But aren't you supposed to go and do right? Of course. By faith, any Jesus follower can access through the Holy Spirit in them, God's sense of right, His motivation to be right and to do right for others. If you are filled with the height, width, length and depth of the love of Christ for you, and of necessity His love for other people as well, your motivation will necessarily be other-directed—loving others and loving toward God. You will want to do right.

So to put this concept in terms used in the *Gospel App*.

> Through Jesus' death, I am made right with God. God can never, will never look at me and even think that something is not right in our relationship. God and I are good (to use a modern slang). Also, Jesus' death and imputation of His right to my account means that the restored relationship is as right, as good as the relationship among the Trinity. God loves me, adores me as He would those who are right, and who have done right to others. He looks at me and can only think "Well done, good and faithful servant." "This is my beloved son with whom I am well pleased." So, God and I are really good. He is not just a judge that declared me right, but still can't stand the sight of me. The Judge and I are good.

Then by faith, through the Holy Spirit, you can actually access the love of God for you and for others. If you access that powerful motivational outward other oriented desire from God—His right—you will be moved to love others as well. Like Solomon before you, you can pray,

> "Endow [your son/daughter] with your [innate rightness], O God, the royal [son/daughter] with your [desire to do good and right for others]. [So that I] will [treat] your people [right, the same way you would], your afflicted ones with [fairness, justice where justice is required, a lack of bigotry and self-centeredness and compassion]." (Ps 72:1-2)

Bibliography

Allender, Dan B. *The Wounded Heart: Hope for Adult Victims of Childhood Sexual Abuse.* Colorado Springs, Co.: NavPress, 1990.

Anderson, E. *Code of the Street: Decency, Violence, and the Moral Life of the Inner City.* W. Norton Company, 1999.

Bascom, Barbara and Carol McKelvey. *The Complete Guide to Foreign Adoption.* New York: Pocket Books, 1997.

Baxter, Richard. *Christian Directory*, Soli Deo Gloria Publications, 1990.

Branden, Nathaniel, *The Six Pillars of Self-Esteem*, Bantam Books, 1995.

Brown, Brené, *Daring Greatly: How the Courage to Be Vulnerable Transforms the Way We Live, Love, Parent, and Lead.* New York: Avery, 2012.

Bunyan, J. *Prayer.* Banner of Truth, 1989.

Calvin, John. *Calvin: Institutes of the Christian Religion 1*, trans. Ford Lewis Battles, ed. John T. McNeill, vol. 20 of Library of Christian Classics (Philadelphia: Westminster Press, 1960).

Enright R.D. and North, J. (ed.) *Exploring Forgiveness.* Madison WI: University of Wisconsin Press, 1998.

Enright, R. D., and the Human Development Study Group. (1996). "Counseling Within the Forgiveness Triad: On Forgiving, Receiving Forgiveness, and Self-Forgiveness." *Counseling and Values*, 40 (1996): 107–126.

Fischer M. L. & Exline, J. "Self-Forgiveness versus Excusing: The Roles of Remorse, Effort, and Acceptance of Responsibility." *Self and Identity*, 5, (2006): 127-146.

Forbes, Heather, and Bryan Post, *Beyond Consequences Logic and Control: A Love-Based Approach to Helping Children with Severe Behaviors.* Boulder, Co.: BCI, 2009.

Fraley, R. C., & Shaver, P. R. "Adult Romantic Attachment: Theoretical Developments, Emerging Controversies, and Unanswered Questions."

Review of General Psychology, 4(2), (2000), 132-154.

Hall, J.H., & Fincham, F.D. "Self-Forgiveness: The Stepchild of Forgiveness Research." *The Journal of Social and Clinical Psychology*, 24 (5) (2005): 621-637.

Hugo, Victor. *Les Miserables*. Penguin Group US. Kindle Edition.

Keck, Gregory C. and Regina M. Kupecky. *Adopting the Hurt Child*. Colorado Springs, Colorado: Pinon Press, 1995.

Keller, T. *Counterfeit Gods: The Empty Promises of Money, Sex, and Power, and the Only Hope That Matters*. Penguin Group, 2009.

Keller, T. *The Freedom of Self-Forgetfulness*. 10Publishing, 2012.

Larson, E. *The Devil in the White City*. New York: Vintage Books, 2003.

Lewis, C.S. *The Great Divorce: A Dream*. Harper San Francisco, 1946.

Lovelace, R. *Dynamics of Spiritual Life: An Evangelical Theology of Renewal*. Inter-Varsity Press, 1979.

Luther, M. *Commentary on Galatians*. Grand Rapids: Fleming H. Revell, 1988.

Machen, J. Gresham. *What is Faith?* The Banner of Truth Trust, 2012.

Mandolfo, C. *Daughter Zion Talks Back to the Prophets: A Dialogic Theology of the Book of Lamentations*. SBL, 2007.

McMurtry, L. *Lonesome Dove: The Novel*. New York: Simon & Schuster, 2010.

Moltmann, Jurgen. *The Trinity and the Kingdom of God: The Doctrine of God*, SCM Press Ltd., 1998.

Morrison, A. *The Culture of Shame*. New York: Ballantine, 1996.

Murray, John. *Redemption Accomplished and Applied*. Michigan: Wm. B. Eerdmans Publishing, 1955.

Murray, John. *The Epistle to the Romans*, Grand Rapids, Wm. B. Eerdmans Publishing, 1977.

Olley, J.W. "'Righteousness'-Some Issues in Old Testament Translation Into

English," *The Bible Translator* 38(3) (July 1987): 307-315.

Peterson, E. *The Message: The Bible in Contemporary Language.* NavPress, 2010.

Peterson, Robert. *Adopted by God.* New Jersey: P&R Publishing, 2001.

Powlison, D. "Idols of the Heart and 'Vanity Fair'" *Journal of Biblical Counseling*, 13(2) (1995): 35-50.

Senna, G. "The Doctrine of Adoption." MA Thesis, Reformed Theological Seminary, 2006.

Senyard, B. *Fair Forgiveness: Finding the Power to Forgive, Where You Least Expect It*. LE Press, 2014.

Swoboda, A.J. *A Glorious Dark: Finding Hope in the Tension Between Belief and Experience*, Grand Rapids: Baker Books, 2014.

Tangney, J. and Ronda L. Dearing, *Shame and Guilt*, New York: Guilford Press, 2002.

Tangney, J., Steuwig, J. & Hafez, L. "Shame, Guilt, and Remorse: Implications for Offender Populations." *The Journal of Forensic Psychiatry & Psychology, 22* (5) (2011): 706-723T.

Tchividjian, T. *One Way Love: Inexhaustible Grace for an Exhausted World*. Chicago: David C. Cook, 2013.

Williams, Neil H. *The Theology of Sonship*, World Harvest Mission, 2002.

Wong, Y., and Tsai, J. "Cultural models of Shame and Guilt." in *The Self-conscious Emotions: Theory and Research*, edited by J.L. Tracy, R.W. Robins, & J.P. Tangney, 209-223. New York: Guilford Press, 2007.

Worthington, E. Jr., *Moving Forward: Six Steps to Forgiving Yourself and Breaking Free From the Past*, New York: WaterBrook Press, 2013.

Worthington, E. L. and Langberg D. "Religious Considerations and Self-Forgiveness in Treating Complex Trauma and Moral Injury in Present and Former Soldiers." *Journal of Psychology and Theology, 40*(4), (2012): 274-288.

The Gospel App Shape

The Gospel App Shape